THANKS FOR
YOUR SUPPORT!

David N. Bossie

David Bossie
President, Citizens United

www.citizensunited.org

THE MANY FACES OF JOHN KERRY

THE MANY FACES OF JOHN KERRY

Why This Massachusetts Liberal
Is Wrong for America

DAVID N. BOSSIE

WND BOOKS
A Division of Thomas Nelson Publishers
Since 1798
www.thomasnelson.com

Published in Nashville, Tennessee, by WND Books.

Library of Congress Cataloging-in-Publication Data

Bossie, David N., 1965–
    The many faces of John Kerry : why this Massachusetts liberal is wrong for America / David N. Bossie.
        p. cm.
    Includes bibliographical references.
    ISBN 0-7852-6075-7
    1. Kerry, John, 1943–   2. Presidential candidates—United States.
    3. Presidents—United States—Election—2004. 4. United States—Politics and government—2001–   I. Title.
    E840.8.K427B67 2004
    973.931'092—dc22

                                                                    2004011321

Printed in the United States of America
04 05 06 07—9 8 7 6 5 4

To *my wonderful family:*
My wife Susan and children Isabella and Griffin. We hope
for a safer tomorrow for all Americans.

In memory of my late mother-in-law Jean Blackwell, a lifelong
Republican whose vote for president will be missed
for the first time in this election.

CONTENTS

CONTENTS

INTRODUCTION

Meet the real John Kerry

JOHN KERRY APPARENTLY DOESN'T LEARN LESSONS. After more than thirty years, he is still using his bully pulpit to endanger the lives of U.S. military personnel fighting overseas, complaining about the sitting president's policies and legislative actions without offering any solutions of his own, and shirking his legislative responsibilities to make headlines.

Only now, after twenty years in the Senate, John Kerry wants to be president. On Capitol Hill, his power is much more limited, his liberal extremism much more tempered by the ninety-nine other voices that share his lofty office. As president, however, he would be in a position to foist his radical extreme-left agenda on a nation that, demonstrably, does not share his mindset. Electing him leader of the free world is not a mistake Americans can afford to make. Of course, that hasn't stopped Kerry from trying the lowest tactics to see that we do.

In the wake of the Iraqi detainee abuse scandal in April 2004, for instance, Kerry campaign head Mary Beth Cahill made fundraising pitches urging Kerry supporters to send money as a sign of support for her boss's demand that Defense Secretary Donald Rumsfeld resign over the scandal.

The tactic led Republican National Committee Chairman Ed

Gillespie to rightfully point out, "The prison images from Baghdad are clearly disgusting, but it's harder to find words to describe those whose first instinct upon seeing them is to raise campaign cash with them."[1]

Gillespie and others are right to condemn these sleazy tactics. The liberal media in the U.S. and around the globe is using every opportunity to stoke anti-American hysteria among the Arab and Muslim world—which hold the primary ethnic and religious groups we're battling in this war on terror. It's a disgrace to see one of our own politicians, a presidential contender, no less, doing the same thing.

But this kind of exploitation for political gain is nothing new to Kerry. As you will read in *The Many Faces of John Kerry*, in the early 1970s after returning from a war zone in Vietnam, Kerry went to great pains to denounce the war in which he took part, helping bring notoriety to an anti-war group and even appearing on the floor of the U.S. Senate to denounce the war as inherently wrong—all the while accusing U.S. troops of committing unspeakable atrocities (which, for the record, he could never substantiate). In the meantime, all Kerry really managed to do, according to an account by former Marine Lieutenant Colonel Oliver North, was feed into North Vietnam's propaganda machine. That in turn led the North Vietnamese to continue their war effort against the South, even though they had suffered great losses, as well as endanger the lives of American POWs being held in dark, dank North Vietnamese prison camps. (Senate colleague John McCain, a former Navy pilot, can attest to this; he spent six years in the infamous "Hanoi Hilton" after being shot down and once claimed Kerry's anti-war rhetoric worsened his treatment.)

Now, as American Marines, sailors, and GIs battle Iraqi insurgents; as U.S. contractors are kidnapped, burned alive, dismembered, beheaded, dragged through Iraqi streets, and hanged from bridges; as the world denounces the U.S. for acting in its own best interests, there is John Kerry, still feeding an enemy propaganda machine with his political opportunism.

MORAL EQUIVALENCY

Senator Kerry and his supporters think naked pictures of otherwise healthy Iraqi detainees can be equated with burning and decapitating non-combatant American civilians. But for those of us who live in the real world, Kerry's blatant disregard for the lives of American military personnel is as disgraceful as it is unforgivable.

America has vast responsibilities. The Bush administration and Congress were elected in part to attend to these responsibilities; the war on terror is this generation's greatest charge, because if we lose it, nothing else—health insurance, gas prices, energy costs, or even jobs—will matter very much. Clearly, our way of life is what President Bush is fighting to preserve. The same will hold true for Kerry, should he win the presidency in November, but based on his political record in dealing with military, defense, and intelligence issues, Americans cannot be certain he'll make the war on terror issue one.

Even if he were to make a priority of the war on terror, there are other problems our nation faces, other issues to address. The following pages outline a number of those issues, and John Kerry's history of addressing—or in many cases flip-flopping—them. What you will see in Senator Kerry is the consummate politician (that's not a compliment), not a consummate leader. You will see a man on a mission, whose positions on the important issues of the day are as malleable as Silly Putty. You will see a man who puts party and personal advancement above principle and doing what is right. You will discover that John Kerry really has no genuine values, no foundation, no moral compass—just a penchant for political expediency.

As John Kerry continues his quest for the White House, and as Election Day nears, keep in mind what you read in the following pages. Understand that this election comes as Americans are engaged in a fight against insidious evil, one which threatens our values, our beliefs, our very way of life. After you read about his history of weak leadership, inability to legislate, and disdain over the years for measures that have helped protect our country, our citizens, and our culture, ask yourself if the United States can afford a leader who has rarely seen a cause worth fighting for except his own political gain.

1

THE EVERREADY BUNNY

Kerry's Clintonian ambition

M ANY OF TODAY'S POLITICIANS aspired to their careers early in life. Each has a story to tell: some talk of personal political experiences; others follow in the footsteps of mothers, fathers, or other family members; and still others see the ascension into national politics as a natural extension of a former professional life, such as those who made careers as lawyers, teachers, or local-level public servants.

As for John Kerry, to many friends and associates it seemed he was aspiring to national politics almost from the time he was old enough to understand the game. It was obvious to some that, early on, he even had his eye on the ultimate prize—the presidency.

At just sixteen years old, he formed the John Winant Society while attending St. Paul's School in Concord, New Hampshire, a group that still exists and which debates major issues of the day. While attending Yale, prior to his enlistment in the U.S. Navy, classmates observed his political ambitions; some would say they were so strong as to be unnerving.

"It was an aura he created," said Harvey Bundy, a Chicago money manager who roomed with Kerry at Yale. "We sat around the room, talking about 'what are our positions going to be in John's cabinet.' I wish I could forecast the market as well."[1]

Others noted Kerry generally began running for the presidency his freshman year. Said a contemporary, "He was obsessed by politics to the exclusion of all else. At that age, it's a bit creepy."[2] The young Kerry volunteered for the senatorial candidacy of Edward Kennedy in 1962, and—while attending Yale—"dated Janet Auchincloss, the half-sister of Jackie Kennedy, the first lady, won the presidency of the Yale Political Union, and was initiated into the Skull and Bones before joining the United States Navy for service in Vietnam," the *London Telegraph* reported.[3] "Perhaps [Kerry's] presidential aspirations were transparent as far back as 1971 when he was interviewed by Morley Safer on CBS' *60 Minutes* about his antiwar protests. Safer asked, 'Do you want to be president?' Kerry, startled by the question, laughed and replied, 'No, that's such a crazy question at a time like this,'" reported *The Hill*—a paper that exclusively covers congressional news.[4]

What is known is that John Kerry sought an early discharge from the Navy—and got it—so he could return to Massachusetts and run for Congress in 1970. "On Jan. 3, 1970, Kerry requested that his superior, Rear Admiral Walter F. Schlech Jr. grant him an early discharge so that he could run for Congress on an anti-war platform," the *Boston Globe* reported in 2003. "I just said to the admiral: 'I've got to get out. I've got to go do what I came back here to do, which is, end this thing,'" Kerry said. His request was granted, and Kerry found himself free of the Navy with an honorable discharge, shaving six months off his service commitment. He gave up on his bid after three months, after losing the Democratic nomination to Catholic priest Robert Drinan.[5]

"KERRYMANDERING"

Kerry decided to make another foray into politics shortly after he severed ties with the anti-war group he helped found. In the early part of 1972, he went looking for a congressional district he

2

believed could be vulnerable and, hence, receptive to his candidacy. The effort was obvious, and it hangs with him to this day. "His ambition tempered only by political naïveté, Kerry tried on congressional districts like suits off the rack," the *Boston Globe* reported. "In less than two months in early 1972, the anti-war leader called three different districts in Massachusetts home. To this day, he bears the brand of opportunist from that brazen district-hopping, which he acknowledges as part of his political 'baggage.'"[6]

The term locally became known as "Kerrymandering," and it not only was the subject of talk around town but also made Kerry the brunt of ire and humor. "A leader of the Vietnam Veterans Against the War, Kerry has brashly surveyed the congressional districts throughout the state during the past two years," reported the Lowell, Massachusetts, *Sun* in March 1972. "He has gone from the Third Congressional District to the Fifth, to the Seventh, to the Fourth and now apparently back to the Fifth. . . . One of the most irritating charges he has set himself up for regardless of where he eventually runs is political carpetbagging or 'district shopping.'"[7]

Much of the angst caused by Kerry's district search was borne by fellow Democrats. He was accused of being an "outsider" who was trying to "buy the election."

"The resentment ran deep among the regular and more conservative Democrats who felt that Kerry was buying the election through money he was able to raise from the liberal establishment in Boston and New York," the *Sun* reported. "Added to the resentment was the awareness that Kerry had been looking at other Massachusetts congressional districts [in which] to run . . . it smacked of opportunism. . . . John Kerry was an outsider to whom many couldn't relate."[8]

Despite his tactics, Kerry was unable to win a seat to the U.S. House of Representatives in 1972, so he decided to move on and attend law school—a career path taken by a host of U.S. politicians before him. He graduated from Boston College Law School in 1976 and, that same year, was elected as assistant prosecutor for Middlesex County, Massachusetts.

For a brief time—1979 to 1982—Kerry was in private law practice, but then served as lieutenant governor for Massachusetts under Governor Michael Dukakis from 1982–84, a platform from which he began campaigning for the U.S. Senate. Once he won in 1984, he settled into Washington and stayed.

FLIPPIN' AND A FLOPPIN'

This vast realm of political experience has had its impact on the junior senator from Massachusetts. One criticism of Kerry that certainly rings true is that he often takes whichever side of an issue is the most politically convenient. He seems to have a long history of such political "flip-flops," as Republican critics call them, dating back to his successful 1984 Senate bid.

"Within a few months of announcing his candidacy, however, [Kerry] was in danger of losing strategic ground to U.S. Representative James M. Shannon of Lawrence, his chief rival in the bruising Democratic primary," the *Boston Globe* reported in 2003. "Kerry had been outscored by Shannon in the endorsement questionnaire of a nuclear disarmament group that vehemently opposed the military buildup under President Reagan. . . . Shannon had outscored Kerry, 100 to 94, on the questionnaire of the group, known as Freeze Voter '84, which favored canceling funds for a slew of major weapons systems."[9]

But enter the world of politics, John Kerry, and raw ambition.

"Then a strange thing happened. Paul F. Walker, Shannon's most prominent backer on the group's executive committee, graded the answers and laid out for Kerry campaign manager Paul L. Rosenberg both the flaws in Kerry's responses and what the 'correct' answers should be," the *Globe* continued. In one internal memo to Kerry, Rosenberg wrote, "Walker was confused about your answer" regarding funding of the Trident submarine, because Kerry had initially hedged opposition to new sub funding. "It is critically important that we get a 100 percent rating," Rosenberg wrote in a memo not previously made public. "You should explain how your position was misinterpreted so that he will correct the rating before it is distributed to the board tomorrow evening," he said, according to the *Globe*. Rosenberg went on to tell Kerry that Walker would be amenable to a change in the grading because "he knows of your strong support for the freeze and knows this is what you must have meant." In response, Kerry changed his answers, thus tying Shannon for a perfect score. Later, at the activists' meeting in late June, the *Globe* reported, Kerry denied Shannon "the 60 percent majority he needed to secure the endorsement for himself. . . . The stalemate for the Freeze Voter '84 endorsement was an important tactical victory for Kerry. But it could be a handicap as Kerry campaigns for president nearly two decades later."[10]

Perhaps one of the most bothersome flip-flops is Kerry's initial pledge—then the violation of that pledge—to not attack President Bush during a time of war. It was a promise that took less than a month for him to violate.

"Senator John F. Kerry of Massachusetts . . . said he will cease his complaints once the shooting starts. 'It's what you owe the troops,' said a statement from Kerry, a Navy veteran of the Vietnam War," the *Globe* reported in March 2003, shortly before Bush ordered U.S. forces to invade Iraq.[11]

Just three weeks later, and with U.S. forces just miles from Baghdad, Kerry violated his pledge and issued a sharp rebuke of the Bush administration. "What we need now is not just a regime change in Saddam Hussein and Iraq, but we need a regime change in the United States," Kerry said at an engagement in Peterborough, New Hampshire.[12]

Kerry premised his Iraq war promise to Bush on his own war experiences—which might explain why he broke it so easily. "I remember being one of those guys and reading news reports from home. If America is at war, I won't speak a word without measuring how it'll sound to the guys doing the fighting when they're listening to their radios in the desert," he said.[13] A critic of Kerry's *measured* "regime change" comment could argue it didn't play well with the men and women of the armed forces who support President Bush—not only as commander in chief but as the nation's leader.

There are many more examples of John Kerry's flip-flops. Regarding Iraq, even Kerry's vote on whether to support the U.S. invasion was the subject of a reversal. Initially, Kerry voted to authorize President Bush to use military force against Iraq.[14] And in the first Democratic presidential candidate debate, he defended his "Yea" vote. "I said at the time I would have preferred if we had given diplomacy a greater opportunity, but I think it was the right decision to disarm Saddam Hussein, and when the president made the decision, I supported him, and I support the fact that we did disarm him," Kerry said in Columbus, South Carolina, in May 2003.[15]

But then Kerry began to change his tune, once he had put his finger to the political wind and realized early competitor Howard Dean was making progress as an anti-war dove. He told reporters when announcing his bid for the presidency, "I voted to threaten the use of force to make Saddam Hussein comply with the resolutions of the United Nations."

And later, in an interview on MSNBC's *Hardball* with Chris Matthews, the following exchange took place:

MATTHEWS: Do you think you belong to that category
of candidates who more or less are unhappy with this
war, the way it's been fought, along with General Clark,
along with Howard Dean and not necessarily in
companionship politically on the issue of the war with

people like Lieberman, Edwards, and Gephardt? Are
you one of the anti-war candidates?

KERRY: I am—yes, in the sense that I don't believe the
president took us to war as he should have, yes,
absolutely.[16]

I have recorded more than sixty flip-flops of John Kerry's
political career, and I have space to highlight only a few more
examples.

In July 2003, Kerry said Democrats—including himself—and
not Republicans had fought long and hard to get rid of the so-
called "marriage penalty" tax. "We fought hard to get rid of the
marriage penalty," he told MSNBC.[17] And, during the early days of
the Democratic primaries, Kerry accused rivals Dean and U.S. Rep.
Dick Gephardt (D-Missouri) of wanting to restore the so-called
"marriage penalty" tax, a policy Kerry himself said he didn't support. "Howard Dean and Gephardt are going to put the marriage
penalty back in place. So if you get married in America, we're going
to charge you more taxes. I do not want to do that," he told *Fox
News* in October 2003.[18]

But in 1998, Senator Kerry voted against eliminating marriage
penalty relief for married taxpayers with combined incomes of less
than fifty thousand dollars per year, which would have saved taxpayers some forty-six billion dollars annually.[19]

Kerry also voted with nearly all U.S. senators to pass the USA
PATRIOT Act by a 98–1 margin in 2001, shortly after the
September 11 attacks.[20] And, at one point, on a campaign stop in
New Hampshire, he even defended his vote, calling it a "necessary"
piece of legislation: "Most of [The PATRIOT Act] has to do with
improving the transfer of information between CIA and FBI, and it
has to do with things that really were quite necessary in the wake
of what happened on September 11."[21]

But that was then. Now, Kerry attacks the PATRIOT Act. "We are a nation of laws and liberties, not of a knock in the night. So it is time to end the era of John Ashcroft. That starts with replacing the PATRIOT Act with a new law that protects our people and our liberties at the same time. I've been a district attorney, and I know that what law enforcement needs are real tools not restrictions on American's basic rights," he said in December 2003.[22]

What about the death penalty for terrorists? Senator Kerry has voiced his support—and opposition—for it.

In 1996, he criticized Massachusetts Governor Bill Weld—who was running for Kerry's Senate seat—for supporting the death penalty for terrorists. "Your policy would amount to a terrorist protection policy. Mine would put them in jail," Kerry said.[23] He also said of the issue, "You can change your mind on things, but not on life-and-death issues."[24]

Really? By December 2002, Kerry was saying he "always" had supported sentencing terrorists to death. "The law of the land is the law of the land, but I have also said that I am for the death penalty for terrorists because terrorists have declared war on your country," he told NBC.[25]

Kerry's flip-flopping on critical issues of national security and foreign policy have a history, especially when it comes to Iraq. For example, when Saddam Hussein invaded Kuwait in 1990, Senator Kerry went both ways in deciding what to do.

First, he voted to deny President George H. W. Bush the authority to eject Iraqi troops from neighboring Kuwait.[26] He even told a constituent he opposed the use of force in Iraq. According to the *Boston Globe*, "On Jan. 22, 1991, Kerry's office sent a letter to a constituent, thanking him for expressing opposition to the deployment of additional U.S. troops in Saudi Arabia and the Persian Gulf. 'I share your concerns,' Kerry wrote, noting that on Jan. 11 he had voted in favor of a resolution opposing giving the president immediate authority to go to war and seeking to give economic sanctions more time to work."[27]

Just one week later, the *same constituent* received a letter from Kerry's office, with the senator claiming he backed President Bush "unequivocally." Reported in the *Boston Globe*, "On Jan. 31, the same constituent received a letter stating that, 'From the outset of the invasion, I have strongly and unequivocally supported President Bush's response to the crisis and the policy goals he has established with our military deployment in the Persian Gulf.' Kerry blamed the mix-up on a computer error and subsequently wrote in defense of his position on the Gulf War: 'The debate in the Senate was not about whether we should or should not have used force, but when force should be used.'"[28]

WHATEVER IT TAKES TO WIN

What is John Kerry willing to do to win the presidency? Some evidence suggests he's ready to do just about anything, and, if his campaign's treatment of rival Democrats is any indication, it could get nasty on the stump—even at the risk of honesty. And though he has since given his support to his one-time rival, former Democratic presidential frontrunner Howard Dean may, deep down, agree; after all, he was the target of Kerry's ire, when he led *all* potential contenders heading into the primary season.

According to *ABC News*, during coverage of the Democratic primaries in January 2004, some of Dean's volunteers and supporters received disturbing campaign phone calls from Kerry's headquarters in Cedar Rapids. One Dean volunteer, Suzette Astley, said one of Kerry's volunteers had unkind and inappropriate things to say about Dean "regarding his foreign policy experience, being from a largely white state, and so-called 'environmental racism.'" Fortunately for Astley, a documentary filmmaker was staying with her, and the exchange with the Kerry volunteer—which was eventually confirmed by the Kerry campaign—was caught on tape.

"Does your candidate know that you're saying these kinds of things, unsubstantiated claims on the phone representing Senator Kerry?" Astley asked the nineteen-year-old volunteer, Jacob Thomas. Before long, she asked to speak with Kerry's regional field supervisor, to whom she complained. "I am just really offended by the call I got tonight," she said. "The person who was talking to me was taking things out of context, repeating unsubstantiated reports to me, and I find that really offensive."

Kerry's campaign responded swiftly with a statement. "The person who made the call is a young volunteer whose remarks were not authorized or condoned by this campaign," said Kerry campaign manager Mary Beth Cahill.

That explanation may have satisfied most, but the Dean campaign said it had been hearing from other Iowans who said they were told very similar—perhaps scripted—things about their candidate from other Kerry volunteers. *ABC News* managed to speak to another Dean supporter from Iowa—Susan Alexander—who had gotten a Kerry campaign phone call the same night as Astley, "which sounded like it came from the same script."[29]

PUSH POLLING

There are other similar incidents. *ABC News* also reported that a third Iowan, Dick Peterson, said he got a phone call two weeks earlier from an organization claiming to be an unaffiliated polling firm—in which pro-Kerry and anti-Dean information was conveyed. The call, "should it have happened, would meet the definition of a 'push poll'—a call purportedly from an objective polling firm that actually seeks to 'push' voters away from candidates by spreading negative information about them," the news service reported. "The Kerry campaign insists it is not using any anti-Dean scripts. 'Not in a million years,' said Kerry campaign spokesman David Wade."[30]

Some Dean supporters said they got calls essentially accusing their candidate of being anti-Semitic. Jay Carson, a spokesman for the former Vermont governor, "said Dean supporters are getting phone calls criticizing Dean for, among other things, claiming to be a Christian when his wife and children are Jewish," the Associated Press reported. "Frances Gehling, a Dean volunteer, said she received a phone call January 16 from a person who identified herself as a Londonderry, N.H., resident who worked for the local Kerry campaign. After Gehling said she supported Dean, the caller asked if it bothered Gehling 'that Dean waffles on the issues.' The caller then asked Gehling about Dean's statement that 'we will learn how to talk about Jesus' when he campaigns in the South. 'She asked how someone who is married to a Jew and raising Jewish children can have Christian values,' Gehring said when contacted by the Associated Press."[31]

Also, Kerry volunteers distorted Dean's record in printed materials before getting caught. "The Dean campaign also said Dean was the victim of misinformation in Michigan, where a poll released Monday shows Dean losing his lead to Kerry in the Feb. 7 caucus," AP reported. "Daren Berringer, director of Dean's Michigan campaign, said the Kerry campaign is distributing a flier that 'distorts and outright lies' about Dean's record on the environment, energy, gun control, the death penalty and higher education. [Kerry spokeswoman Stephanie] Cutter said the fliers were distributed by volunteers and once the Kerry campaign officials found out, they stopped it."[32]

PROFESSIONAL POLITICIAN

Unquestionably, many underhanded and scheming things go on in professional politics. John Kerry is not the exception. However, he is an absolute reflection of his elitist upbringing and political ambition. "The rap on John Kerry is that he is an aloof politician who lacks a core. Part of his personal story feeds the image: Kerry is a man without geographic roots; his youth stretched through a dozen towns across two continents. He enjoyed the cachet of illustrious family names but not always the bonds of a household. By the time he was 10 years old, he was shipped off for an eight-year odyssey at boarding schools in Switzerland and New England, where 'home' was a dormitory or an aunt's estate," said his own local paper, the *Boston Globe*.[33]

Born and bred for the selfishness of liberal politics? Some would argue yes.

When he first began attending St. Paul's at thirteen, he "was mocked by some . . . as a Kennedy wannabe," the *Globe* reported. "He'd sign his papers and wear his Oxford cotton shirts embossed with his initials, 'JFK,' as if the political affinity were preordained. Behind his back, classmates rolled their eyes and, as one said, joked that the initials stood for 'Just For Kerry.'"[34]

Others say he's been emulating Kennedy since childhood. "It is true that from his earliest days in public life—a career that seems to have begun in prep school—even John Kerry's closest friends have teased him about his overactive sense of destiny, his theatrical sense of gravitas, and his initials," said the *New Yorker*.[35]

And, Franklin Foer wrote in the *New Republic*:

High school social status, of course, should be meaningless in a presi-dential race. But, in at least one way, Kerry's boarding-school years do matter: They contradict the conventional portrait of him . . . Kerry's middle name is Forbes, as in the Forbes shipping fortune. Winthrop blood ties him to the earliest days of the Massachusetts Bay Colony. And, at every stage in life, the establishment has seemingly renewed his membership; first by admitting him to one of its fanciest boarding schools, then by accepting him to Yale, and then again by tapping him to join Skull & Bones.[36]

Some of his boarding school friends say the labels don't fit, that his worst critics often are relying on old-school hearsay and unsubstantiated rumor. But what is more clear is his record in the political spotlight and, given that history, even his friends would be hard-pressed to deny he possesses a strong sense of opportunism—though no doubt, on the campaign trail, they will try.

2

LET THEM EAT CAKE!

Digging up Kerry's elitist background

LEGEND HAS IT FRENCH QUEEN Marie Antoinette, when told the peasantry had no bread to eat in the days prior to the French Revolution, responded, "Let them eat cake!"

While the quote attributed to her has been disputed over the years, what has been demonstrated time and again by the ruling elite in countries all over the world is their callousness towards the needs of the ruled, as well as arrogance and indifference to suffering. In the case of Antoinette, at the time of her alleged slight, the French citizenry was being overtaxed for wars and other indebtedness incurred by the French government, most often as a result of bad choices, poor fiscal discipline, and a taste for the exquisite and opulent.

Antoinette provides valuable insight into the minds of the elite when they are faced with problems of the common man—problems they aren't able to identify with.

During Marie Antoinette's 1770-era France, early British subjects living in "The New World" complained often about the high cost—economically, socially, and culturally—of taxes. "No taxation without representation," was a rallying cry which incited colonists to rebel against Great Britain during the Revolutionary War. Now, after the passage of a few hundred years, millions of Americans find themselves in a paradox of sorts: We are no longer unrepresented in government, but we're heavily taxed to fund a plethora of central government activities never envisioned by our early revolutionaries nor codified in the Constitution they wrote. And nowhere is this paradox more evident than between ordinary Americans and the elite of the Democratic Party—which includes Senator John Kerry of Massachusetts. And here's another contradiction: Kerry *does* represent a small number of American citizens living in Massachusetts, but his consistent votes to raise taxes and oppose tax cuts affect all of us.

In a free society that thrives on the creative efforts of entrepreneurs, the worst thing political leaders can do to their people is seize a large portion of any wealth they create—one of the prime motivations and rewards for creative effort. Remove the financial motivation and rewards and such a confiscatory economic policy not only leads to an eventual stifling of growth but can also sap the entrepreneurial spirit that stimulates a country's wealth to begin with. President George W. Bush and many Republicans agree with this principle, and that's why they moved early on in Bush's first term to cut taxes—*three times*. This is a principle, however, that Kerry the multimillionaire doesn't believe. In his own words, as president he would punish the entities who fund ingenuity, provide jobs to Americans and a future to the country.

"As president, I will scrub the tax code . . . to remove every single loophole, every single incentive, every single provision that rewards Benedict Arnold CEOs and corporations for moving profits and American jobs overseas," he declared in Iowa.[1]

Benedict Arnold? For those whose memories fail, Arnold was a Revolutionary War-era general who wanted to give West Point to the British, in exchange for British-supplied rewards. Kerry is essentially calling outsourcing CEOs *traitors*.

National Review editor Rich Lowry had the following words for Kerry's corporate CEO description, as well as the Massachusetts senator's alternative "scrub the tax code" anti–Benedict Arnold plan: "One would think it would involve jail, or re-education camps, or at least the mandatory recitation of the Pledge of Allegiance—sans the phrase 'under God,' of course—by everyone heading an American business. Instead, Kerry is proposing changing the mix of tax incentives for American corporations. On Kerry's own terms, this is absurd—like offering Benedict Arnold increased child tax credits, free dental care and college aid for his five children to try to keep him from betraying his country."[2]

Lowry continues, noting that one reason U.S. corporations seek overseas climates for their operations has much to do with the kinds of taxes Kerry and Democrats have, in the past, supported. But there are a number of other, non-traitorous reasons for relocating overseas, two of which Lowry explains: "to be closer to foreign customers and to achieve efficiencies that make them more productive. Why this is considered a bad thing is not clear—except that it makes for an easy pander to economically illiterate voters."[3]

Also, it should be noted that a great many corporations Kerry claims are run by "Benedict Arnold CEOs" are, in fact, donors to his campaign. "Kerry has accepted money and fundraising assistance from top executives at companies that fit the candidate's description of a notorious traitor of the American Revolution," the *Washington Post* reported in February 2004. "Executives and employees at such companies have contributed more than $140,000 to Kerry's presidential campaign, a review of his donor records shows. Additionally, two of Kerry's biggest fundraisers, who together have raised more than $400,000 for the candidate, are top executives at investment firms that helped set up companies in the world's best-known offshore tax havens, federal records show."[4]

KETCHUP

But what about the H.J. Heinz Corporation, of which the senator's wife—Teresa Heinz-Kerry—is an heiress and owns a significant amount of stock? What is that corporation's job retention and overseas job creation record? Heinz Corporation is guilty of the same tax loopholes and displacement of workers Kerry is contingent upon using for his own campaign rhetoric.

For instance:

- Heinz laid off seventy workers in Pittsburgh and cut an additional thirty salaried positions that were unfilled in 2001.[5]
- Three hundred twenty-five workers in California were laid off in 2001 after the closure of a pet food factory.[6]
- Four hundred workers in Pennsylvania and Idaho were let go in 1998.[7]
- In 1997, Heinz Ketchup closed a plant in California, causing three hundred full-time and one hundred eighty seasonal workers to lose their jobs.[8]
- Three hundred fifty jobs were eliminated in Utah in 1996.[9]
- Two hundred Heinz employees lost their jobs in Oregon in 1995 after Heinz closed a plant in Eugene.[10]

Were all of these jobs lost forever? Hardly. Most were simply moved overseas. "A United States-based multinational foods company, H.J. Heinz, is to set up a joint operation in South Africa. Heinz Foods South Africa will use Heinz's world-class technology to manufacture products locally," reported one South African paper in 2003. "Andre Hanekom, Pioneer Foods managing director, said: 'By manufacturing products previously only imported into South Africa, the venture will create jobs and provide export opportunities to other African countries.'"[11]

That wasn't the only off-shoring done by the Heinz corporation:

- In 1997, two hundred twenty jobs were relocated to Canada.[12]

- In 1997, two hundred jobs were added in Ireland.[13]

- In 2000, Heinz added two hundred jobs in New Zealand.[14]

- In 2000, sixty more jobs were moved to Ireland.[15]

The Heinz corporation has directly and intentionally cut U.S. jobs to move them to another countries. "Heinz Bakery Products has selected [Mississauga, Ontario, Canada] over a U.S. location for its North American Sweet Goods Center, a move that should create about 220 new jobs. . . . Heinz Bakery, a subsidiary of Pittsburgh-based H.J. Heinz Co., announced two months ago its Mississauga plant, which employs 240, and its Buffalo plant, which employs 80, would be shut down to consolidate operations at a new location," said the *Toronto Star*, in a 1997 story regarding the move.[16]

Obviously the Heinz company is not the only corporation to downsize in the U.S. while expanding overseas operations. However, many Americans would view it as hypocritical for Kerry to criticize other corporations for similar moves while simultaneously blaming the Bush administration for corporation relocation, when his wife's company is doing exactly the same thing.

Worse, Kerry's own presidential campaign has "outsourced" jobs, using centers in Canada to make campaign calls to prospective voters. The *Milwaukee Journal Sentinel* reported, "The presidential campaign of Sen. John Kerry on Tuesday dumped a firm it hired to make automated phone calls to Wisconsin voters—after it learned the calls were routed through Canada. The action came quickly, following criticism earlier in the day that the Kerry calling effort was exporting American jobs."[17]

CLASS*LESS* WARFARE

Kerry—like many modern-day Democrats—plays the class warfare card, especially when it comes to economics and taxes. He has

18

claimed the Bush White House has, through its tax-cut policies, put the poor and middle class on hold, at the expense of so-called wealthy Americans and corporations.

"If you're a corporate crony calling for another tax giveaway, they'll put you right through. But if you're a middle-class family call[ing] for some tax fairness, you'll have to leave a message," Kerry said in Iowa in January 2004.[18]

"[T]his is a case of 'here we go again,' back to 1981 with Ronald Reagan. The American people have a clear choice. We can go back to Reaganomics, where you cut much more than you can, give a big tax cut mostly to the wealthy at the expense of a lot of people at the lower end," he told CNN in 2001.[19]

During his 2004 presidential campaign, Kerry has also said he'll fight legislative proposals to raise taxes on the middle-class.[20] "George W. Bush has supported tax cuts for the wealthiest Americans and corporations with the false promise that some of that money might one day trickle down to middle-class families and bolster our economy—but the Bush policies are a proven failure," the Kerry campaign said in August 2003.[21]

"Under this administration, America's middle class has been abandoned, its dreams denied, its Main Street interests ignored, and its mainstream values scorned by a White House that puts privilege first, and we must change that," he told an audience at the University of Toledo in February 2004.[22]

Senator Kerry has even attempted to frighten people—especially older Americans—into believing the Bush tax cuts did not include middle-class and working-poor families: "[W]e have the wealthiest people in the country getting yet another tax break, which doesn't come out of a surplus. *It comes out of Social Security*. It's being transferred from the payroll tax of most average Americans to the wealthiest people in the country," he said in an interview on MSNBC's *Hardball* with Chris Matthews in February 2004.[23]

But will Kerry, the multimillionaire, really be a voice for the commoner, especially regarding the taxes working families pay? To do so, he would have to buck decades of tradition enshrined by the modern Democratic Party, which prefers higher taxes to support more social spending.

"Kerry will have to expend an awful lot of time and money to convince people that he's not the classic Massachusetts liberal," said Larry Sabato, a University of Virginia political analyst. "And that's going to be tough, because mainly he is."[24]

What Kerry chooses not to admit—and instead spin to the American people—is that the Bush tax cuts, in fact, shifted more of the tax burden from the lower and middle classes to the upper class of wage earners. According to assessments by the Tax Foundation and Citizens for Tax Justice—two groups that monitor tax policy and its economic effect on citizens and businesses—the group of zero-tax filers grew from 29 million in 2000 to a record 44 million in 2004, a huge increase.[25] The reason? "Such families owe nothing because they don't earn enough to pay income taxes or because they will have more credits from government programs than they owe in income taxes," the Washington Times reported. And those figures applied before Congress acted on a separate measure to give 6.5 million families "who are already off the tax rolls" an additional $400 per child tax credit, which brought that total figure to $1,000 per child. The latter measure "would extend the full $1,000-per-child credit to married couples making up to $150,000, eliminating the eligibility 'marriage penalty,'" the Times said.[26]

Historically, when Republican administrations have cut taxes, the burden usually shifts to upper-income families and wage earners. "The number of families that have fallen off the tax rolls has more than doubled since 1980, when there were 18.6 million— about 20 percent of those filing—who had no liability, according to numbers from the Tax Foundation," said the paper.[27]

Ronald Reagan was elected president in November 1980 and reelected in 1984. During his tenure, he signed the "Reagan tax cuts," embodied in the Economic Recovery Tax Act of 1981 and the Tax Reform Act of 1986. Bill Clinton, alternately, raised tax rates, even though his own economic council found in 1994 that "[i]t is undeniable that the sharp reduction in taxes in the early 1980s was a strong impetus to economic growth." The Reagan cuts reduced marginal tax rates *across the board* to taxpayers of all income levels, but the Congressional Joint Economic Committee found in April 1996 "that after the high marginal tax rates of 1981 were cut, tax payments and the share of the tax burden borne by the top 1 percent climbed sharply. For example, in 1981 the top 1 percent paid 17.6 percent of all personal income taxes, but by 1988 their share had jumped to 27.5 percent, a 10 percentage point increase." The conclusion: "The Reagan tax cuts, like similar measures enacted in the 1920s and 1960s, showed that reducing excessive tax rates stimulates growth, reduces tax avoidance, and can increase the amount and share of tax payments generated by the rich. High top tax rates can induce counterproductive behavior and suppress revenues, factors that are usually missed or understated in government static revenue analysis."[28]

The cuts made by the Bush administration weren't even as extraordinary as Reagan's. Federal Reserve Chairman Alan Greenspan has described them as "average."[29] The Reagan cuts in the 1980s and cuts made by Democrat John F. Kennedy in the early 1960s were larger.[30]

NUMBERS DON'T ADD UP

Regardless, Kerry is looking at raising taxes—at least on those he deems "wealthy." He says he wants to increase taxes on people who earn more than $200,000 a year. At the same time, Kerry wants to increase spending on a host of old and new domestic programs—spending that won't be covered by his other fiscal policies, as pointed out by ABC's Diane Sawyer:

SAWYER: [H]oward Dean . . . said . . . repeal the Bush
tax cut, period. And yet you say, just repeal those on
people over $200,000, which doesn't amount to much
money.

KERRY: That's correct. I think Howard Dean is absolutely
wrong. I want to protect the middle class. He doesn't. I
guess he's prepared to ask everybody in the middle class
to pay another $2,000 in taxes. I'm not.

SAWYER: I'm sorry. But if you only repeal those above
$200,000, we calculate that it comes to some $40
billion against a potential of $470 billion deficit.
What does it gain?[31]

The same numbers were also calculated by the *National
Journal*: "[Kerry has] thus far shown little inclination to avoid the
kind of new spending ideas. . . . Kerry's economic plan consists of
higher federal spending and more tax credits, but no commitment
that these measures be offset by higher taxes. . . . Kerry's campaign
hasn't crunched the numbers, but additional revenue from wealthy
Americans likely would not cover all of the spending in his economic plan."[32]

Such an imbalance has led the Bush campaign to declare Kerry
would have to raise taxes by at least $900 million.[33]

The final insult came during tax time in 2004, when Teresa
Heinz-Kerry announced that, unlike her husband, she would not
make her tax returns public. "As she is not a candidate for any office,
she will not be making additional disclosures," said Jeff Lewis, Heinz-
Kerry's chief of staff.[34] Granted, she is not the candidate. However,
though her vast wealth is no secret, some believe it has already
become an issue. In December 2003, Kerry mortgaged one of the
homes he owns with his wife—in Beacon Hill in Boston—to finance
his presidential bid.[35] Also, the *Boston Herald* reported, "Heinz-
Kerry's personal wealth has been an issue in Kerry's campaign—with

opponents suggesting repeatedly the Bay State senator is likely to dip into his wife's wealth if he falters against President Bush."[36]

TAX MAN

In truth, Kerry himself has rejected past opportunities to ease the tax burden on the working poor and middle classes. In 1995 he voted for a resolution that declared middle-class tax cuts unwise.[37] Throughout his Senate career, he has often demonstrated he is no friend of *any* taxpayer, no matter which economic class. His record proves he's voted 350 times for higher taxes—in a sense, he's supported a staggering $2.3 trillion in tax increases.[38] Highlights of Kerry's Senate career include:

- 2003 vote to raise income taxes by $90 billion.[39]
- 2003 vote to increase Superfund taxes by $15.6 billion.[40]
- 1999 vote to increase tobacco taxes by $133 billion to pay for prescription drug benefits.[41]
- 1998 vote to raise taxes $755 billion by increasing cigarette tax by $1.10 a pack and by increasing tobacco company payments.[42]
- 1998 vote to increase payroll taxes by $2 billion.[43]
- 1998 vote to raise taxes by $311 million on hard-rock mining companies.[44]
- 1997 vote to raise marketing assessment on tobacco by $34 million.[45]
- 1997 vote to raise personal and corporate income taxes by $16 billion.[46]
- 1996 vote to raise taxes by $65 billion, by extending expiring taxes, closing corporate tax loopholes, and closing other tax expenditure loopholes.[47]

- 1995 vote to raise income taxes for individuals by $74 million.[48]

- 1993 vote for fiscal year 1994 budget resolution, which increased income taxes by $295 billion.[49]

In the mid-1980s, shortly after becoming Massachusetts' junior senator, Kerry voted for a series of bills that would have raised personal income taxes by nearly $12.7 billion, had they all passed.[50] A separate bill would have raised more than $51 billion in *new* taxes—and all this after the Reagan tax cut early in his first term had already begun producing economic benefits and dividends for a recession-struck society.[51]

WHATEVER YOU WANT TO HEAR, BABY

Of course, on the campaign trail, Kerry has made a number of tax-relief pledges to lower- and middle-class earners, including a promise to fight to keep tax relief in place for married couples.[52] But his actions as senator do not support such pledges. In 1998, Kerry voted against eliminating the marriage penalty for couples with combined incomes of less than $50,000—well within the economic structure he says he intends to protect from higher taxes.[53]

He has also claimed to be in favor of ending double taxation of dividends, only to later oppose them. In May 2003, the American Shareholders Association highlighted this hypocrisy in a press release:

Just five months ago, and one month prior to the President's call for ending this unjust double taxation, Kerry delivered a speech calling for eliminating the double taxation of dividends, yet, he has now gone silent on the issue to curry favor with the liberal spending interests he needs to win the Democratic nomination for president. In fact, Kerry called for eliminating the double taxation of dividends as well as a capital gains reduction, which is similar to the House of Representatives' plan that will be voted on tomorrow. . . .[54]

In Kerry's own words about the dividends tax: "And to encourage investments in the jobs of the future—I think we should eliminate the tax on capital gains for investments in critical technology companies—zero capital gains on $100 million issuance of stock if it's held for five years and has created real jobs, and we should attempt to end the double taxation of dividends."[55]

On top of the flip-flopping, Kerry's even claimed to be "proud" of some of his pro-tax votes. In May 1996, the *Boston Globe* quoted him as saying he was "'very proud' of his vote to increase the [gas] tax by 4.3 cents per gallon. . . ."[56] In short, he was "proud" he raised taxes on the very income groups hit hardest by such taxes—and groups he claims he wants to protect—the working-poor and middle-class wage earners.

New York Times writer John H. Cushman Jr. explained in 1993 that many of the Clinton-era tax hikes Kerry supported would hurt lower income taxpayers. "[M]any people who are not wealthy will be affected by the tax increases, some in ways that have been widely heralded, but others in ways that may come as a surprise. Gasoline taxes are going up; so are taxes on many people's Social Security benefits. . . ."[57]

CLAIMING CREDIT

Oddly, Kerry has also, at times, claimed credit for providing tax cuts—only they weren't *his* cuts, nor were they even sponsored by the Democratic Party. In a Democratic presidential candidate debate in Detroit in the fall of 2003, Kerry took credit for providing so-called "middle-class tax cuts"—which were really part of the Bush administration's tax-cut plan.

"When Governor [Howard] Dean just said, 'What middle-class

tax cut,' let me tell him what middle-class tax cut. [One family] in Colfax, Iowa earned $70,000. But under [Dean's] plan, they are going to pay $2,178 more in taxes because they lose the child credit to raise their children, they pay a penalty for being married again because [Dean] puts it back, and they lose the 10 percent bracket, as everybody else here does. So you begin to be taxed at 15 percent, not 10 percent. Those aren't Bush Republican cuts, those are the Democrat cuts that we worked hard to put in place to protect the middle class."[58]

But, according to a White House description of President Bush's tax-cut plans, the goal was to enable more Americans to *enter* the middle class, as well as ensure those who are already there don't take a step backward: "Across-the-board tax relief does not happen often in Washington D.C. . . . Tax relief is a great achievement for the American people. . . . Tax relief is an achievement for families struggling to enter the middle-class. . . . Tax relief is an achievement for middle-class families squeezed by high energy prices and credit card debt," President Bush said when signing his first round of cuts in June 2001.[59]

In a separate debate, Kerry also falsely claimed Democrat credit for setting the lowest tax rates, as laid out by the Bush plan: "And I have to tell you, both Governor Dean and [Rep. Richard] Gephardt [of Missouri] have said they want to get rid of the whole Bush tax cut. If you get rid of the whole Bush tax cut, you're getting rid of the Democratic part of the cut that we put in, the 10 percent bracket. You're going to pay more tax if you do what they want."[60]

Even the *Washington Post* noted the 10 percent figure was initially part of the Bush plan. "For example, the first $43,050 of a married couple's taxable income is now taxed at 15 percent. Under the Bush plan, the first $12,000 would be taxed at 10 percent and the next $31,050 at 15 percent," the paper said in 2000.[61]

And, still as Candidate Bush, the Texas governor extolled his plan during the Republican National Convention in 2000: "On principle . . . no one in America should have to pay more than a third of their income to the federal government, so we will reduce tax rates for everyone, in every bracket. On principle . . . those with the greatest need should receive the greatest help, so we will lower the bottom rate from 15 percent to 10 percent and double the child credit."[62]

Kerry—on behalf of fellow Democrats—has falsely claimed credit for other Republican-led tax-cut ideas. In 1996, he said Democrats, not the GOP, were responsible for child tax credits and marriage penalty relief. "We fought hard in the 1990s, we Democrats, real Democrats. We balanced the budget, paid down the debt, created 23 million jobs, and we did it without raising taxes on middle-class Americans. We fought hard to get rid of a marriage penalty. We fought hard to get a child-care credit."[63]

LABOR PAINS

In a likely play to his Big Labor base, Kerry has also made an issue of job loss (mostly in manufacturing) since the recession began, shortly before Bush won office in 2000.[64] He says he will work for policies that keep jobs in the U.S., instead of those which have led to corporations relocating jobs overseas. But even Kerry's "solution" conflicts with itself. For example, while decrying the loss of tax base from corporations that have moved overseas, in order to either woo them back or to convince those that remain to stay in the U.S., Kerry would provide them with "new tax breaks."

"Over 2.7 million manufacturing jobs have been lost since President Bush took office," claims Kerry's Web site. "John Kerry will save jobs by ending the unpatriotic practice of U.S. corporations moving offshore simply to avoid paying their fair share of our nation's tax burden. To create new manufacturing jobs Kerry will provide new tax breaks to manufacturers who produce goods and create jobs in the United States."[65]

There's more. Kerry has also proposed other "targeted tax cuts" for corporations—entities he so often criticizes as greedy—such as the Crane-Rangel-Hollings legislation, which would have provided reductions in income taxes for manufacturers that made their goods in the U.S.[66]

TAX UNTO OTHERS

When it comes to "taxes for the rich," however, Kerry isn't so willing to pony up his own money. In one campaign statement, the Massachusetts senator said this: "In my first hundred days in the White House, I will roll back George Bush's tax cut for the wealthiest."[67] But when it came to voluntarily paying higher income tax rates in his own state, Kerry was missing in action.

"[W]hen John Kerry had a chance last year to voluntarily pay an extra $687 in Massachusetts state income taxes, he went AWOL," wrote *Boston Herald* columnist and area talk radio host Howie Carr. "[H]ere in Massachusetts we have a provision on our state income-tax form that allows all concerned citizens to pay their taxes at a higher rate than is required by law. It's something you can volunteer to do. . . . It's a choice each state taxpayer must make on Line 22—whether to pay at the 5.35 percent rate, set by 2 million mean-spirited voters at the ballot box in 1998, or at the old Dukakis-era 5.85 percent rate. . . . [L]ast year [Kerry] reported $137,480 in total taxable income for 2002, which means that paying at the higher rate imposed by Gov. Dukakis, whom he served under, would have cost him an additional $687. . . . But when it came Sen. Kerry's turn to buy a round, he was . . . invisible. . . ."[68]

Carr said a call to the Kerry campaign revealed a candidate befuddled about the provision. "Michael Meehan returned it, telling me that indeed the senator did pay at the 5.35 percent rate. He appeared unfamiliar with the 5.85 percent option available on

Line 22. 'You're kidding,' he said. 'People can choose to pay higher taxes? How many people pay at the higher rate?'"[69]

Not Kerry—even though he wants American taxpayers to fork over more of *their* money.

FLIP-FLOPS: TAXES

Kerry has also flip-flopped on the issue of whether or not the middle class has actually been helped—or hurt—by the Bush tax cuts. In one breath he says Bush tax cuts have hurt the middle class; in another, he claims they have helped. "[T]he average American is actually paying more taxes than they were before George Bush," Kerry said during an interview on NBC.[70]

In his book, *A Call to Service*, Kerry writes, "With every passing day it's clearer that the administration's tax cuts for privileged Americans will represent a major redistribution of the tax burden from the top to the middle."[71]

Yet, a short while later, Kerry was asked about the effects on taxpayers if there were a return to Clinton-era taxes—taxes he supported with "yea" votes in the Senate. "[T]he fact is that going back to the Clinton tax cuts doesn't create another job; it puts a burden on current predicament of middle-class Americans. They lose their current revenue," he said during a Democratic presidential debate in New York.[72]

Kerry also has said he supported the child-care tax credit, but when it was time to put pen to paper, he backed away from it.

In May 2001, he said on the floor of the Senate, "I want to commend the chairman of Finance Committee, Senator Grassley, and the ranking Democrat, Senator Baucus, for their good faith efforts to craft a tax bill. . . . I have enormous respect for their hard work and the extent to which they each listened to members from both sides of the aisle. I am particularly grateful to see that the Finance Committee included a proposal advocated by myself . . . which would extend the child tax credit to perhaps as many as an additional 16 million children. The legislation's new child credit refundability provision amounts to nearly $70 billion in expanded relief for working families with children. That is truly an accomplishment."[73]

A child-care credit was included in President Bush's tax cuts, but Kerry voted a number of times to repeal those cuts and, in essence, the child-care cuts as well. In 2003, Kerry sponsored an amendment that would have rolled back the Bush tax cuts by $200 billion.[74] In 2001, Kerry—in one instance—voted to roll back the tax cuts by $448 billion over ten years.[75] In another case the same year, he voted to repeal the tax cuts by $100 billion.[76]

RECESSION FINGER-POINTING

Democrats have generally blamed George W. Bush for the economic recession that struck the nation in 2000, months before he took office in 2001. Kerry, for his part, has blamed Bush for the loss of millions of jobs in the U.S. since taking office—job losses he has not necessarily tied to the recession but certainly to the Bush administration.

"[W]e know what is wrong with George Bush," Kerry said stumping in New Hampshire. "He holds the national presidential record for job destruction—three million lost jobs in less than three years. We have the weakest economic growth in more than fifty years."[77]

He told the *Washington Post*, "The economy in this country is in the worst shape it's been in many, many years. It's the worst jobs record since Herbert Hoover was president. It is the worst growth record since World War II and the Bush administration policy is dead wrong. . . ."[78]

The fact that the economy is in recovery *under Bush* has hardly slowed down candidate Kerry. When forced to acknowledge the recovering economy, Kerry insists it is only benefiting wealthy

Republicans. While campaigning in Iowa on January 14, 2004, Kerry said, "Last weekend, the president of the United States gave a speech suggesting that his tax cuts have created an enormous economic recovery in America. Yes, it's a recovery if you're a Republican with a rich stock portfolio; it's a recovery for Wall Street and a 40 percent increase in the profit of corporations. . . . This is truly a Bush-league recovery."[79]

Yet analyses and research have shown the recession actually began in the waning months of Bill Clinton's final term. "The recession started in December 2000," says Victor Zarnowitz, a member of the Business Cycle Dating Committee of the Cambridge, Massachusetts-based National Bureau of Economic Research; the committee is responsible for officially charting the timing of America's business cycles.[80]

Curiously, Kerry has openly admitted Bush was not responsible for the recession of 2000. "Secondly, I think it would be unfair, almost silly for any of us to sit here and say it's all George Bush's fault. I—I'm not—I'm not saying that. Clearly there is a cyclical aspect to what's happening in the economy. And some of this began some time ago, and I think there was some anticipation of a change," Kerry told a CBS television audience.[81]

There was also a push by experts, pundits, and media—perhaps one even Kerry could not ignore—to credit the growth of the economy in the latter part of 2003 (revised U.S. gross domestic product figures showed the economy grew 8.2 percent in the third quarter—the strongest growth in twenty years) to the Bush tax cuts.[82]

"There was one other gift under the Christmas Tree this year: A robust economy," said a December 2003 editorial in Pennsylvania's *Lancaster New Era*. "It's a gift, courtesy of President Bush, whose tax cuts and general handling of the economy are widely credited with the strong upswing."[83]

"Critics can say what they want, but the Bush administration's tax cuts are stimulating the resurgent national and state economy, one of the biggest success stories of the year," said another editorial in the *Home News Tribune* of East Brunswick, New Jersey.[84]

Some Democrats even admitted the tax cuts were a good idea for the economy. In an op-ed for the *Wall Street Journal*, James J. Cramer wrote:

> I'm a Democrat. . . . But I'm also an objective financial commentator. With stocks at two-year highs and interest rates . . . near all-time lows, I can't help reach a different conclusion from Mr. Bush's critics: The economic policies pursued by this president have been a stunning empirical success. . . . The Bush economic policies have worked beyond what anyone could have hoped for. Or, to put it in parlance my party might understand, *This time it's not the economy stupid.*[85]

Kerry himself has admitted the economy began to see some stimulus benefits from Bush economic policies, including the tax cuts. "There's a huge amount of stimulus in our economy right now and we're beginning to see some of the impact of that," Kerry said in December 2003, well after both Bush tax cuts had been enacted by Congress.[86]

Perhaps Kerry didn't have a choice. Some of the nation's best economics thinkers were pronouncing the cuts a huge success and, more importantly, were producing the hard facts and data to back up their claims. Perhaps even more inconvenient for Kerry was the fact that economic and job growth figures began to seriously reverse their previous downward slides well before the official kickoff of the 2004 election cycle. By mid-March, the nation's unemployment rate had fallen to 5.7 percent, new jobless claims had hit post-Clinton lows, and the GDP had topped 4.1 percent for the final quarter of 2003. In March 2004, the economy added 308,000 jobs.[87] All of the data supported making the tax cuts permanent, though Kerry opposes that.

"Bush administration supply-siders who argued in favor of permanent tax incentives to grow the investment side of the economy are being proven exactly right. . . . The Bush combination of lower tax rates to ignite economic recovery at home and a determined policy to inflict punishment on our enemies abroad is almost exactly the same as Ronald Reagan's program two decades ago. In each case, peace and prosperity were achieved," *National Review* said in December 2003.[88]

The Bush economic strategy and, more importantly, its results, left Kerry and his supporters grasping at straws. His hopes of riding a message of a Bush administration economic failure into the White House in November may have all but vanished.

That hasn't kept him from trying. Kerry has even gone so far as to proclaim that Bush's economic policy was a "false god": "The Clinton administration founded its economic strategy on the four pillars: fiscal discipline, open trade, support for innovation, and investment in the knowledge and skills of the American people. The Bush administration has torn down those four pillars one by one and in their place erected a single pillar. This pillar is an idol, really, so fiercely and faithfully it is brought out for every occasion. On it the sum total of the president's fiscal and economic policies have been inscribed: namely, tax cuts for the wealthiest Americans. The idol is a false god."[89]

Kerry has also accused the Bush White House of having no coherent economic strategy, save for tax cuts. "[The Bush administration] has monomaniacally focused on the role of the wealthy in creating economic growth by inflexibly demanding lower taxes on high earners, big investors, and the inheritors of huge estates. If the Bush administration has any long-term economic strategy apart from tax cuts for this class, I haven't heard about it, and I've definitely been paying attention. . . . [L]ower- and middle-class families have become the forgotten majority and the passive pawns in the Bush administration's view of the economy," he wrote in his book, *A Call to Service.*[90]

ECONOMICS 101

But what would President Kerry's economic strategy be? According to the candidate, he suggests it will be a group effort: "I will hold economic policy summits once a week for the first six months of my administration, aimed at developing targeted strategies to create jobs in key regions and key industries."[91]

President Bush has economic advisors too. And there are questions about whether Kerry will make his "policy summits" public, as Kerry himself demanded Vice President Dick Cheney do, regarding the vice president's closed-door energy task force meetings.[92]

Regarding taxes, Kerry says he'll keep marriage penalty relief, the 10 percent bracket, and child-care credits—tying each into "the middle class," though all of those cuts were initiated by President Bush and passed by a Republican-controlled Congress.

"I don't believe that we should be raising taxes on the middle class. Specifically, I want to protect the increases in the child tax credit, the reduced marriage penalty, and the new 10 percent tax bracket that helps people save $350 on their first level of income," he said.[93]

The *Washington Post* summarized Kerry's plan: He will "repeal the Bush tax cuts for those making $200,000 or more a year, which would result in higher income tax rates and bigger tax bills on dividends and estates for those wage earners. . . . [W]ill oppose Bush's plan to make permanent the tax cuts enacted under his watch. . . . Kerry and congressional Democrats instead will press to make permanent only those tax cuts benefiting families with incomes of less than $200,000. This includes tax breaks for married couples and parents, as well as lower rates for all taxpayers."[94]

But what about other taxes that benefit all levels of taxpayers—not simply "the rich"? Kerry would keep some and eliminate some, such as the so-called "death tax" on estates. "Mr. Kerry would certainly not allow the estate tax to be canceled, and he would return the top tax rate, now 35 percent, to 39.1 percent, where it was in 2001," reported the *New York Times*.[95]

Kerry, playing the role of the stereotypical Democrat, also wants to increase spending on social programs. Yet, according to assessments, his plans to pay for those increases remain murky and, in the end, may actually involve tax increases, if for no other reason than money doesn't grow on trees: "Kerry's economic plan consists of higher federal spending and more tax credits, but no commitment that these measures be offset by higher taxes," said the *National Journal* in January 2004.[96] Generally speaking, Senator Kerry has said, as president, he would seek to raise taxes on people with incomes of $200,000 or more, while cutting taxes on everyone else. But this idea is not new; Kerry was preceded by one of the most famous of all recent Democratic tax-raisers, Bill Clinton. Stephan Moore of *Human Events* wrote:

This claim that "my tax plan only raises taxes on those with incomes over $200,000" has been proved false before. Remember? This was almost precisely Bill Clinton's campaign gambit that sounded so enticing and fooled so many voters in 1992. No sooner was Clinton sworn into office than he was tossing over the side of the ship of state his middle-class tax cut and instead raising taxes on millions of the non-rich who receive Social Security benefits or happen to drive a car, or use electricity for that matter (remember the infamous BTU tax?). When liberals say they only want to "tax the rich" what is sometimes lost in translation is that they define "rich" as anyone who actually has a job. . . .[97]

Kerry has also proposed a further tax cut for workers on the first $10,000 of income, but he's flip-flopped on that promise too. "[W]e should give every working American some tax relief now. I propose a payroll tax holiday on the first $10,000 of income. Every worker in America would immediately receive a $765 tax cut and every two-income family would get a cut of $1,530," he said during a speech in Cleveland in December 2002.[98]

And, during a Democratic presidential debate in January 2004, Kerry continued to talk up his payroll tax "holiday." Noting that millions of Americans don't pay income taxes as it is, "the only way to get them a benefit so they actually got some money back in their pocket and could pay their bills was to give them a refundable payroll tax credit on a one-year basis."[99]

Just two days after that statement, Kerry backpedaled on the issue, in an interview on CNBC:

> GLORIA BORGER: But you're also talking about providing workers with a one-year payroll tax holiday.
> KERRY: No, actually that was the alternative that I proposed to the Bush tax cut at the time when we were voting on it some time ago now.
> BORGER: Right.
> KERRY: That is not appropriate at this moment in time and I've not suggested it right now. . . .
> BORGER: And so now you don't want to do that?
> KERRY: Not at this moment in time. . . .[100]

If he were to remain serious about offering a "tax holiday," which doesn't at all seem certain now, Kerry claimed he wouldn't have to take the rebate funds from Social Security.[101] But he does say the federal government, compliments of American taxpayers, would have to come up with the money *somewhere*. "Unlike most so-called stimulus plans, a payroll tax holiday would help every working American. . . . Every working American would receive a tax break as soon as the IRS could mail the check. The plan would be paid for out of general revenues, so it wouldn't touch a dime slated for Medicare and Social Security," Kerry said in a December 2002 op-ed piece.[102]

The Bush economic plan differs substantially. According to White House officials and President Bush, cutting tax rates for *all* Americans has led to real growth in terms of gross domestic product. As long as GDP climbs, so too, does the government's tax rolls. So, in essence, Uncle Sam manages to collect more money based on current levels of taxation, but Kerry—as he has admitted—wants to actually *raise* taxes, be they on "the rich" or other classes. Republicans like Bush shun this approach because "the rich"—corporations, entrepreneurs, and various capital investors—*create* business ventures with their money, businesses which hire workers. Taxing them more, as Kerry and fellow liberals propose to do, reduces the amount of investment capital these higher wage earners have to spend on new businesses—endeavors which could create more jobs, more *taxpayers*, and, hence, more revenue for Washington, all under current Bush administration tax rates.

Also, Kerry's economic plans will rob Americans of incentive; people realize that, under Democrat Kerry's economic plans, the better they do, the more money a Kerry-led government will take from them in the form of taxes.

Case in point: In order to "pay" for the domestic programs he is advocating, Kerry proposes to take the money from the very "rich" who tend to create jobs. "[H]ere's what I do. Number one, I provide a four thousand dollar tuition tax credit. . . . I provide it for all four years. Secondly, I will provide an increase in the child-care credit, so parents can get afterschool programs to help their children be able to advance education. Thirdly, I provide a healthcare reduction of almost a thousand dollars per individual, which goes mostly to the middle class and will help businesses be more competitive. . . . And it's affordable within the money that I get back from rolling back George Bush's tax cut for the wealthiest Americans."[103]

But, of course, he can't sustain any of it because the entrepreneurs, the job creators, scale back their efforts either because they have less capital to create jobs or because they are less motivated since Tax Man Kerry is waiting to skim a substantial portion of their take.

HOORAY FOR TAXES!

Yet for all his bluster about cutting taxes for "the middle class" and lower wage earners, it's difficult to put any stock in Kerry. A year before the current campaign season began in earnest, the junior senator from Massachusetts said "no" to *any* new tax cuts: "I say no new tax cuts and that includes the new Bush tax cuts that are set up in what we passed a year ago. . . . The country can't afford it. . . . It doesn't pass muster," he said in January 2003.[104]

The campaign of early presidential candidate Senator Joseph Lieberman (D-Connecticut) at one time accused Kerry of stealing the senator's jobs plan. Lieberman spokeswoman Kristin Carvell hinted that Kerry was emulating her boss, who unveiled his plan for manufacturing in Salem, Massachusetts, on the campaign trail in 2003. "Glad we could save the Kerry campaign some hard work, but it will ultimately be a Lieberman administration that will lead to more jobs here at home for America's workers," she said, according to the Associated Press.[105]

Kerry's career in the Senate, despite his campaign rhetoric, has been a twenty-year period of support for raising taxes, as well as efforts expended trying to block any tax cuts—a feat noticed by his own constituents. In one instance, a Red Sox baseball fan "queried" Kerry on the subject. Joan Vennochi has the story:

> Fenway Park, end of the sixth inning, during a backs-to-the-wall playoff game: senator John F. Kerry gets up from his seat behind home plate, walks to the path that separates the elite from everyone else, and stands chatting with a well-connected Boston lawyer. Recognizing their junior senator, the Sox fans in the stands start to

murmur. In classically ornery Boston style, someone calls out: "You gonna raise our taxes, John?" The scattered laughs send Kerry scuttling back to his to-die-for vantage point during Boston's . . . showdown with Oakland.[106]

Kerry has even said it was necessary to forego tax cuts. In 1999, his office issued a press release explaining his position: "This amendment safeguards that we do not return to the misguided era of runaway deficit spending. These fiscal spending choices are never easy, but they are the right choices," Kerry said about his measure, which he claimed promoted "fiscal responsibility" by prohibiting "a return to deficit spending" to pay for any tax cuts in the 1999 budget. "This kind of fiscal discipline has built the foundation for these past six years of economic expansion and must continue if we are to keep our economy strong well into the next century. Without this important safeguard, the tax breaks of today may jeopardize the future of our national priorities, such as education, and health-care programs."[107]

Like other liberal Democrats, Kerry couched his opposition to tax cuts under the guise of fiscal responsibility. But in reality, his position was the same as it's always been regarding taxes: the more, the better.

TAX AND SPEND

Maybe Kerry can't help himself. Before he arrived in Washington, as an elected official for the state of Massachusetts, Kerry was a tax-and-spend liberal.

"Our administration will join other Northeastern and Midwestern governors in fighting for federal policies that promote private investment and help arrest the flight of people and capital from the Frostbelt to the Sunbelt," Kerry—a lieutenant governor candidate with gubernatorial candidate Michael Dukakis—said.

"We will join with governors from other industrial states to fight for continued federal support of . . . vital public commitments."[108]

The Dukakis-Kerry ticket also backed other big-spending plans. "We will organize a 'campaign for computer literacy.' . . . We will fight to increase state support for public higher education. . . . We will appoint a special assistant to the governor for Educational Affairs. . . . We will continue to oppose federal cutbacks in funding for community-based health and nutrition programs," said campaign literature from the pair.[109]

Would President Kerry truly support programs that evoke fiscal responsibility on the federal level, or would he continue to back programs and plans that would involve higher taxes and more federal control? Democrats have a history of the latter, and after all, if Kerry is anything he is a quintessential Democrat. Perhaps the best advice comes from *Human Events'* Stephan Moore: "When Kerry says he wants to be a fiscal conservative and cut taxes for working people, voters must remember the wise words of Ronald Reagan: Trust but verify. If Kerry fools us with his seductive rhetoric, just the way Clinton did 12 years ago, we should not say shame on him, we should say: shame on us."[110]

In other words, if Kerry is elected, Americans should hold on to their wallets.

3

THIRTY-YEARS WAR

Manipulating Vietnam for profit and power

B ETWEEN 1962 AND 1975, scores of men and women served in
the United States military during the Vietnam War. Not all went
to Southeast Asia, but in a very real sense all were subjected to
deployment there. In the words of many combat vets who served
tours in Vietnam, just putting on the uniform—especially as a volunteer—was a great sacrifice for the nation.

Included in the Vietnam-era group of military vets were
President George W. Bush and John Kerry. While each served dur-
ing the Vietnam War, only one—Kerry—served *in country*, the term
Vietnam vets gave to time spent in Vietnam itself.

The senator from Massachusetts volunteered for the U.S. Navy
in 1965 and, after graduating from Yale University in 1966, entered
the service as a junior officer. He eventually became commander
of two swift boats in the Mekong Delta in Vietnam, earning a Silver
Star, Bronze Star with "V" decoration, and three Purple Hearts for
wounds in battle.

Bush—also a graduate of Yale—alternatively served in the Air
National Guard during the latter portion of the Vietnam War. But
according to Kerry's presidential campaign, a young Lieutenant
George W. Bush only joined the National Guard to get out of "regular" active duty service overseas. In fact, Bush volunteered for

overseas duty; he was, however, turned down because he didn't have enough flight time as a combat pilot in the F-102 interceptor, which he flew for the Texas National Guard. Bush, the *Washington Post* reported, "tried to volunteer for overseas duty, asking a commander to put his name on the list for a 'Palace Alert' program, which dispatched qualified F-102 pilots in the Guard to Europe and the Far East, occasionally to Vietnam, on three- to six-month assignments. He was turned down on the spot. 'I did [ask]—and I was told, 'You're not going,' Bush said." He was told only pilots with "extensive" flying time—one thousand hours or better—would be sent overseas to Vietnam, and the future president didn't have that kind of time in the cockpit. Moreover, "the Air Force . . . was retiring the aging F-102s and had ordered all overseas F-102 units closed down as of June 30, 1970," the *Post* reported.[1] So unless he was trained on another aircraft—not likely, given the extent of his F-102 training and the time it would take to get up to speed on another aircraft—Bush wouldn't be ready to go to Vietnam in time.

Still, Bush's mission in the 111th Fighter Interceptor Squadron of the Texas Air Guard was an important one and, as it turns out, the equivalent of flying homeland security duty in 2004. The Convair F-102 "Delta Dagger," the United States' first all-weather, delta-winged jet interceptor, was first incorporated into the Air Force's Air Defense Command in 1956. It was designed to intercept incoming enemy aircraft—specifically Soviet Air Force nuclear bombers en route to the United States.

Kerry, attempting to portray President Bush's National Guard service as less honorable than other military service, insulted a large number of soldiers who served and are presently serving the country in the National Guard—a serious and foolish action for someone vying for the role of commander in chief. Moreover, Kerry's assumption that Bush's Guard service was unimportant compared to his own, or that Bush joined the Air Guard to get out of Vietnam or other important duty, is simply not true—a point confirmed by a former pilot who served with Bush in a 2004 letter to the editor of the *Washington Times*:

> In the Cold War, the air defense of the United States was borne primarily by the Air National Guard, by such people as Lt. Bush and me and a lot of others. Six of those with whom I served in those years never made their 30th birthdays because they died in crashes flying air-defense missions," wrote Col. William Campenni, U.S. Air Force/Air National Guard (Ret.), of Herndon, Virginia. While most of America was sleeping and Mr. Kerry was playing antiwar games with Hanoi Jane Fonda, we were answering 3 A.M. scrambles for who knows what inbound threat over the Canadian subarctic, the cold North Atlantic and the shark-filled Gulf of Mexico. We were the pathfinders in showing that the Guard and Reserves could become reliable members of the first team in the total force, so proudly evidenced today in Afghanistan and Iraq. . . . Lt. Bush was a kid whose congressman father encouraged him to serve in the Air National Guard. We served proudly in the Guard. Would that Mr. Kerry encourage his children and the children of his colleague senators and congressmen to serve now in the Guard.[2]

DISMISSING THOSE WHO SERVED

It's also noteworthy to mention Kerry has changed his mind on the importance of serving in Vietnam at all. In 1992, for instance, when Democrat Bill Clinton was running against incumbent President George H. W. Bush and receiving loads of criticism for dodging his Vietnam draft obligation—and then lying about it—Kerry defended Clinton, saying service during the war shouldn't matter.

From the Senate floor February 27, 1992, Kerry complained Vietnam had been "inserted into the campaign."[3]

"What saddens me most is that Democrats, above all those who shared the agonies of that generation, should now be re-fighting the many conflicts of Vietnam in order to win the current political conflict of a presidential primary. . . .We do not need to divide America over who served and how," he said.[4] Again, this time in October 1992, Kerry blasted the elder Bush for criticizing Clinton's draft dodging and war protesting: "Mr. President, you and I know that if support or opposition to the war were to become a litmus test for leadership, America would never have leaders or recover from the divisions created by that war."[5]

GOOD FOR THE GANDER

However, when he began his campaign for president, he changed his tone on the importance of debate regarding Vietnam service. Suddenly, Vietnam service should be deemed important for presidential platforms, and Kerry challenged Bush to a debate over the issue in February 2004. "As you well know, Vietnam was a very difficult and painful period in our nation's history, and the struggle for our veterans continues. So, it has been hard to believe that you would choose to reopen these wounds for your personal political gain. But, that is what you have chosen to do," Kerry wrote to the president in a letter.[6] While campaigning in Georgia at the same time, Kerry also issued this statement: "As [Republicans] did with John McCain in South Carolina in 2000 and as they did with Senator Max Cleland, they have again questioned my commitment to the defense of our country. . . . I'd like to know what it is Republicans who didn't serve in Vietnam have against those of us who did."[7]

Then again, the Bush campaign was not questioning Kerry's Vietnam service. Rather, as the Bush-Cheney campaign explained, it is Kerry's record on issues of defense and national security that was being criticized—issues which the Bush-Cheney campaign said it believes are fair game during a presidential election. If there was any questioning of military service, however, it could be said Kerry was questioning Bush's service, not to mention insulting hundreds of thousands of National Guardsmen and women. In published statements Kerry likened National Guard service to dodging the draft and opposing the war. "If people went to Canada, if people opposed the war, if people chose to be in the Guard, that's their choice, and I've never raised that in an issue," he said in one statement.[8] "I've never made any judgments about any choice somebody made about avoiding the draft, about going to Canada, going to jail, being a conscientious objector, going into the National Guard. Those are choices people make," he said in another statement.[9]

However, in 2003–2004, there were 8,866 National Guard troops serving in the Iraq war, with scores more being tapped for service in the overall war on terror.[10] As of mid-January 2004, about one-fifth of the 130,000 soldiers in Iraq—28,000—were members of the National Guard and Reserve.[11] In addition, in Afghanistan, Air National Guard and Reserve units comprised between 60 and 80 percent of Air Force personnel who liberated the country from its Taliban rulers.[12] Air National Guard members have participated in nearly every conflict fought by the United States since World War I.[13]

Clearly, Guard units—like the one George W. Bush volunteered for to become a fighter pilot—have played key roles in our nation's defense over the decades, a fact John Kerry would do well to acknowledge, lest he alienate a sizeable voting block of Guard vets more than he already has.

VIETNAM OPPORTUNISM

While many vets and non-vets on both sides of the political aisle don't feel comfortable criticizing aspects of Kerry's Vietnam service, some questions do arise as to Kerry's own actions to seemingly exploit his service for later political gain. One such exploitation involves the shooting of videos by Kerry showcasing some of his in country feats:

"Vietnam. The Mekong Delta. February 1969. . . . And Kerry just happens to have captured it all on film," writes Charles Sennott, for the *Boston Globe* in 1996. "The films have the grainy quality of home movies. In their blend of the posed and the unexpected, they reveal something indelible about the man who shot them—the tall, thin, handsome Naval officer seen striding through the reeds in flak jacket and helmet, holding aloft the captured B-40 rocket. The young man so unconscious of risk in the heat of battle, yet so focused on his future ambitions that he would reenact the moment for film. It is as if he had cast himself in the sequel to the experience of his hero, John F. Kennedy, on the PT-109. 'John was thinking Camelot when he shot that film, absolutely,' says Thomas Vallely, a fellow veteran and one of Kerry's closest political advisers and friends."[14]

Kerry has also brought along images of his Vietnam experience on the 2004 campaign trail. "The latest TV ad from Sen. John Kerry, (D-MA), uses Vietnam-era footage to showcase the White House hopeful's combat experience and opposition to President Bush's policies. The 60-second spot, which went on the air Tuesday, opens with clips of Vietnam," said a 2003 report on NationalJournal.com.[15]

Don Bendell, a Vietnam veteran who served as an officer in four Special Forces groups, is also a best-selling author, with over 1.5 million copies of his books in print worldwide. He chastised Kerry for his anti-war activities after returning from only a four-month stint in country in the June 2004 issue of *Soldier of Fortune* magazine. In an op-ed piece in which he labeled Kerry "Hanoi John . . . a phony, opportunistic hypocrite," Bendell went on to write:

> The old hurts are surfacing and the feelings of betrayal by fellow citizens, and their leader stirring them up, are breaking my heart again. How did we who served in Vietnam suddenly become cold-

blooded killers, torturers, and rapists, of the ilk of the Nazi SS or the Taliban? Most of us were American soldiers who grew up idolizing John Wayne, Roy Rogers, and all the other heroes. . . .[16]

Bendell went on to blast Kerry for his remarks before Congress in 1971, in a speech in which Kerry claimed he witnessed or heard about a plethora of tragedies allegedly committed by U.S. troops:

My children and grandchildren could read your words and think those horrendous things about me, Mr. Kerry. You are a bald-faced, unprincipled liar, and a disgrace, and you have dishonored me and all my fellow Vietnam veterans. Sure, there were a couple of bad apples, but I saw none, and I saw it all, and if I did, as an Army officer, it was my obligation to stop it, or at the very least report it. Why is there not a single record anywhere of you ever reporting any incidents like this or having the perpetrators arrested? The answer is simple. You are a liar.[17]

THE "ANTI-WAR" CANDIDATE

If Kerry's war experiences were heroic—he was awarded three Purple Heart medals for combat-related injuries, plus the Bronze and Silver Star medals for action under fire—his behavior upon returning from Vietnam was, in the eyes of many, far less so.

Kerry's overarching goal was to enter politics, and he wanted so badly to begin, he sought—and gained—permission from the Navy to be relieved of his duties early. President Bush also received an early discharge from the Texas Air National Guard so he could attend Harvard Business School, and Kerry supporters have made use of this discharge to further belittle Bush's service. (Kerry, interestingly enough, has done little to take supporters to task for their criticism of Bush, though both men were honorably discharged from service *before* their commitments were completed.) Like Bush,

Kerry was ready to get on with his life, but unlike Bush, Kerry was still preoccupied with Vietnam. As noted in Chapter One, in 1970 Kerry requested an early release so he could pursue anti-war politics. "I just said to the admiral: 'I've got to get out. I've got to go do what I came back here to do, which is, end this thing,'" Kerry recalled. Out six months early, Kerry ran for Congress.[18]

Perhaps Kerry was thinking political office would give him a more stable platform to launch his anti-war views, but as a returning vet in 1970, he was a political unknown and didn't get far. "He gave up on a three-month 1970 bid for Congress in Massachusetts' Third District, which at the time stretched from Newton to Fitchburg, when it became clear the Rev. Robert F. Drinan would instead get the Democratic Party nomination," the *Globe* reported.[19] There was a more popular spokesman for Kerry's viewpoints; Drinan was a liberal Democrat who was also dovish on the war. Drinan went on to defeat Phil Philbin, who had held the seat since Kerry was born. Kerry, meanwhile, was the first Vietnam vet with a dovish war platform, and he was convinced he could beat Drinan. He was wrong. Still, when Drinan won the caucus, Kerry worked hard for Drinan's victory.[20]

VIETNAM VETERANS AGAINST THE WAR

Kerry's ambitions were so prevalent they were also noticed—and resented—by some members of a group he adopted: Vietnam Veterans Against the War. Founded in 1967, the VVAW—which still operates today—demonstrated against the war and, according to information posted on its Web site, "exposed the shameful neglect of many disabled vets in VA Hospitals and helped draft legislation to improve educational benefits and create job programs."[21]

Some group members eventually came to view Kerry as a power-grabbing elitist, and it became "a source of internal friction within the antiwar movement," the *Globe* noted. "[Kerry's] patrician image was derided by others in the group, which was mostly composed of working-class veterans. [VVAW member Scott] Camil said Kerry showed up in ironed clothes, while most of the others were rumpled. Camil said a member had tried to reach Kerry by telephone and was told by someone, presumably a maid, that 'Master Kerry is not at home.' At the next meeting, someone hung a sign on Kerry's chair that said: 'Free the Kerry Maid.'" Other members of the group viewed him as an opportunist.[22]

His pampered life continued to show through in other aspects of his activism. For instance, during an organized veteran's protest at the National Mall in Washington D.C. in April 1971, most marchers camped out at the Mall, but not Kerry: "For days, the Nixon White House attempted to block them from using the Capitol grounds, and 100 were arrested. Kerry was a leader among this angry band, but also not quite part of the group. Most were more outwardly rebellious, with longer hair and much more willingness to confront the powers that be. While they stayed in tents, Kerry spent most nights at a Georgetown townhouse owned by the family of George Butler, an old college friend and fellow veteran," the *Globe* reported.[23]

Years later, when he began to campaign for the White House, Kerry would tell Americans he was at the Mall—not in Georgetown. "And I could not be more proud of the fact that when I came back from that war, having learned what I learned, that I led thousands of veterans to Washington. We camped on the Mall, underneath the Congress, underneath Richard Nixon's visibility. He tried to take us to the Supreme Court of the United States. He did. He tried to kick us off. And we stood our ground and said to him, 'Mr. President, you sent us 8,000 miles away to fight, die and sleep in the jungles of Vietnam. We've earned the right to sleep on this Mall and talk to our senators and congressmen.'"[24]

As a point of clarification, Kerry's implication here is that President Nixon, a Republican, was responsible for invading

Vietnam. But in reality, President John F. Kennedy, a Democrat, first ordered American-crewed helicopters to Vietnam in 1961, to support the Democratic forces of South Vietnam. The war effort was increased by Lyndon B. Johnson after he became president following JFK's assassination. Johnson got congressional authorization for the war, and it was during his tenure, in 1965, the first major U.S. combat troops were introduced (more than 125,000) in country and fighting seriously intensified. The Tet Offensive—January 31, 1968—was the high-water mark for U.S. troops (about 500,000). Serious anti-war protests had already begun (1967), and when Nixon took office (January 1969), he had inherited a massive problem. Rather than starting the invasion, it was Nixon who initiated a phased withdrawal of U.S. forces from Vietnam.[25]

FAMOUS APRIL 22, 1971, SPEECH

Kerry gave perhaps the most famous speech of his political life on April 22, 1971. Speaking before a packed Senate Foreign Relations Committee, surrounded by television cameras and veterans, Kerry called the war in Vietnam a "mistake." "With his thatch of dark hair swept across his brow, Kerry sat at a witness table and delivered the most famous speech of his life, the speech that defined him and made possible his political career. 'How do you ask a man to be the last man to die in Vietnam?' Kerry asked. 'How do you ask a man to be the last man to die for a mistake?'"[26]

During the speech, Kerry accused U.S. soldiers of wrongdoing, citing a litany of alleged events of cruelty and torture, blaming their actions on the country. Citing alleged testimony from veterans at an earlier gathering of vets in Detroit, known as the 1971 "Winter Soldier Investigation," Kerry said U.S. troops "ravaged" South Vietnam: "It is impossible to describe to you exactly what did happen in Detroit, the emotions in the room, the feelings of the men who were reliving their experiences in Vietnam, but they did. They relived the absolute horror of *what this country, in a sense, made them do.* They told stories that at times they had personally raped, cut off ears, cut off heads, taped wires from portable telephones to human genitals and turned up the power, cut off limbs, blown up bodies, randomly shot at civilians, razed villages in fashion reminiscent of Genghis Khan, shot cattle and dogs for fun, poisoned food stocks, and generally ravaged the countryside of South Vietnam in addition to the normal ravage of war, and the normal and very particular ravaging which is done by the applied bombing power of this country."[27]

In the weeks following his famous testimony, other veterans criticized Kerry's characterization of military behavior in Vietnam; in response, he called them "blind" and accused them of lying.

"Former Navy Lieut. John F. Kerry said last night his critics in a new pro-administration veterans group must have been 'blind' to what they saw in Vietnam and were in fact not telling the truth when they said they never took part in war crime activities in Southeast Asia. . . . 'These guys are kind of blind,' [Kerry] said, 'and it's a shame we have to square off but the overwhelming evidence points to the fact there were in fact war crimes committed,'" a Lowell, Massachusetts, paper reported in June 1971.[28]

"WINTER SOLDIER" INVESTIGATION

As more facts about the Winter Soldier Investigation began to stream out in spring and summer of 1971, it became increasingly clear some of the "facts" cited as evidence by Kerry in that famous speech were embellished at a minimum and outright fabricated at worst.

"I would like to talk, representing all those veterans, and say that several months ago in Detroit, we had an investigation at which over one hundred and fifty honorably discharged and many very highly decorated veterans testified to war crimes committed in Southeast Asia, not isolated incidents but crimes committed on a day-to-day basis with the full awareness of officers at all levels of

51

command," Kerry said during his Senate testimony.[29]

For one, it was later discovered the investigation was bank-rolled by actress Jane Fonda, perhaps the most infamous of all anti-war protestors—who would become notorious among veterans and other Americans for posing with a North Vietnamese anti-aircraft crew in Hanoi a year later, in 1972.

The Winter Soldier probe "was put together amid strains between many veterans and Jane Fonda and her adviser, Mark Lane. Because Fonda was paying the bills, she won the arguments, including the decision to move the hearings to Detroit, a site she considered somehow more authentic than Washington D.C.," said a May 2001 *Los Angeles Times* piece.

It was also discovered that the investigation itself was a sham. For instance, many of the so-called "witnesses" never served in Vietnam. A January 2004 account in *National Review* summed it up this way:

> [Kerry] said in essence that his fellow veterans had committed unparalleled war crimes in Vietnam as a matter of course, indeed, that it was American policy to commit such atrocities. *In fact, the entire Winter Soldiers Investigation was a lie. . . .* When the Naval Investigative Service attempted to interview the so-called witnesses, most refused to cooperate, even after assurances that they would not be questioned about atrocities they may have committed personally. Those that did cooperate never provided details of actual crimes to investigators. The NIS also discovered that some of the most grisly testimony was given by fake witnesses who had appropriated the names of real Vietnam veterans.[30]

In essence, for all his bluster, Kerry really didn't provide Congress with proof of his accusations—that abuse by U.S. soldiers in Vietnam was widespread and common.

Kerry had other opportunities to elaborate—for the record—

about the atrocities. Instead, he declined. A number of weeks after testifying on Capitol Hill about the alleged atrocities, Kerry was booked to appear on the *Dick Cavett Show*. He told Cavett he hadn't actually witnessed any of the atrocities he described to lawmakers, but he did say he himself had committed war crimes. "I personally didn't see personal atrocities in the sense I saw somebody cut a head off or something like that," Kerry said. "However, I did take part in free-fire zones, I did take part in harassment and interdiction fire, I did take part in search-and-destroy missions in which the houses of non-combatants were burned to the ground. And all of these acts, I find out later on, are contrary to the Hague and Geneva Conventions and the laws of warfare. So in that sense, anybody who took part in those, if you carry out the application of the Nuremberg Principles, is in fact guilty. But we are not trying to find war criminals. That is not our purpose. It never has been."[31] The facts show that Senator Kerry did, indeed, lie to the United States Congress—no proof ever came forward to light to show Kerry was telling the truth.

ANGRY VETERANS TURN ON KERRY

A number of returning Vietnam vets—including members of his own patrol boat crew—also were not pleased with Kerry's statements, his position on the war, and the things he was accusing them of doing.

Writes Douglas Brinkley in his book, *Tour of Duty*, "As could be expected, when Ted Peck, fully recovered from his combat injuries, living in San Francisco, and working as a salesman, turned on the TV and saw Kerry's face, his 'stomach turned.' Bill Zaladonis of PCF-44, who was living in Pittsburgh, couldn't believe his eyes when he saw Kerry on national television denouncing President Nixon. 'I just about fell out of my chair,' he recalled. . . . The loyal James Wasser of PCF-44 caught part of Kerry's testimony on the nightly news. 'I love John, but I was pissed,' Wasser recalled."[32] (PCF-44 was one of two boats Lt. John Kerry commanded while in Vietnam; the second was PCF-94.)

His own Navy shipmates believed he was the type to use the war for political opportunity. "[Michael] Bernique, the swift boat skipper who so admired Kerry's courage in battle, said his congressional testimony was 'pure unadulterated bull——. It's my personal feeling that had the political climate been different John could have returned as a right-wing Republican. But I think John is an opportunist and he saw an opportunity.'"[33]

Other vets were more pointed. Some thought Kerry was merely using the anti-war cause as a political launching pad. "The memory still rankles retired Colonel Jerry Morelock, a West Point graduate and 30-year Army veteran who now directs the Winston Churchill Memorial and Library at Westminster College in Fulton [Missouri]. 'When Kerry was testifying before Congress in 1971 about all the war crimes going on in Vietnam, I was in Vietnam,' recalled Morelock, who served as a field artillery battery commander. 'I guess I missed the briefing because I didn't see all these war crimes that were supposedly being committed on a routine basis.' 'I thought he was just stabbing the rest of us in the back,' Morelock adds, 'with all this B.S. about so-called war crimes. I thought he was using it just as a platform to launch a political career,'" he told the St. Louis Post-Dispatch.[34]

Other vets—especially those who served with him overseas—said Kerry, while still in country, never voiced opposition to the war. "To some veterans, including some of those who served alongside Kerry, [his complaints were] too much. They thought they had served honorably, and they had seen Kerry as a gung-ho skipper who led the charge and didn't voice such opposition on the battlefield."[35]

Says Jug Burkett, author of the epic Vietnam War history, Stolen Valor, in comments to NewsMax.com in February 2004, "Any Vietnam veteran who knows what Kerry did after he came home from Vietnam is definitely not a fan of John Kerry."[36]

FBI PROBE: UNDER SUSPICION

Right or wrong, a number of anti-war protesters were monitored in the late 1960s and early 1970s by the FBI, for possible activity that could have led to subversive action against the U.S. government. John Kerry was among those monitored by the FBI. The files, newly disclosed in March 2004, "reveal that the bureau's agents and informants closely followed Kerry, now the presumptive Democratic nominee for president, and other leaders of Vietnam Veterans Against the War, infiltrating meetings, recording speeches and filing reports to Director J. Edgar Hoover and President Richard Nixon," reported the *New York Times*.[37]

When the news broke, Kerry dismissed it as "ancient history" and acknowledged he knew the bureau had tracked him in 1971 until mid-1972, when he left the anti-war group he founded to run for Congress. But he admitted he didn't know the surveillance was as extensive as it turned out to be. According to the *Washington Post*, Kerry said that while "today's FBI isn't the FBI of J. Edgar Hoover," the knowledge of having been spied on for protest activity "makes you respect civil rights and the Constitution even more."[38]

Despite Kerry's indignation, the FBI had cause to monitor all anti-war activity because—while most was admittedly non-violent—some aspects of protesting the war did indeed lead to violence. Following the Tet Offensive in 1968, "American public opinion shifted dramatically, with fully half of the population opposed to escalation," wrote Mark Barringer, for *The Oxford Companion to American Military History*. "Dissent escalated to violence. In April protesters occupied the administration building at Columbia University; police used force to evict them. Raids on draft boards in Baltimore, Milwaukee, and Chicago soon followed, as activists smeared blood on records and shredded files. Offices and production facilities of Dow Chemical, manufacturers of napalm, were targeted for sabotage. The brutal clashes between police and peace activists at the August Democratic National Convention in Chicago typified the divided nature of American society and foreshadowed a continuing rise in domestic conflict."[39]

The anti-war movement "regained solidarity following several disturbing incidents," Barringer adds. "In February 1970 news of the My Lai massacre became public and ignited widespread outrage. In April President Nixon, who had previously committed to a planned withdrawal, announced that U.S. forces had entered Cambodia. Within minutes of the televised statement, protesters took to the streets with renewed focus. Then, on May 4, Ohio National Guardsmen fired on a group of student protesters at Kent State University, killing four and wounding sixteen. Death, previously distant, was now close at hand."[40]

Besides escalating violence, the FBI was also concerned about underground plots by anti-war activists to target political leaders. And, while Kerry himself was never implicated in such a plot, there is evidence he attended one meeting in 1971 where the possible assassination of U.S. senators was discussed. Kerry at first denied attending the November 1971 meeting of the Vietnam Veterans Against the War, which took place in Kansas City, Missouri. But after being contacted by newspapers about his attendance, which was verified by FBI surveillance records, his campaign changed its position, the *Kansas City Star* reported. "In a prepared statement . . . however, [Kerry presidential] campaign spokesman David Wade, traveling with the candidate in Idaho, said: 'John Kerry had no personal recollection of this meeting 33 years ago. John Kerry does recall the disagreements with elements of VVAW leadership . . . that led to his resignation. If there are valid FBI surveillance reports from credible sources that place some of those disagreements in Kansas City, we accept that historical footnote in the account of his work to end the difficult and divisive war.'"[41] The paper continued, reporting that details of the Kansas City meeting and internal VVAW correspondence clearly indicated Kerry was an active mem-

ber of the group, though mostly as a major draw on the lecture cir-
cuit of universities and civic groups in September 1971, just months
before the November meeting. "One FBI report suggests that
despite his resignation from leadership, Kerry was willing to work
for the group after November 1971. . . . None of the records show
any indication of what then-Florida organizer Scott Camil dubbed
a 'domestic Phoenix Program' he was promoting to the Vietnam
veterans group. Camil [said] that his idea—modeled after a U.S.
military effort to hollow out the leadership of Viet Cong sympa-
thizers in South Vietnam—would have made targets of pro-war
politicians to force the withdrawal of American troops from
Vietnam," the paper reported.[42]

Insight magazine further reported, "For years Kerry claimed
that he had resigned after a July 1971 meeting in St. Louis and had
not been present for the Kansas City meeting that was moved from
venue to venue to try to avoid FBI surveillance of the group's most
secret plans. The reason official confirmation that he did not leave
the group until after the Kansas City meeting is important, say spe-
cialists on radical activities during the Vietnam era, is that the FBI
documents confirm earlier reports by those present that Kerry participated in a closed-door discussion of a proposal to assassinate
seven U.S. senators who were special targets of Hanoi, with whose
agents selected leaders of VVAW had been meeting."[43]

"HANOI" JANE

One of the most anguished of all associations between Kerry and
his past was his connection to actress Jane Fonda. It is an association that still breeds anger and disgust among many, especially
Vietnam War vets.

David Thorne, brother of Kerry's first wife, Julia—also a Kerry
presidential campaign advisor, Yale buddy, and fellow Skull and
Bones Society member—briefly tried to put some distance between

his ex-brother-in-law and Fonda. He was asked on *Fox News'* *Hannity & Colmes* show in February 2004 point-blank if either of the two anti-war activists had any relationship. "No," Thorne replied. However, he immediately qualified his answer by adding Kerry and Fonda had "met each other, they knew each other a little bit." But Thorne still insisted: "John was never part of what Fonda did."[44]

Thorne, who also co-edited Kerry's anti-war creed, *The New Soldier*, was supported in his account by Kerry campaign spokeswoman Stephanie Cutter, who described Kerry and Fonda as mere acquaintances at the time. "What's important to understand here is two things: He met her before she went to Vietnam, and he did not approve of her very controversial trip," said Cutter.[45]

But the documented accounts of Kerry and Fonda appearing together at events, as well as her financial support of his anti-war veterans' group and its Winter Soldier Investigation, give the appearance of a much closer relationship.

For one, both appeared and spoke at a September 7, 1970, anti-war protest in Valley Forge, Pennsylvania. "Skinny-dippers frolicked in the Delaware River. Their long hair, ripped jeans, army-surplus-store canteens, and toy guns gave VVAW the look of a ragtag band of Haight-Ashbury refugees. . . . [A]ctress Jane Fonda, standing on the bed of a pickup truck, denounced the Nixon Administration as being a beehive for cold blooded killers. . . . But it was John Kerry who stole the day. . . . 'We are here because we above all others have earned the right to criticize the war on southeast Asia,' Kerry shouted into the microphone," writes David Brinkley in *Tour of Duty.*[46]

Brinkley also mentions that Fonda, enamored with Kerry's anti-war message and group, took both under her wing: "On the popular culture front, the winter soldier hearings also strengthened VVAW support. Jane Fonda . . . personally adopted the group as her leading cause," he writes.[47]

And later, Fonda would admiringly recall the actions of the future Massachusetts junior senator, as well as his words. "Some 150 sweat-soaked members of Vietnam Veterans Against the War ended their three-day trek at Valley Forge, Pa., on Sept. 7, 1970. Huddled around a flatbed truck, they listened to remarks by Jane Fonda and a reading from Donald Sutherland. Between the main acts came a floppy-haired former Navy lieutenant who had won a fistful of medals on the bloody canals of the Mekong Delta. Tall and self-assured, 27-year-old Yale graduate John Kerry read from a rumpled sheaf of papers in the ringing voice that had commanded men on gunships. Condemning the tactics and morality of the war, Kerry was 'brilliant,' Fonda says today," the *Chicago Tribune* reported in December 2003.[48]

In 1989, Kerry and Fonda again found themselves at the same event. "What a week it was in Aspen, Colo., where the sunshine pouring down is the golden color of money. . . . The house rented by Ethel Kennedy was packed with Kennedy cousins. Ted Kennedy Jr. was at that New Year's Eve party; so were Jane Fonda and Tom Hayden, with her daughter Vanessa Vadim, Sen. John Kerry and Julianne Phillips," *USA Today* reported.[49]

Recently, even Fonda has tried to put space between the two, criticizing anyone who attempts to tie Kerry with her own previous anti-war activities.

"The American people have had it with the big lie. Any attempts to link Kerry to me and make him look bad with that connection is completely false. We were at a rally for veterans at the same time. I spoke, Donald Sutherland spoke, John Kerry spoke at the end. I don't even think we shook hands. And they're also saying this organization, Vietnam Veterans Against the War, was a Communist organization. This was an organization of men who risked their lives in Vietnam, who consider themselves totally patriotic," she told CNN in February 2004. "And anyone who slams that organization, and slams Kerry for being part of it, is doing an injustice to veterans. How can you impugn, how can you even suggest that a Vietnam veteran like Kerry or any of them were—are not patriotic? He was a hero there. And this is the kind of big lie that's coming out of this current administration that I think the American people are sick of. And I don't think it's going to work."[50]

Does it really matter if Fonda's assessment is correct, or whether she and Kerry had a bigger relationship than they are willing to admit? Many Americans today may say it doesn't, but what if their efforts—together and separately—helped Vietnam win the war? Would that change Kerry's own anti-Vietnam rhetoric which, some claim, was used to good propaganda effect by North Vietnam?

Kerry, his campaign, and his supporters have often suggested Kerry's anti-war activities should be excused because of his military service. As he said at the Valley Forge anti-war rally, "We are here because we above all others have earned the right to criticize the war on Southeast Asia." But Kerry's war record—admirable and honorable by any measure—is not the issue, nor is his right to speak his mind in opposition to the war so much in question. Rather, what may be the most important aspect of his anti-war activities, and those of Fonda, is the manner in which it may have offered aid and comfort to America's enemy: North Vietnam.

According to former Marine Lieutenant Colonel Oliver North, now a *Fox News* correspondent and analyst, a 1985 memoir of General Vo Nguyen Giap, the North Vietnamese commander that eventually drove American forces from his country, said that if it weren't for organizations like Kerry's Vietnam Veterans Against the War, Hanoi would have surrendered to the U.S. "People are going to remember General Giap saying if it weren't for these guys, [Kerry's group], we would have lost," North told *Fox News'* Sean Hannity, during Hannity's nationally syndicated radio show in February 2004. "The Vietnam Veterans Against the War encouraged people to desert, encouraged people to mutiny—some used what they wrote to justify fragging officers," North—who earned two Purple Hearts in Vietnam—said. "John Kerry has blood of American soldiers on his hands."[51]

Giap wasn't alone in recognizing the power of winning the public relations battle—in his home country, in the U.S., and abroad. Arizona Republican Senator John McCain, a Navy fighter pilot who was shot down over Vietnam and spent six years as a prisoner of war in the brutal and infamous "Hanoi Hilton" prison, noted in a *U.S. News & World Report* article in 1973 his North Vietnamese guards would taunt him and other prisoners with anti-war rhetoric from Kerry and others. "[A]fter he was released from the Hanoi Hilton in 1973, McCain publicly complained that testimony by Kerry and others before J. William Fulbright's Senate Foreign Relations Committee was 'the most effective propaganda [my North Vietnamese captors] had to use against us,'" said one report, citing McCain's story. "All through this period," wrote McCain, his captors were "bombarding us with anti-war quotes from people in high places back in Washington." Again he claimed, "This was the most effective propaganda they had to use against us."[52]

Later, McCain biographer Paul Alexander chronicled the Arizona Republican's angst for many years towards Kerry, during their early years in the Senate together. "For many years McCain held Kerry's actions against him because, while McCain was a POW in the Hanoi Hilton, Kerry was organizing veterans back home in the U.S. to protest the war," Alexander wrote in McCain's 2002 book, *Man of the People: The Life of John McCain*. Alexander says the two Vietnam veterans finally reconciled in the early 1990s after having "a long—and at times emotional—conversation about Vietnam" during a mutual trip to Kuwait.[53]

Though Kerry is trying to pass himself off as a war hero—he did volunteer, he did serve in combat, and he was wounded in action, to be sure—what he did when he returned was more than just dishonor his fellow soldiers, sailors, and airmen, many of whom were still fighting and dying in Vietnam (or, in the case of

POWs, fighting to survive captivity). It was a despicable and opportunistic betrayal of America at a vulnerable time when the nation was at war with an elusive enemy and, some say because of the actions of people like John Kerry, nearly at war with itself.

4

INTERNATIONALIST
MAN OF MYSTERY

Kerry's very foreign policy: Let the UN do it!

PERHAPS THE BEST WAY to describe John Kerry's foreign policy is this: let the United Nations, *not* the United States, handle it. If elected, Kerry says he'll make a trip to the United Nations before the end of his first hundred days in office. It is often these first days that define a presidency or, at a minimum, a president's priorities. So it is in that vein Americans should view Kerry's trip. At a time when the U.S. is engaged in a global war to eradicate terrorism, a prospective commander in chief says it is vitally important for him to subjugate Americans to the whims of an international body comprised of nations which may or may not have an interest in seeing the U.S. succeed. "[I]n the first hundred days in office, I will go to the United Nations—I will go in the first weeks—and I will travel to our traditional allies to affirm that the United States of America has rejoined the community of nations," Kerry told the Council on Foreign Relations in a December 2003 speech.[1]

Kerry, in criticizing President Bush's Iraq strategy in April 2004, defined that statement himself. Responding to Bush's April 13, 2004, prime-time news conference, Kerry said the president "made it clear that he intends to stubbornly cling to the same policy that has led to a greater risk to American troops and a steadily higher cost to the American taxpayer. We need to set a new course in Iraq. We need to internationalize the effort and put an end to the American occupation. We need to open up the reconstruction of Iraq to other countries."[2] Though Bush explained that "other nations and international institutions are stepping up to their responsibilities in building a free and secure Iraq," Kerry went further in his insistence that the effort begun by American willpower to confront evil be handed over to inter-national interests. "We need a real transfer of political power to the [United Nations]," Kerry said.[3]

Kerry's vision of a "bold" diplomatic and foreign policy strategy for the present and future has never been Amerocentric—that is to say, he has too often failed to quickly acknowledge threats to *our* country, and he does not consider it a natural right for the U.S., as the most powerful and free nation on earth, to relish its role as guarantor of those rights for other nations too weak to secure them. In the past, he has even had trouble identifying terrorists for who and what they are. "One person's terrorist is someone else's freedom fighter," he said at a hearing on the updated British-American extradition treaty in 1985.[4]

TERRORISM BUILD-UP

There had been a number of terrorist attacks on American assets prior to September 11, but those attacks failed to galvanize the Clinton administration or the nation itself. Post 9/11, terrorism became the number one foreign policy and homeland security priority and will likely remain so for the foreseeable future. For his part, President Bush identified the threat shortly after his inauguration in January 2001, and in the spring began pressing his newly minted administration—no members of which were in place yet—to begin devising a more aggressive strategy to deal with international terrorist threats, and specifically Osama bin Laden's al Qaeda group. Said former counterterrorism chief Richard Clarke: "President Bush told us in March to stop swatting at flies and just solve this problem, then that was the strategic direction that changed the NSPD (National Security Presidential Directive) from one of rollback to one of elimination."[5] In fact, dealing with the threat of terrorism and bin Laden was Bush's *first* presidential directive to his staff.

In the years leading up to those attacks, there were ample warning signs militant Islamic factions increasingly targeted U.S. interests. For some, the threat began in earnest on November 4, 1979—during President Jimmy Carter's term—when Muslim extremist students overran the U.S. Embassy in Iran, keeping fifty-two Americans hostage for 444 days. In April 1980, President Carter ordered a rescue mission, but it failed when a number of the rescue helicopters crashed in the Iranian desert. The Carter administration continued to negotiate for the release of the hostages, but to no avail; they were finally released minutes after President Ronald Reagan's inauguration in January 1981.

Here's a brief description of other attacks on U.S. forces and interests by Muslim extremists:

- In 1982, the U.S. Embassy in Beirut, Lebanon, was bombed; a year later, after President Reagan had sent in U.S. Marines, their barracks were bombed, killing more than two hundred Marines; the U.S. eventually withdrew.

- In 1985, the *Achille Lauro*, an Italian cruise ship, was seized, and an American passenger, Leon Klinghoffer, was murdered and thrown overboard.

- In April 1986, a nightclub frequented by U.S. military personnel in West Berlin, West Germany, was bombed by Muslims from the Libyan Embassy in East Berlin.

- In December 1988, Libyan extremists blew up Pan Am Flight 103 over Lockerbie, Scotland.

- In December 1992, Yemenese terrorists targeted U.S. Marines in two separate bombing attempts.

- In February 1993, the World Trade Center was attacked the first time when a truck bomb detonated in the underground parking area of the twin towers, killing six people and injuring hundreds more.

- In October 1993, eighteen U.S. Army Rangers were killed in a bloody battle with Muslim militia extremists in Somalia; eventually the U.S. withdrew.

- In November 1995, a car bomb detonated in Saudi Arabia, killing five Americans and wounding thirty more.

- On June 25, 1996, extremists detonated a truck bomb in front of two Khobar Towers, a U.S. Air Force housing complex in Saudi Arabia, killing nineteen U.S. servicemen.

- In 1998, U.S. embassies in the East African countries of Kenya and Tanzania were bombed, killing 258 and wounding 5,000.

- In October 2000, the U.S.S. *Cole* was attacked while at port in Yemen, killing seventeen Navy seaman.

- The World Trade Center was destroyed, the Pentagon was attacked, and another plane crashed in Pennsylvania in a simultaneous terrorist attack on September 11, 2001, killing nearly 3,000.

Where was John Kerry on each of these incidents? How did he propose to respond to these threats to American security, both overseas and at home?

For one—and despite two declarations of war against the U.S. by Osama bin Laden—Kerry questioned the growth of the intelligence community. "Now that the [cold war] struggle is over, why is it that our vast intelligence apparatus continues to grow. . . ?" he asked in support of the same earlier contention by colleague Senator Patrick Moynihan (D-New York) on the Senate floor in May 1997.[6]

In 1997, Kerry wrote a book on transnational crime, scarcely mentioning terrorism and never mentioning bin Laden, not even once. In the same book, he referenced only once the ruling Taliban government of Afghanistan, known by then to be a harbor for bin Laden and the terrorist training camps he operated. "In the autumn of 1996, Taliban fighters . . . called for a return to Islamic purity and a repudiation of opium trafficking. But Western intelligence analysts immediately detected evidence that the public statements were a sham to mask continued [drug] smuggling. . . ."[7]

A book reviewer for the *Cleveland Plain Dealer* wrote that Kerry's book lacked "any new ideas" regarding the fight against terrorism. "With a laundry list of examples to make his point—the New York World Trade Center bombing, the bombing of the federal building in Oklahoma, the nerve gas attack on the Japanese subway—Kerry posits that terrorists will increasingly force society to bargain away its freedoms. . . . Kerry will probably receive some criticism for his book's failure to advance any new ideas for dealing with international crime," wrote Phillip Morris. "Other than his declaration that nations must work more closely together to identify and apprehend criminals and their assets, Kerry seems to be lacking for solutions to the criminal scourge he so skillfully documents."[8]

Even the liberal magazine *The New Republic* recognized that Kerry's recipe for handling the war on terror was flawed. "Kerry must be assuming no one will go back and actually read his [1997] manifesto [*The New War*], because his description of it is awfully selective," wrote Michael Crowley in February 2004. "Yes, Kerry briefly considered the possibility of a terrorist catastrophe on American soil. But *The New War* was almost entirely focused on the threat of global crime—not terrorism. If the future Kerry predicted really had arrived, we'd currently be locked in a vicious cyberwar with CD-pirating Japanese yakuza, Chinese kidney-traders, and

Italian mobsters—not hunting Islamic fundamentalists potentially armed with weapons of mass destruction." Crowley went on to say few had predicted 9/11 or that Islamic fundamentalism would be the newest threat to U.S. security following the cold war. But, he argued, "the ways in which *The New War* missed the mark are nevertheless revealing. They show the extent to which Kerry was influenced by the criminal investigations of his early Senate career, his preference for viewing post-cold-war security more as a matter for law enforcement than the military, and his tendency to describe problems *ad nauseam* without offering a clear and bold course of action."[9]

Conversely, President Bush has forged an alliance with multiple nations around the world who have committed to assisting the U.S. in combating the terrorist threat. In addition, Bush has tied up terrorist financial resources and assets, as well as located and either arrested or killed known terrorists and their allies. Bush has also pledged to find terrorists wherever they hide, no matter where.[10]

These are all successful plans of action that presidential candidate Kerry now criticizes, though at one time he recommended and endorsed the very same course.

Immediately following the African embassy bombings in 1998, Kerry-the-politician appeared angry and decisive: "Those who strike out against us with terror have to understand we will pursue them and do everything in our power to protect American citizens and interests," he said.[11] But he voiced concern over threats to punish Iraq using military force a few weeks later, when Baghdad ejected United Nations' weapons inspectors—using the African embassy attacks as cover. "And now, given what's happened in Kenya and Tanzania, we have to do that in a climate where the United States may have to even ask itself whether we're prepared to be a country that's perceived as just willing to drop some bombs on Muslim nations without the support of other people in the world," he said during a joint hearing between the Senate Armed Services and Foreign Policy Committees.[12]

Continuing in the meek vein, Kerry has also suggested the U.S. could not—and should not—go it alone against the global terrorist threat. He told CNN in 1999, in response to a question about whether the Clinton administration was doing enough to deal with worldwide terrorism: "They are doing a huge amount at this point. I mean, could we all do more? Probably we could. But the fact is there are certain limitations at this point in time. I mean, one of the problems is, for instance, Russia, and the capacity to get full cooperation there. We've had difficult relations with the Chinese. We are also seeking better cooperation there. So we are working with very great international difficulties and constraints. . . ."[13]

Leading observers to question whether the senator really understands the scope of the problem and the threat to American security, even now, after over ten years of attacks on U.S. interests and soil, Kerry says the terrorist threat is *exaggerated*. NBC News' Tom Brokaw, in a Democratic presidential candidate debate in Greenville, South Carolina, in January 2004—a month before the Madrid bombings and not even three years since 9/11—asked Kerry whether he believed the terrorist threat was being inflated by the Bush administration, as the Europeans have suggested, or whether the White House was correct in stating the threat is high and in dire need of attention. Kerry replied, "I think it's somewhere in between. I think that there has been an exaggeration and there has been a refocusing. . . . I will renew our alliances. I will rejoin the community of nations. I will build the kind of cooperative effort that we need in order to be able to win. . . . And I think this administration's arrogant and ideological policy is taking America down a more dangerous path. I will make America safer than they are. . . ."[14] Since this statement, there have been a number of other terrorist bombings worldwide; the deadly attack on train stations in Madrid killed 190 people and left some 1,200 others wounded.

Though he promises to make the nation safer, some familiar with his congressional voting record might question how he intends to fulfill his promise. Besides voting consistently to curb the U.S. military's budget, Kerry has also voted to cut the amount of money for U.S. federal law enforcement and intelligence agencies tasked with tracking threats and helping to win the terror war:[15]

- After the World Trade Center bombing in 1993, Kerry proposed a $45 billion cut in defense and intelligence spending.

- In 1994 Kerry proposed cutting $1 billion from intelligence spending and freezing the budget at that level through 1998.

- In 1995 following an attack on the Saudi National Guard barracks, Kerry proposed cutting $1.5 billion in intelligence spending over five years.

- Kerry wanted to cut $4.8 billion from defense in 1999.

- After the U.S.S. *Cole* bombing in 2000, he sought a reduction in defense spending by $10 billion.

- Following 9/11, Kerry sought $10 billion less in defense spending.

COPS AND COURTHOUSES:
KERRY'S WAR ON TERRORISTS

President Bush has placed intelligence gathering and military force first and foremost—and on a near-equal footing—in fighting the war on terror. In fact, some analysts have even speculated the terror war is, in reality, World War III.[16] But Kerry has different ideas about what should be made priorities in the terror war. (Note: The military isn't top on Kerry's list, which should come as no big surprise as the next chapter proves.)

In comments to the Senate Banking, Housing, and Urban Affairs Committee in September 2001—just two weeks after 9/11—Kerry suggested sharing financial information was key. "[I]f you are going to be serious about fighting a war on terrorism—and we should be, obviously, and must be—the first order of priority is to implement an extraordinary diplomatic effort to raise the international standards of accountability and transparency and exchange of information."[17]

While Kerry says he believes intelligence is important, he also believes it is *more so* than direct intervention and action. "[T]he most important weapon in this war . . . is not a direct military weapon; it's intelligence and intelligence gathering," he told CNBC in May 2002—hinting further the U.S. should not be waging the war alone. "And there are a whole series of things that we could begin to do with respect to our relationship with countries, our foreign policy that would begin to change our capacity to fight this war."[18]

In fact, Kerry suggested the military shouldn't be used much at all—perhaps as a last resort. The terror war "is much more an intelligence and law enforcement effort," he said in May 2002. "Soldiers are then used in key moments once the intelligence is attained."[19] Adds the *Boston Phoenix*, Kerry "has been content to define the war on terrorism as a law-enforcement and intelligence effort."[20]

The Massachusetts senator has even suggested the war isn't a war at all. "[W]hat I think all of us need to focus on is the fact that the rhetoric of this war is overblown in some ways and not focused properly in others. This is not a war as we have known it. This is not a war in which there's a front-line or the troops are going out every day on patrol. This is fundamentally an intelligence operation and [a] law enforcement operation and a diplomatic operation. . . ."[21]

His stance hasn't changed two years later, either. In a *New York Times* interview on March 6, 2004, Kerry said, "the final victory in the war on terror depends on a victory in the war of ideas, much more than the war on the battlefield. The war—not the war, I don't want to use that terminology. The engagement of economies, the economic transformation, the transformation to modernity of a whole bunch of countries that have been avoiding the future. And that future's coming at us like it or not, in the context of terror, and in the context of failed states, and dysfunctional economies, and all that goes with that. . . ."[22]

Through eight years of the Clinton administration—which Kerry praised as "doing a huge amount" in the fight against terrorism[23]—little effective military action was employed against the terrorist threat, even though the World Trade Center bombing in 1993, the attacks on U.S. military bases in Saudi Arabia, and the bombing of the U.S.S. *Cole* all happened on Clinton's watch. What action *was* employed often occurred when turmoil struck the administration, such as when former White House intern Monica Lewinsky, with whom Clinton admitted sexual contact, was scheduled to testify before a grand jury, or immediately prior to the House of Representatives' moves to impeach him—e.g., lobbing million-dollar cruise missiles at tents in Afghanistan and at a baby formula factory in the Sudan.

In fact, during Clinton's tenure, terrorist attacks against the U.S. grew exponentially. Transversely, President Bush employed primarily direct military action against known terrorist forces, and subsequently attacks against U.S. assets at home and abroad have largely diminished. According to the State Department's 2002 global terrorism report, "international terrorists conducted 199 attacks in 2002," a significant drop (44 percent) from the 355 attacks re-corded during 2001. Also, "the number of anti-U.S. attacks was 77, down 65 percent from the previous year's total of 219."[24]

Yet Kerry remains wedded to the failed terrorism policies of past eras. He wants to approach the war on terror as though it's a law enforcement problem, not plainly a battle for freedom, liberty, and security the world over. He wants to remain "engaged" in the Middle East, though every administration since the 1950s has tried to bring peace and stability to the region. And he believes any effort by the United States, the world's sole remaining superpower, should be approved by the "international community."

"The war on terror is less—it is occasionally military, and it will be, and it will continue to be for a long time," Kerry said during the Democratic presidential debate in Greenville, South Carolina. "But it's primarily an intelligence and law enforcement operation that requires cooperation around the world—the very thing this administration is worst at."[25]

Even Kerry's own foreign policy advisor has praised Bush's terror war strategy. "If there's one thing Americans are willing to credit President Bush with, it's that he's willing to confront our enemies and destroy them," Will Marshall, president of the Progressive Policy Institute, said in May 2003. And he discounted the notion put forth by Kerry and other Democrats that Bush's invasion of Iraq in March 2003 somehow took the initiative away from other aspects of the war on terror. "[Democrats have] an uphill fight . . . in asserting that the Iraq war in some way put the fight against terrorism on the back burner. . . . We captured a number of high-ranking al Qaeda figures during the war. If anything, the war shed more light on the incestuous relations of various Middle Eastern terror groups," admitted Marshall.[26]

KERRY'S REVOLVING DOOR POLICY ON IRAQ

Regarding the U.S.-led invasion of Iraq, Kerry has flip-flopped on his position several times. His opinion has ranged from believing Iraq, under Saddam Hussein, was a hotbed of terrorism, to believing the Iraq invasion took the administration's focus dangerously away from the terror war.

In 1998, Kerry said in a press conference, "Saddam Hussein has already used these weapons and has made it clear that he has the intent to continue to try, by virtue of his duplicity and secrecy, to continue to do so. That is a threat to the stability of the Middle

East. It is a threat with respect to the potential of terrorist activities on a global basis. It is a threat even to regions near but not exactly in the Middle East."[27]

But after the war on terror began and once he moved closer to his presidential candidacy, Kerry downplayed the importance of any Iraqi terrorist connection, if not Saddam himself. "I believe the capture of Saddam Hussein is helpful and it's a great moment. But it's a moment," he said in December 2003. "And it is not the central part of the war on terror. We need a president that understands the real war on terror is not Iraq."[28]

But the very next day, in response to a statement on the unimportance of the status of Iraq in the global war on terror made by Democratic presidential rival Howard Dean, Kerry switched sides again: "Iraq may not be the war on terror itself, but it is critical to the outcome of the war on terror. And therefore any advance in Iraq is an advance forward in that. And I disagree with the governor [Howard Dean]."[29]

A few weeks later, Kerry—during a Democratic debate in Iowa—changed his stance once again by accusing the Bush administration of using Iraq and Saddam's capture to distract the country from the terror war. "Saddam Hussein was way down the list, with respect to the targets, even on the Pentagon's own list of targets. And what they did was supplant Iraq for the real war on terror, which is Osama bin Laden, al Qaeda, and terror across the world," Kerry said.[30]

Not that much of this matters for Kerry should he become president, because the senator believes the U.S. should relegate all authority and action in Iraq to the United Nations. According to his campaign Web site, Kerry "believes that we must obtain a new Security Council resolution to give the United Nations authority in the rebuilding of Iraq and the development of its new constitution and government." He also says as president he would "work to expand participation and share responsibility with other countries in the military operations in Iraq," though the Bush administration has already built a coalition of dozens of nations which contributed troops and assistance to rebuilding Iraq.[31]

Even though the men and women of the United States military took the biggest risks, bore the brunt of the invasion, and took on the most casualties by toppling—then capturing—Saddam Hussein, Kerry believes the "international community" should ultimately decide the fate of Iraq's former dictator. Why? Because if the U.S. does it alone, he doesn't think it would be "fair." Says his campaign Web site, "John Kerry believes that a mixed tribunal, in which international judges, prosecutors, and investigators work alongside Iraqis, would meet the needs of the Iraqi people as well as that of the United States and the international community for a process that is valid and fair."[32]

INTERNATIONAL MAN

Kerry has, at times, voiced what may sound like an "America-first" foreign policy. For example, he has spoken confidently regarding North Korea's nuclear weapons program, insisting the U.S. won't allow Pyongyang to create, then proliferate, nuclear weapons or nuclear weapons materials. "I'd make it very clear I'm prepared to do whatever's necessary to not have nuclear weapons," he told the *New York Times*. "Make no mistake, and this is very important: North Korea should never doubt the resolve of the United States to be serious about proliferation."[33]

However, as a presidential candidate, Kerry suggests that a take-action approach to terrorism is bad foreign policy.

"The line of attack comes naturally. Throughout his nearly 20 years in the Senate, the Massachusetts Democrat has expressed a deep commitment to negotiation and international institutions as a way to advance U.S. interests, according to interviews with the candidate and his aides and a review of his speeches, floor statements and votes," says Glenn Kessler of the *Washington Post*.[34] During his career, he pushed for dialogue and engagement with the Sandinistas in Nicaragua. He pushed the same approach in communist Vietnam, as well as with the Muslim extremists in Iran. During the 1990–91 Gulf War, he criticized President George H. W. Bush for assembling a coalition to eject Iraqi forces that had invaded neighboring Kuwait. And, says Kessler, Kerry "has criticized the incumbent president for bungling the war in Iraq by failing to enlist the United Nations and key allies in the enterprise."[35]

Such positions fit well with Kerry. He says his father—a longtime diplomat with the State Department—taught him "the benefit of learning how to look at other countries and their problems and their hopes and challenges through their eyes, to a certain degree, at least in trying to understand them." According to the senator, "We don't always do that that well. We often tend to see other people in the context of our history, our own hopes, our own aspirations."[36]

That pained logic could explain why, in April 2004, Kerry defended a Muslim extremist in Iraq who was responsible for insurgents killing scores of American troops. According to reports, Kerry said a newspaper owned by Moqtada al-Sadr, a radical Shiite cleric who U.S. officials said was responsible for an insurgency that killed scores of American soldiers, was a "legitimate voice" in the Arab nation. Kerry, in an interview with National Public Radio, said of al-Sadr's newspaper, which was shut down in March 2004 after it urged violence against U.S. troops, "They shut a newspaper that belongs to a legitimate voice in Iraq." He then quickly corrected himself, saying, "Well, let me . . . change the term legitimate. It belongs to a voice—because he has clearly taken on a far more radical tone in recent days and aligned himself with both Hamas and Hezbollah, which is a sort of terrorist alignment."[37] *Sort of?* Both Hamas and Hezbollah are well-documented terrorist organizations.

Kerry has been a member of the Senate Foreign Relations Committee since he first won office in 1984. As the *Washington*

Post notes, Kerry has more foreign policy experience than any candidate trying to unseat an incumbent president since Richard Nixon in 1969. "Kerry, however, never headed the committee and generally focused on somewhat eclectic issues, such as pressing for normalizing relations with Vietnam or cracking down on globally organized crime," Kessler wrote. "Kerry's aides cannot recall whether he ever sketched out a broad foreign policy vision before he sought the presidency. Indeed, many of Kerry's speeches during his Senate years were lengthy and subtle, reflecting an understanding of complex issues but also a tendency to sketch so many shades of gray that the reasoning for his position became opaque."[38]

Some pundits believe Kerry, in anticipation of a presidential run, has—in recent years—tried to toughen his foreign policy persona, transforming it from "International Man" into something more Amerocentric. But it may not have worked; his sentimentalities likely continue to reside in the anti-Vietnam War era of his life. "My sense is his heart is in the anti-Vietnam, '70s-'80s left," says Robert Kagan, senior associate at the Carnegie Endowment for International Peace.[39]

Overall, Kerry has adopted a "blame America first" attitude, implying the U.S. is the rogue nation that has been shunned by the "community of nations" and, hence, should beg permission to "rejoin." Kerry wants to rely on foreign bodies to manage U.S. foreign policy, and the Massachusetts senator has expressed support for global treaties—which are bad for American businesses and commerce and threaten America's ability to defend itself—and for international courts of law that have a history of superseding the U.S. Constitution.[40]

PURE PARTISANSHIP

Americans expect their politicians to be loyal party members in virtually all manner of politics. The exception is during times of war or national emergency; then, most people expect lawmakers to drop the partisanship and band together to do what's right and necessary to defend the nation. But President Clinton made that expectation difficult because he repeatedly ordered military operations to distract attention away from his scandals, and millions of Americans understood that. Needless to say, they also understood, then, when Republicans jumped on Clinton during those times of manufactured national crisis; the GOP did not necessarily bash Clinton over the use of American military power, but rather the timing of it.

Despite the genesis for the scandal-inspired attacks, Kerry still chastised GOP colleagues for criticizing Clinton during those times, but he (1) never publicly questioned why Clinton ordered such military strikes during times of personal crisis; even worse, (2) has since broken his own vow not to condemn President Bush during (and over) the current terror war, especially in the absence of any personal scandals allegedly committed by Bush. In short, Kerry continues to put partisanship over the nation's foreign policy priorities.

Immediately after the U.S. launched its invasion of Iraq in March 2003, Kerry pledged to hold his criticism of Bush. "You know, we're beyond that now. We have to come together as a country to get this done and heal the wounds," he said. "There will be plenty of time here to be critical about how we arrived here."[41] But he broke his pledge just weeks later, declaring, "What we need now is not just a regime change in Saddam Hussein and Iraq, but we need a regime change in the United States."[42]

But consider his tone back in 1998, when Kerry blasted Republicans for criticizing Bill Clinton's China policies on the eve of the president's visit to Beijing. "It isn't just horrendous, it's dangerous; it's damaging. It diminishes the ability of the president to go with the sense that he's got a clear playing field," Kerry said.[43] And during Clinton's four-day bombing campaign against

Saddam Hussein in 1998—as the House was beginning impeach-ment proceedings—Kerry defended the president: "I believe that everybody who has been involved with the issue of Iraq under-stands that a day of reckoning has been a long time coming for Saddam Hussein. . . . This is not contrived, and it has nothing to do with impeachment."[44]

But in January 1991, after voting against a resolution authoriz-ing President George H. W. Bush to use military force to oust Saddam Hussein's army from Kuwait, Kerry said no one should "draw the line" between parties or the White House and Congress. "In an interview last week, [Kerry] said that it would be 'a mistake for anyone to draw the line' too sharply between the administration and Congress or between Democrats and Republicans on the gulf. 'It's the same policy, applied differently. Both seek the same goal and both would approve the use of force,' Kerry said."[45] In reality, those who know his political modus operandi know he would never have sought nor authorized force; rather, he would have elected to stick with economic sanctions, a tactic not credited with much success but used often during the Clinton administration. As he said in an interview regarding the crisis in Haiti in 1993, during the Clinton administration: "We have used economic sanctions against South Africa, and to great avail. We have used them against Iraq and other countries. They are a tool of diplomacy and of international affairs, and it is appropriate that that be applied here."[46] Later, Kerry said sanctions in Haiti didn't work only because they weren't enforced: "[Thugs] saw what happened in Somalia. They saw the United States, in essence, have a few people killed, and decide that it didn't like its strategy and turn around. Within a week, the thugs appeared on the dock in Haiti and turned the Harlan County around. That sent them a second, dramatic message about our intent. They saw the sanctions over a course of months not truly enforced and biting, and that sent them a message."[47] Still speaking of Haiti, Kerry—writing in the *New York Times*—repeated the call for enforced economic sanctions: "We need to pursue an aggressive diplomatic course, to escalate sanctions and to impose a total naval blockade if necessary."[48] But by 2003, Kerry wasn't a stalwart of sanctions, as noted by his actions regarding Myanmar, formerly known as the country of Burma. Kerry missed both Senate votes on a bill that would "prohibit the importation of any products from Myanmar, the country formerly known as Burma, and freeze the regime's assets in U.S. financial institutions. The bill also would extend a current U.S. visa ban against members of the ruling military junta and authorize the president to assist pro-democracy activities in Myanmar."[49]

Surprisingly, Kerry also dramatically used Saddam Hussein's weapons of mass destruction to defend Clinton's bombing campaign—even though now, as he campaigns for the presidency, he repeatedly questions the Bush administration's quest to locate evidence of Iraqi WMDs. "[A]mericans need to really understand the gravity and legitimacy of what is happening with Saddam Hussein. He has been given every opportunity in the world to comply. The president does not control the schedule of [the United Nations Special Commission]," Kerry lectured at a press conference. "The president did not withdraw the UNSCOM inspectors. And the president did not, obviously, cut a deal with Saddam Hussein to do this at this moment. Saddam Hussein has not complied. Saddam Hussein is pursuing a program to build weapons of mass destruction."[50]

Kerry continued, pleading with Americans to "come together" and put aside partisan differences at a crucial time. "It seems to me that it is even more perilous for a president who is facing impeachment to consider at this time trumping up some kind of use of the armed forces," said Kerry. "If ever there might be something to invite impeachment, that would be it. So I believe that Americans ought to come together, understanding the larger interests that are at stake in the Gulf."[51]

REGIME CHANGE

Kerry has support for his presidential campaign from some unlikely sources—including a few "rogue" nations who believe they'd have it easier if the White House was under the direction of the Massachusetts liberal. One such country, according to some analysts, is North Korea.

"North Korea is waiting for its own regime change—in D.C.," says Pang Zhongying, professor of international relations at China's Nankai University.[52] Reported the *Financial Times* in March 2004, "In the past few weeks, speeches by the Massachusetts senator have been broadcast on Radio Pyongyang and reported in glowing terms by the Korea Central News Agency (KCNA), the official mouthpiece of Mr. Kim's communist regime. The apparent enthusiasm for Mr. Kerry may reflect little more than a 'better the devil you don't know' mentality among the North Korean apparatchiks. Rather than dealing with President George W. Bush and hawkish officials in his administration, Pyongyang seems to hope victory for the Democratic candidate on November 2 would lead to a softening in U.S. policy towards the country's nuclear weapons program."[53]

North Korea's Stalinist government controls the flow of information to its people through the KCNA. Recently, Radio Pyongyang has broadcast Kerry speeches bashing President Bush. "Mr. Kerry was first introduced to North Korea's information-starved people in early February, when Radio Pyongyang reported that opinion polls indicated he was likely to defeat Mr. Bush. A few days later, the station broadcast comments by Mr. Kerry criticizing Mr. Bush for deceiving the world about Iraq's elusive weapons of mass destruction," the *Financial Times* reported. "Later . . . [the Korean Central News Agency] welcomed Mr. Kerry's pledge to adopt a more 'sincere attitude' towards North Korea if elected. 'Senator Kerry, who is seeking the presidential candidacy of the

Democratic Party, sharply criticized President Bush, saying it was an ill-considered act to deny direct dialogue with North Korea,' said the news agency. Pyongyang's friendly attitude towards Mr. Kerry contrasts with its strong anti-Bush rhetoric."[54]

It should be noted that the Democratic administration of Bill Clinton advocated much the same diplomatic "talk first, last, and always" approach with North Korea, Libya, Iraq, Iran, and other enemies of the United States. Though the problems with these rogue nations intensified during eight years of Clinton, many have been addressed and solved in just under four years of a George W. Bush term:

- Pariah nation Libya, led by Col. Moammar Gadhafi, isolated throughout the 1990s, agreed in 2003 and 2004 to renounce its nuclear weapons program (and other programs to create weapons of mass destruction) and allow international inspectors in to verify such; admitted responsibility for the Pan Am Flight 103 bombing over Lockerbie, Scotland, in 1988; and has pledged to rejoin the "community of nations"—all with the Bush administration's guidance.

- Saddam Hussein was ousted from his dictatorship over Iraq, and while violence still continues there, the country is no longer a threat to Mideast peace, harbor of terrorism, and hub of anti-American sponsorship.

- The Bush administration has put Iran on notice it will not tolerate the growth of its nuclear weapons program; the get-tough approach may have convinced Tehran to promise in early April 2004 to stop manufacturing centrifuges used in nuclear weapons production.

- North Korea remains a thorn in the side of a world hungry for peace, but the Bush administration has managed to at least engage Pyongyang in six-way negotiations (which include South Korea and China) in a bid to convince the Stalinist nation to give up its weapons of mass destruction programs.

The fact is John Kerry is a proponent of relinquishing control of the fate of U.S. interests and U.S. international security to the United Nations. He believes diplomacy is the best weapon to wage against terrorists who have declared war on this country and are responsible for the worst attack on U.S. soil this country has ever seen. His weak defense record underscores his aversion to decisive, brave, definitive action.

5

KERRY'S DEFENSE-LESS RECORD

Cutting budgets and crippling the U.S. military

WOULD A PRESIDENT John Kerry be an effective commander in chief of the most powerful armed forces in the world? Only if you believe his election year rhetoric. Based on Kerry's past positions on funding, development, and improvement of the American military, it's a sure bet U.S. forces would not even be a contender in the war on terror.

That's because John Kerry, one of the Senate's preeminent liberals, voted against funding increases for military personnel, weapons systems, and defense innovation. Despite denials on the campaign trail, it's a fact he often opposed Pentagon initiatives and programs that have led to spectacular U.S. military victories in Afghanistan, the Philippines, Iraq, Serbia, and elsewhere over the past decade.

Perhaps detecting his own weakness in the area of military and defense issues, in December 2003 Kerry proposed an increase in the armed forces by forty thousand troops, as a relief valve for a U.S. military spread thin throughout the world fighting terrorism. "As we internationalize the work in Iraq, we need to add 40,000 troops—the equivalent of two divisions—to the American military in order to meet our responsibilities elsewhere, especially in the urgent global war on terror," he told a crowd at Drake University in Des Moines, Iowa. "In my first hundred days as president, I will move to increase the size of our armed forces. Some may not like that. But today, in the face of grave challenges, our armed forces are spread too thin. Our troops in Iraq are paying the price for this everyday. There's not enough troops in the ranks of our overall armed forces to bring home those troops that have been in Iraq for more than a year."[1]

Then, in January 2004, as the Democratic primary season was set to get underway—and Kerry was still behind then-favorite Howard Dean—he came out boasting of his record on all matters military, telling CNN he's "always fought" for a strong national defense. "I've always fought all my life for a strong military, for the strongest armed forces in the world, and for the defense of our nation," he said. "And I've spent the last twenty years trying to defend our nation as a member of the Foreign Relations Committee, as chairman of the Narcotics Terrorism Committee. I stood up and fought against Ronald Reagan's illegal war in Central America. I stood up and fought in order to hold Oliver North accountable and expose what he was doing."[2]

Great campaign sound bites, but Kerry's thirty-four-year, anti-military record does not support his current campaign rhetoric.

THE 1970s

Looking back to the beginning of Kerry's long political career, funding the U.S. military has never been one of his priorities. Whether it is his bitterness over Vietnam or other factors, the truth is the public should question any potential commander in chief who has done so little to strengthen America's military.

At an early point in his political career, Kerry managed to oppose a military draft, an all-volunteer force, and a professional army. According to a candidate questionnaire he answered for his 1972 House bid, Kerry wrote, *"I am opposed in principle to the concept of a draft. But I am opposed also to a volunteer army* which given present conditions in this country is, I think, a greater anathema. I am convinced a volunteer army would be an army of the poor and the black and the brown. . . . *I also fear having a professional army* that views the perpetuation of war crimes as simply 'doing its job.'"[3]

Eventually he settled on supporting an all-volunteer military, like that which exists today, but he couched that support under the provision the government would "create controls for it."[4]

Kerry also believed the U.S. military should be controlled by other governments or entities and not by the United States. "Kerry said that the United Nations should have control over most of our foreign military operations," reported the *Harvard Crimson.* Said Kerry, "I'm an internationalist. I'd like to see our troops dispersed through the world only at the directive of the United Nations."[5]

During his 1972 campaign for the U.S. House, Kerry vowed to vote against military appropriations.[6] His answer to ensuring the "country's security" was "real cuts" in military spending, according to a newspaper questionnaire:

QUESTION: What are your views concerning military spending and your position concerning the country's security?

KERRY: It is very important that this country maintain an adequate posture. Threats do exist in the world and they are not going to disappear. But the question really revolves around adequacy. What is an adequate defense that permits the U.S. to defend itself against any real threat? There are very real cuts that can be made not only in future programs but in present procurement and administration costs in the Department of Defense. I truly believe that the U.S. is in a superior enough position that only our initiative can guarantee a world-wide mitigation and reduction of defense spending. Now is the time to take the initiative.[7]

THE 1980s

Campaigning for Massachusetts' lieutenant governor, on the ticket with fellow ultra-liberal Michael Dukakis, Kerry also took the position that the U.S. should negotiate with the Soviet Union for its own security. According to a campaign flyer, both men believed "in a mutual, verifiable freeze on the proliferation of nuclear weapons with the Soviet Union as the best way to begin the urgent business of curtailing the arms race. Imagine the student aid and social programs we could fund with the money now going to unnecessary and wasteful military expenditures," the flyer said.[8]

Both men also pledged to fight Reagan's defense spending. "[Dukakis/Kerry] will be leaders in the fight against Reaganomics—against . . . a *record* $1.6 trillion increase in defense spending coupled with *record cuts* in domestic social programs," proclaimed campaign literature.[9]

During President Reagan's military build-up in the early 1980s—a build-up that is, in part, credited in ending the cold war and breaking the will of Soviet Union[10]—Kerry, as Massachusetts' lieutenant governor, in a letter to a constituent, wrote, "What we as citizens can tell our government is that President Reagan should reorder his priorities. We don't need expensive and exotic weapons systems."[11]

In the early '80s, Kerry continued to campaign not on a platform of military strength but instead one of compromise and capitulation. "[In 1982] I became the first candidate for statewide office in Massachusetts to promote the adoption of the freeze," he said in a 1984 senatorial campaign questionnaire.[12] His campaign literature for the Senate race chirped the same tune: "During his campaign for Lt. Gov. in 1982, John Kerry made the nuclear freeze a central issue of that race, attending rallies in support of the freeze in Massachusetts and New York, and running advertising about the freeze. . . ."[13]

Once lieutenant governor, he continued to use his political position to oppose Reagan defense initiatives. "As Lieutenant Governor, John Kerry has spoken out against the Reagan defense increases, and, in his capacity as head of the state's Office of Federal/State Relations, has criticized the Reagan administration for spending federal resources on dangerous and wasteful weapons systems," 1984 campaign literature enthused.[14]

When he ran for the U.S. Senate in 1984, he continued his anti-military spending rhetoric. "I believe in a mutual and verifiable freeze on the testing, production, and future deployment of nuclear warheads, missiles, and other delivery systems," candidate Kerry told *Gender Watch*, a women's rights publication, in June 1984. "The notion of nuclear superiority is without meaning. A strong defense does not require the United States to develop space-based anti-ballistic or 'Star Wars' weapons, MX missiles, B-1 bombers, or other weapons which are overly complicated, extraordinarily expensive, ultimately unreliable, and strategically destabilizing. The United States can and must have a defense which is both strong and less expensive. This nation can choose a national defense that is efficient and affordable by a careful understanding of the role of conventional forces in the nuclear age, and a scrupulous review of each and every military dollar we spend."[15]

As he continued his Senate race, Kerry expounded upon his anti-military spending position. "We are continuing a defense buildup that is consuming our resources with weapons systems that we don't need and can't use," claimed campaign literature.[16] In fact, Kerry implied the more the U.S. spent on defense, the less safe it was. "The biggest defense buildup since World War II has not given us a better defense. Today, Americans are more threatened by the prospect of war, not less so," he told the *Boston Globe* in May 1984.[17]

"I want you to know that I will fight to cut the overall defense budget. . . . As your Senator, I will not be reluctant to support cuts in the Pentagon budget," Kerry said in a 1984 letter to supporters.[18] He added, "There's no excuse for casting even one vote for unnecessary weapons of destruction and as your Senator, I will never do so."[19]

Kerry also told the *Boston Globe* he didn't support "annual increases in the military budget above the rate of inflation."[20] In the same campaign, he remarkably said President Reagan's military expenditures were out of proportion with the Soviet threat: "The defense expenditures of the Reagan administration are without any relevancy to the threat this nation is currently facing."[21]

Believing the Reagan White House was wasting money funding defense initiatives, Kerry pledged to supporters he would become a "force" within the Senate to fight such expenditures. "A senator must promote real reductions of nuclear weapons by introducing amendments to appropriations bills to delete specific weapons systems. But he must do more than this—he must be a force within the Senate to achieve a change in the way Congress looks at defense and weapons systems and arms control, so that Congress never again engages in wholescale [sic] adoption of systems that make no sense in any context," he said in a Senate questionnaire.[22] Believing the U.S. could talk its way into national security with regards to the Soviet Union, Kerry suggested, "Now is not the moment merely to control the arms race, but to stop it. Implementation of a freeze can be achieved through (1) negotiations with the Soviets; (2) a moratorium by the U.S. on the production, testing, and deployment of nuclear weapons . . . (3) and curtailing appropriations for new weapons systems."[23]

Kerry thought peace could be achieved by unilateral disarmament. To make his point, he "recommended that funding be cut off for new nuclear weapons as a first step toward reaching agreement with the Soviet Union on a mutually verifiable freeze."[24] His support for this strategy was confirmed in his 1984 Senate questionnaire

when he answered yes to the question, "Will you vote for the proposed mutual Arms Race Moratorium Act ('quick freeze') which
cuts off funding for nuclear weapons activities that are generally
agreed to be verifiable . . . if within a 90-day period the Soviets agree
to do likewise?"[25]

In the budget for Fiscal Year 1985, Kerry wanted to trim $54
billion—a down payment on a larger $200 billion cut in the defense
budget over four years. "[Kerry] recommended cancellation of 27
weapons systems including the B1 bomber, the cruise missile, MX
missile, Trident submarine, Patriot air defense missile, F-15 fighter
plane, Sparrow missile, stealth bomber and Pershing II missile," the
Boston Globe reported. "He recommended reductions in 18 other
systems including the joint tactical air system, the Bradley fighting
vehicle, the M1 Abrams tank and the F-16 fighter plane."[26] Despite
those cuts, which were deep, Kerry suggested there could be others.
"There is nothing cast in stone about this list. . . . It is an effort to
create a dialogue in this campaign. It may be that *there could be
additional cuts.*"[27]

WEAPON MODERNIZATION

Kerry also opposed simple modernization of key strategic weapons
systems—weapons programs which had kept the U.S. safe for years
but which were being outpaced by technological advances by the
Soviets and other potential U.S. enemies. In his 1984 Senate questionnaire, he opposed important military upgrades: replacing the B-
52 with the Stealth bomber or the B-1, replacing the Minute-man
missile with the Midgetman or MX missile, replacing the Poseidon
SLBM (submarine-launched ballistic missile) with the Trident I or
II.[28] The Poseidon SLBMs were introduced in 1971 and, upon manufacture, were initially plagued with "severe reliability problems,"
which "affected many components, including the nuclear warheads, some of which were defective to the point which would have

prevented detonation." The problems were not all corrected until 1974. Beginning in October 1979, the Poseidon was gradually replaced by its successor, the UGM-96 Trident C-4.[29]

Despite its many problems, Kerry would have delayed deployment of Poseidon's replacement. "I believe the United States should maintain its current submarine capacity by replacing Poseidon submarines with Trident submarines as the Poseidons become obsolete," he said in his 1984 Senate questionnaire—ignoring the need to get a more reliable sub in the water immediately. "This means replacement in the ordinary course of obsolescence, 20 to 25 years following the commission of each Poseidon, so long as replacement of old submarines by new ones does not (1) increase the number of nuclear submarines currently deployed by the U.S. or (2) increase the nuclear submarine capabilities of the U.S."[30]

Before all was said and done, Kerry proposed even more cuts. He told the *Cape Codder* newspaper in September 1984 he had expanded his list to include "specific cuts in sixty categories." They included the SSN-688 Los Angeles class nuclear attack submarine, Trident I submarine, Trident I missile, Trident II submarine-based missile, Midgetman missile, Pershing II missile, DDG-51 Aegis air defense destroyer, and CG-47 Aegis air defense cruiser.[31] (An historical sidenote: the *Cape Codder* published Kerry's recommended cuts seventeen years to the day before the September 11, 2001, attacks.)

Worse than opposing modernizations and advancing cuts, Kerry's 1984 Campaign Defense Position Paper actually called for the outright cancellation of a number of weapons systems: The MX missile, B1 bomber, anti-satellite system, Strategic Defense Initiative ("Star Wars"), AH-64 Helicopters, Patriot air defense missile, Aegis air-defense cruiser, battleship reactivation, AV-8B (Harrier) vertical takeoff and landing aircraft, F-15 fighter aircraft, F-14A fighter aircraft, F-14D fighter aircraft, Phoenix air-to-air missile, and the Sparrow air-to-air missile. It also called for a 50 percent reduction of Tomahawk cruise missile funding.[32]

In all, the cuts formed Kerry's defense "strategy," according to his campaign. "Joining Kerry was Michael Nacht, chairman of Kerry's foreign policy task force and an instructor at Harvard's John F. Kennedy School of Government, who said Kerry's proposal was 'unique' because it was an overall defense strategy, not just a pro or con statement about certain Reagan administration programs," the *Berkshire Eagle* newspaper reported.[33]

"We must secure the abandonment of destabilizing theories of defense, too, including anti-ballistic missile and 'Star Wars' defense," Kerry said in his 1984 Senate questionnaire.[34]

Interestingly, Kerry didn't even want the U.S. to develop weapons to protect American satellites from Soviet anti-satellite weapons. He viewed it as a potential system that might upset the Soviets: "John Kerry believes that testing and deployment of anti-satellite weapons (ASAT) is a dangerous escalation of the arms race. . . . John Kerry believes that Congress must not allow the Reagan Administration to continue the testing of these space-based weapons. . . . Congress must stop appropriating money for ASAT weapons."[35] If elected Kerry said he "would be a strong advocate to prevent these expenditures and to hold the Senate accountable."[36]

Immediately after winning his 1984 race, Kerry wasted no time in attacking the Reagan administration's defense spending. "[W]e are watching an administration walk away from any sense of trying to deal with what weapons systems we need to really maintain a legitimate level of defense, versus what they are willing to simply fund and fund and fund, out of their willingness to fund any weapons system. They've never met one they don't like," Kerry told an audience at a political action convention in January 1985.[37]

According to the congressional record, Kerry's first speech in the Senate, on March 19, 1985, was in opposition to the Reagan administration's push to build twenty-one MX missiles.[38]

In time, he would even blame economic recession on Reagan's

military spending. "In a far-ranging address to the Greater Boston Chamber of Commerce, Kerry . . . proposed a series of measures aimed at reversing the nation's slide toward economic mediocrity—a decline he blamed partly on military spending which does little economic good," the *Middlesex News* reported. "An end to the arms buildup 'could release enormous sums of money,' Kerry said. With that diverted to civilian use, 'this country would just take off.'"[39]

In all, Kerry has voted to cut, transfer, or otherwise reduce the defense budget over the years at least thirty-eight times—including cuts in many weapons systems that have saved the lives of many U.S. soldiers in military engagements like Iraq, Afghanistan, and elsewhere.[40]

The *Boston Globe* reported in June 2003 that Kerry "supported cancellation of a host of weapons systems that have become the basis of U.S. military might—the high-tech munitions and delivery systems on display to the world as they leveled the Iraqi regime of Saddam Hussein in a matter of weeks."[41] Speaking of Iraq (and, perhaps, Kerry's history of military misjudgments), the Massachusetts senator objected to the sale of forty U.S.-made F/A-18 fighters to Kuwait, just two years before Saddam Hussein invaded the tiny Arab nation, triggering the first Gulf War. "The F-18, that's our most sophisticated, latest technology . . . I'm concerned about it. I just don't see a need for it at first blush," said Kerry.[42]

THE 1990s—AND BEYOND

Campaigning for the presidency, Kerry says he wants to increase the number of U.S. troops, but his policies to cut military programs over the last twenty years are inconsistent with his claim. In 1993, he introduced a plan to cut numerous defense programs, including a measure that would reduce the number of Navy submarines and their crews; cut the number of light infantry units in the Army down to one; reduce tactical fighter wings in the Air Force; terminate the Navy's coastal mine-hunting ship program; and force the retirement of no less than sixty thousand members of the armed forces in one year.[43]

Following the cold war, Kerry has consistently questioned the need for continued levels of military spending. "So you can look at all the potential threats of the world, and when you add the expenditures of all of our allies to the United States of America, you have to stop and say to yourself, 'What is it that we are really preparing for in a post-cold-war world?'"[44] This statement came about one month before nineteen U.S. Air Force personnel were killed and 372 wounded in a terrorist attack on Khobar Towers, a U.S. military housing complex in Dhahran, Saudi Arabia, and six months after terrorists struck the Saudi National Guard.

But it isn't just the weapons our war fighters use to protect our country he has opposed. Senator Kerry has voted against raising the standard of living for our personnel. He's voted at least twelve times as a senator against increasing military pay.[45]

Throughout the 1990s—and into the new millennium—Kerry voted against military programs the Pentagon (and, in some cases, even former President Clinton) felt were necessary. Some highlights include:

- Kerry voted in 1993 to kill a bill to increase defense spending over five years by $67.4 billion.[46]

- That same year, he voted to cut missile defense funding by $400 million.[47]

- In 1994, Kerry voted to cut missile defense funding even more—by $513 million.[48]

- In 1995, he voted to freeze defense spending for seven years, slashing $34 billion from Defense Department funding, transferring the savings to education and "jobs training."[49]

- He voted against an $11.1 billion military construction bill, which included $4.3 billion for military family housing—

one of only fourteen senators to vote against the bill.[50]

- He voted to cut funding for B-2 bombers.[51]

- He voted again to slash another $300 million from missile defense research and development.[52]

Kerry also voted against the 1996 Defense Appropriations Bill, which was enacted and provided more than $44.5 billion for procurement of the following weapons and weapons systems:

- six F-15E Strike Eagles
- six F-16 Fighting Falcons
- four Aegis-equipped destroyers
- eight C-17 transport planes
- missile defense systems
- two SR-71 Blackbirds
- one LHD helicopter carrier
- one Seawolf class submarine
- $777 million in National Guard and Reserve equipment

Kerry hardly met a cut he didn't like. On July 10, 2001—just two months before the September 11 attacks—Kerry voted again to cut $150 million from defense funds to give to low-income heating assistance.[53]

"PEACE DIVIDEND"

Liberal-leaning publications have attempted to liken the defense budget cuts of some past Republican administrations to Kerry's record of budget cuts. In the February 25, 2004, issue of online newsmagazine Slate, Fred Kaplan wrote, "Before George W. Bush's political operatives started pounding on John Kerry for voting against certain weapons systems during his years in the Senate, they should have taken a look at" how George H. W. Bush and Dick Cheney, as his secretary of defense, cut weapons systems.[54]

Kaplan quoted Bush the elder, who said in his 1992 State of the Union address: "After completing twenty planes for which we have begun procurement, we will shut down further production of the B-2 bomber. We will cancel the small ICBM program. We will cease production of new warheads for our sea-based ballistic missiles. We will stop all new production of the Peacekeeper [MX] missile. And we will not purchase any more advanced cruise missiles. . . . The reductions I have approved will save us an additional $50 billion over the next five years. By 1997 we will have cut defense by 30 percent since I took office."[55]

Kaplan also quoted Dick Cheney, speaking before the Senate Armed Services Committee the same month: "Overall, since I've been secretary, we will have taken the five-year defense program down by well over $300 billion. That's the peace dividend. . . . And now we're adding to that another $50 billion . . . of so-called peace dividend."[56]

The cuts made by the prior Bush administration came in the aftermath of the Soviet Union's demise. *The* primary threat to world peace at that time, as U.S. military planners saw it, was a well-armed Moscow. When the Soviet Union crumbled, it was—as Cheney said—no longer necessary to continue procuring weapons systems developed and built *specifically* to counter the Soviet threat. In contrast, Kerry sought massive defense cuts during the height of the Soviet threat. His defense cuts are starkly different from the "peace dividend" made possible by America's victory over the Soviet Union in the cold war. Kerry's proposed cuts would have made it difficult, if not impossible, to achieve that victory. And while a large standing military may be unnecessary in peacetime, the U.S. currently is not at peace; it is fighting a global war on terror, so added military expenditures are vital to continue the effort. Kerry, whose voting record in the Senate proves he is a well-established anti-military voice, would be a detriment to the war on terror and, hence, to U.S. national security.

OUT IN LEFT FIELD

Kerry's record is so far out of the mainstream that some of his fellow Democrats have been among his most vocal critics. In 1994, when he wanted to trim $43 billion from the defense, intelligence, and science budget, "he encountered some harsh resistance," the Associated Press reported. "The cuts would threaten national security. U.S. fighter pilots would be endangered. And the battle against terrorism would be hampered, opponents charged," AP reported. "And that's just what Kerry's fellow Democrats had to say."[57]

Decorated World War II veteran Senator Daniel Inouye (D-Hawaii) said Kerry's proposal would have gutted intelligence. "We are putting blindfolds over our pilots' eyes," Inouye said. The Senate ended up defeating Kerry's plan by a vote of 75–20.[58]

At the time, Kerry tried to explain his position, claiming his was a champion to balance the budget. Ten years after the vote, Kerry's presidential campaign tries to respond to his voting record with good sounds bites that have little meaning: "Unlike George Bush, John Kerry does not support every special project defense contractors like Halliburton and others want," said campaign spokesman Chad Clanton. "John Kerry absolutely voted against business as usual in our intelligence community."[59]

Typical of a professional politician like Kerry, he makes broad statements that make for good campaign sound bites, but he never introduces specifics. AP noted when Kerry introduced his plan, he didn't mention much about the funding he wanted to eliminate from the defense and intelligence budgets. "What we have offered to the Senate is an opportunity to register our votes for real choices, for a set of choices that reflect what the American people would really like to be spending their money on as opposed to being forced to spend it by the continuation of programs that the president has asked to have cut; that the National Academy of Sciences boards have said are worthless; that most of what the evaluations say are wasteful," he argued.[60]

A handful of senators joined Kerry, but several of his fellow senior Democrat senators were at odds with the proposal. "The amendment offered by the senator from Massachusetts would reduce the fiscal year 1994 budget for national defense by nearly $4 billion," said Senator Robert Byrd (D-West Virginia), then the powerful Appropriations Committee chairman. "We have already cut defense spending drastically. . . . Cutting another $43 billion is simply unwise and insupportable."[61]

Senator Inouye, arguing against Kerry's proposed cuts, said they would ignore the current and future threats of North Korean proliferation and terrorism, stating, "These issues include nuclear proliferation by North Korea . . . peacekeeping efforts in Bosnia and Somalia, as well as terrorist threats against American citizens and property."[62]

"If we expect the 1 percent of our nation to risk their lives and stand in harm's way," added Inouye, "the least we can do is to provide them with all of the resources necessary so that they can carry out their mission and get home to their loved ones. We cannot do any less. This [Kerry-proposed defense cutting] amendment would take away their protection, and I am not prepared to do that."[63]

Kerry's historic opposition to the funding of existing nuclear weapons, as well as the funding of new types of nuclear weapons programs, also bothered fellow Democrats, many who believed the Massachusetts senator was not only risking the lives of U.S. military personnel abroad, but those of Americans at home. Senator Dennis DeConcini (D-Arizona), in a speech on the Senate floor in 1994 criticizing Kerry's proposed defense cuts, reminded colleagues of the threat still posed to the U.S. by such weapons of mass destruction, even after the fall of the Soviet Union: "Yes, the world has changed. We no longer face the same sort of threat to our survival that we faced during the cold war. But the world remains a dangerous place. . . . There are still nuclear weapons out there which are targeted against the United States, and whose control we worry about. There are countries not friendly to us which seem bent on developing their own weapons of mass destruction."[64]

Kerry has also supported the degrading of U.S. intelligence-gathering. DeConcini, then the Intelligence Committee chairman, criticized Kerry for his recommendation to reduce intelligence spending by $6 billion over six years. He said the reduction in intelligence spending would, at the time, "leave Americans vulnerable while facing problems such as the war in Bosnia, nuclear proliferation and terrorism," according to AP. "It makes no sense for us to close our eyes and ears to developments around the world," DeConcini added, wondering aloud why Kerry didn't raise the idea of his cuts with the committee first.[65]

In all, Kerry served eight years on the Senate Intelligence Committee, in which time he voted on three occasions to cut the intelligence budget, while never once voting to increase it.[66]

As our country faces a brand new type of war defending the homeland against terrorism, hunting down international terrorists, and preventing other nations from supporting and harboring terrorist networks, a large number of the weapons systems in place right now would simply not exist if Kerry's military cuts were adopted.

When questioned about his more than twenty-year defense history, Kerry doesn't think his votes regarding defense spending are legitimate issues, because he thinks they are personal attacks. However, this record speaks for itself. The American people should know that Kerry is not the better of the two candidates at leading the war on terror. President Bush has a proven record in fighting terrorism. Kerry, on the other hand, has a proven record in opposing measures necessary to help the U.S. fight terrorism.

6

HOMELAND INSECURITY

Making America a safer place for terrorists

FOLLOWING THE TERRORIST attacks of September 11, 2001, the issue of securing the American homeland became the federal government's first priority. But what many Americans do not know is that there was some effort to secure the homeland years before terrorists destroyed the World Trade Center Towers and a portion of the Pentagon using airliners as missiles.

In the decades preceding the twenty-first century, the most serious threat faced by the U.S. was destruction via nuclear war with the former Soviet Union (and, to a lesser extent, the People's Republic of China). To that end—and despite some government efforts to plan for such a contingency—John Kerry opposed preventative legislation.

In fact, his opposition to disaster planning dates back to his earlier political days. In 1982, as he campaigned for lieutenant governor in Massachusetts, Kerry said he was opposed to evacuation plans for the state in case of nuclear conflict. "During my [1982] campaign, I called on the state to abandon planning for nuclear evacuation, calling such evacuation plans a sham intended to deceive Americans into believing they could survive a nuclear war," he said in a Senate campaign questionnaire in 1984.[1] Once elected lieutenant governor, Kerry kept his pledge, drafting an executive order that cancelled all evacuation planning. "As Lieutenant Governor, I have [carried] forward my campaign promise that the Commonwealth cease planning for evacuation and relocation during a nuclear war, and drafted an Executive Order condemning such planning," he said in the 1984 Senate questionnaire.[2] The order was eventually signed into law by ultraliberal and 1988 Democratic presidential nominee Governor Michael Dukakis:

> Whereas, the only effective defense against the horrors of nuclear weapons lies in their elimination and in the prevention of nuclear war or attacks . . . I, Michael S. Dukakis, Governor of the Commonwealth . . . hereby rescind Executive Order No. 31 of 1956 and order as follows: . . . Henceforth, the Commonwealth will continue to develop the concept of Comprehensive Emergency Management to deal with major disasters or emergencies in the Commonwealth, with the qualification that the Commonwealth shall not engage in crisis relocation planning in preparation for nuclear war. . . . No funds shall be expended by the Commonwealth for crisis relocation planning for nuclear war.[3]

Such opposition was not limited to his days as lieutenant governor or his early political career or even in the absence of horrific terrorist attacks on U.S. soil. Years later, in 2002—and in spite of the 9/11 attacks—Kerry opposed President Bush's plan for the creation of the Department of Homeland Security, an agency developed specifically to better prepare the country against such horrific attacks in the future.

Kerry led the fight against the agency, which was backed by President Bush and Republican lawmakers, as well as a number of Democrats. In order to attract the most qualified candidates to ensure the country's national security, a key point of Bush's plan was to gain the "flexibility hiring and acquisition practices at the new department," and he asked Congress "to give the new Secretary of

Homeland Security the power to do away with the current pay structure, labor-management rules and performance appraisal system," reported *Government Executive* magazine.[4] Kerry put politics ahead of national security and sided with labor unions against the Bush plan, which delayed the creation of the Department of Homeland Security by months.[5] Although Kerry after months of stalling by majority Democrats, finally voted to create the Department of Homeland Security,[6] he then skipped a 2003 vote to fund the new agency.[7]

IMMIGRATION: OPEN THE GATES!

Another major concern regarding homeland security is the porous nature of America's borders, both the Mexican and Canadian borders.[8] Miles and miles of the border with Mexico and Canada are virtually unguarded, poorly protected, and under little surveillance. This problem has a number of security and immigration reform experts worried, and—with the threat of terrorism looming large—it is an issue which concerns our leaders as well as the electorate. According to his Senate voting record, Kerry, during his years in the Senate, has regularly voted to further weaken U.S. immigration laws and reward criminal lawbreakers who illegally enter the country.

In 1985, Kerry voted for a broad amnesty for illegal aliens. During debate on such an amnesty proposal, Kerry supported a measure "to make illegal aliens who were in the United States prior to January 1, 1981, eligible for legal status, and to delete a proposed commission that would study the 'legalization' issue." The language of the Kerry-backed amendment was far less strict than the underlying bill and was soundly defeated.[9] Two years later, Kerry supported an amendment granting amnesty "to the spouses and children of aliens eligible for legal residency in the United States, even if the spouses and children are not themselves eligible."[10]

Even more worrisome than an amnesty break, not all aliens sneaking into the U.S. are from Mexico or even Canada. According to border residents, some may be from Islamic nations which are known to sponsor terrorism. In February 2003, Sierra Vista, Arizona, resident Walter Kolbe "was chasing some wild animals away from his home . . . when he stumbled upon" a backpack that contained a diary with Arabic writing. Upon examining the book, Mr. Kolbe and his wife "noticed two names and telephone numbers—one listing in Canada and the other Iran—and confirmed the beginning numbers were the international codes for those two countries." The couple notified the FBI of their find.[11]

KERRY PROPOSES INTELLIGENCE CUTS

Members of Kerry's own party have often felt ill at ease with their Massachusetts colleague's political decisions regarding homeland security issues. Dating back to 1994—during a time when the global threat of terrorism was on Washington's radar screens—Democrats criticized Kerry for seeking huge budget cuts in defense and intelligence capabilities.

As mentioned in the previous chapter, Democratic Senator Dennis DiConcini of Arizona complained in 1994 about Kerry's quest to cut the U.S. intelligence budget. He said cuts from the previous year were likely "as deep as the intelligence community can withstand."[12]

"Overall," he said, "intelligence resources have been reduced in real terms more than 13 percent compared with 1989 appropriations." DiConcini compared those cuts to other, earlier cuts made in military spending and urged his Senate colleagues to consider future military deployments before cutting any more: "We still face the possibility that U.S. military forces might be deployed around the globe to accomplish a variety of missions." And, he warned, "we no longer seem immune from acts of terrorism in the United States"—prophetic words indeed—while claiming a Kerry amendment to cut further intelligence spending could hamper global threat identification efforts.[13]

Democratic Senator Daniel Inouye also criticized the 1994 Kerry amendments to cut defense, security, and intelligence spending even further.

"[T]he intelligence budget has already been cut by almost 18 percent over the past two years," he said from the Senate floor. "An additional reduction . . . would severely hamper the intelligence community's ability to provide decision makers and policymakers with information on matters of vital concern to this country." Inouye went on to say, "Congress has worked in close partnership with the intelligence community to refine the intelligence budget without detrimentally affecting this country's national security. . . . [Kerry's proposal to further reduce funding] would result in a termination of programs and activities that are essential to the security of this nation."[14]

Seventy-five senators—including ultra-liberal Senator Ted Kennedy—voted against the Kerry 1995 proposal to cut more from intelligence.[15]

As explained previously, "peace dividend" cuts made in the latter 1980s and early 1990s by President George H. W. Bush and then-Defense Secretary Dick Cheney were much more responsible than the haphazard cuts sought by Kerry. The administration of the first President Bush sought to eliminate excess weapons systems that were deemed vital against cold war enemies like the former Soviet Union but not so vital in the new kind of low-tech, limited warfare envisioned by the first Bush administration and which the second Bush administration is currently fighting.

DOES KERRY HAVE A TERROR PLAN?

Despite his record of votes to weaken U.S. national security, during his presidential campaign Kerry has said the Bush administration has not done enough to ensure the safety of the nation. He says Bush "hoodwinked the American people" and that the Texas Republican is "not making the world safer." He adds, "I do not believe this administration is doing the job of protecting Americans."[16]

Specifically, Kerry says "the priorities and choices of this administration are wrong."[17] And he says he believes the Bush White House "has given too short shrift to the needs of homeland security, ignoring the advice of their own experts, doing the job on the fly and on the cheap. To this administration, homeland security is a fine political weapon, but not high enough a priority to force a reassessment of their tax cuts to the rich and the special interests."[18]

Kerry also claims the Bush administration hasn't done enough to give Americans the opportunity to make their homeland safer. "Americans want to serve and contribute. President Bush told us to go shopping. I believe we are better than that—that all of us still want to make a difference and all of us will enlist in the cause of a safer nation."[19]

A lot of his campaign rhetoric makes for good sound bites, but what, specifically, does Kerry propose to do to make this country safer?

1. During his campaign, Kerry has said he wants to increase funding for local emergency responders, as one way to handle the crisis of new terror attacks: "Our first defenders should never come in last in the budget. Firefighters are first up the stairs and John Kerry believes they deserve to be first in line when we decide our spending priorities."[20]

2. Kerry also wants to implement a national service plan, "asking more of Americans" while employing the National Guard in a domestic protection role. "He would start by: Enlisting the National Guard in Homeland Security. . . . Expanding Americorps to Make Homeland Security a Core Mission. . . . Creating a New Community Defense Service. . . . Calling on the Private Sector to Help Bring Technological

Innovations to the War on Terrorism," says the Kerry campaign Web site.[21]

3. At the same time, Kerry says the country "needs an independent intelligence capability that focuses explicitly on domestic intelligence."[22]

The Bush administration, however, has already accomplished many of these proposals. And one major accomplishment—enactment of the USA PATRIOT Act, which Kerry voted for—is now under assault by him.

Among other things, the USA PATRIOT Act would expand law enforcement's power to investigate suspected terrorists. It allows disclosure of wiretap information among certain government officials, authorizes limited disclosure of secret grand jury information to certain government officials, and permits the detention of foreigners suspected of having ties to terrorism. The act also makes it easier for law enforcement to track voice and Internet communications using surveillance techniques and strengthens laws to combat money laundering. But many of the act's intelligence-gathering provisions could sunset as early as December 31, 2004.

When the USA PATRIOT Act was first enacted, Kerry voted "Yea."[23] Indeed, he even spoke publicly in praise of some of the bill's most controversial provisions. In an interview on MSNBC's *Hardball*:

CHRIS MATTHEWS: Let's talk about Ashcroft, the attorney general. Conservative fellow, wants more wiretap authority. What do you make of that? Are you for that kind of approach, tougher surveillance?

KERRY: I am for tougher surveillance. I think you've got to do it, obviously, in keeping with the liberties of our country. But you can do these things, many of them. For instance, it's absolutely outdated to have a wiretap linked only to a telephone number in a modern age where you throw one away and use another ten minutes later. So I think it's absolutely legitimate to track the wiretap to a specific individual. There are other kinds of things that we absolutely must do in order to modernize.[24]

But now, as the election approaches, Kerry is attacking the legislation, saying the Department of Justice has somehow gone "overboard" in applying the law. The *Kansas City Star* reported:

Kerry campaign spokesman Robert Gibbs said the senator not only voted for the [PATRIOT] act, but also helped write some of its provisions to thwart money laundering. But he said the Justice Department under Ashcroft has gone overboard. "No one imagined the degree to which the envelope would be pushed," Gibbs said.[25]

And, in an interview with National Public Radio, Kerry said, "If you are sensitive to and care about civil liberties, you can make provisions to guarantee that there is not this blind spot in the American justice system that there is today under the PATRIOT Act."

Yet in typical Kerry fashion, he also defended his vote, despite his alleged problems with the legislation. "I voted for the PATRIOT Act right after September 11—convinced that—with a sunset clause—it was the right decision to make," he told an audience at Iowa State University in December 2003. "It clearly wasn't a perfect bill—and it had a number of flaws—but this wasn't the time to haggle. It was the time to act."[26]

FIRST RESPONDERS

Senator Kerry has also criticized the Bush administration for supposedly doing too little to provide funding for "first responders"— men and women who man local police, fire, and emergency medical systems who will be the first on the scene of any new terrorist attacks in the U.S. But the truth, Americans should know, is that the administration has done as much as Congress—which Kerry is a part of—has approved.

"My first responsibility as your president is to protect the American people and to provide a strategy that not only protects the American people, but should there ever be another incident, provides response, quick response for the American people," President Bush told an audience at the Georgia Institute of Technology in Atlanta, after witnessing a mock response of Georgia First Responders in March 2002.[27] Since the 9/11 attacks, Bush's administration has kept pace with that responsibility.

To begin with, Bush has promoted dramatically increased federal funding of local first responder organizations—specifically police, fire, and emergency medical services agencies—because they will be relied upon to initially respond to any disaster or attack. In 2002 and 2003, some $2.4 billion in grants was made available to local governments for first responder funding.[28] In all, under Bush, the federal government has spent $41.4 billion to beef up domestic security during the fiscal year ending in September 2004.[29]

"NORTHCOM"

The Bush administration has also increased the role and capability of the military to defend the United States. The administration and the Pentagon created the U.S. Northern Command [NORTH-COM] in 2002, a brand-new command whose mission specifically is homeland defense. "U.S. Northern Command provides military assistance to civil authorities . . . [which] includes domestic disaster relief operations that occur during fires, hurricanes, floods, and earthquakes. Support also includes counter-drug operations and consequence management assistance, such as would occur after a terrorist event employing a weapon of mass destruction," says the NORTHCOM Web site.[30]

INDEPENDENT INTELLIGENCE CAPABILITIES

Whereas the Bush White House has begun to provide better protection of Americans at home, it has also taken the offensive abroad to root out terrorists *before* they can gather, plan, and execute. "Along with the sweeping transformation within the FBI, the establishment of the Department of Defense's U.S. Northern Command, and the creation of the multi-agency Terrorist Threat Integration Center and Terrorist Screening Center, America is better prepared to prevent, disrupt, and respond to terrorist attacks than ever before," said the White House on March 2, 2004—the first anniversary of the creation of the Department of Homeland Security.[31]

Bush National Security Advisor Condoleezza Rice, in an effort to refute claims made by former counterterrorism czar Richard Clarke in early March 2004 that the White House had not done enough to protect the country from terrorism, said Bush met with CIA Director George Tenet forty-six times before 9/11 about the terrorism threat, which was thought to be primarily overseas. Though she admitted the administration "would not be honest with the American people if we said that before 9/11 this country was on war footing" during an interview on CBS's *60 Minutes*, she added, "What the president did after 9/11 was to declare war on al-Qaeda in ways that had not been done before."[32] Noted UPI, "Rice said that early in the administration, efforts were made with Pakistan's president to get him to join the effort in eliminating al-Qaeda and its Taliban protectors in Afghanistan, which Pakistan was then supporting."[33]

In opening remarks to the federal panel investigating the 9/11 attacks April 8, 2004, Rice said:

THE MANY FACES OF JOHN KERRY

The terrorist threat to our nation did not emerge on September 11th, 2001. Long before that day, radical, freedom-hating terrorists declared war on America and on the civilized world. . . . The terrorists were at war with us, but we were not yet at war with them. For more than twenty years, the terrorist threat gathered, and America's response across several administrations of both parties was insufficient. . . . [T]ragically, for all the language of war spoken before September 11th, this country simply was not on a war footing. . . . At the beginning of the Administration, President Bush revived the practice of meeting with the Director of Central Intelligence almost every day in the Oval Office— meetings which I attended, along with the vice president and the chief of staff. At these meetings, the president received up-to-date intelligence and asked questions of his most senior intelligence officials. . . . We also moved to develop a new and comprehensive strategy to eliminate the al-Qaeda terrorist network. . . . This new strategy was developed over the Spring and Summer of 2001, and was approved by the President's senior national security officials on September 4. It was the very first major national security policy directive of the Bush Administration—not Russia, not missile defense, not Iraq, but the elimination of al-Qaeda.[34]

She said President Bush had informed her he was tired of "swatting at flies," leading her to believe he wanted a comprehensive strategy to go after terrorist groups rather than hit-and-miss with specific individuals.[35]

Since 9/11, says constitutional lawyer and syndicated columnist Ann Coulter, the Bush administration "has won two wars against countries that harbored Muslim fanatics, captured Saddam Hussein, immobilized Osama bin Laden, destroyed al-Qaeda's base, and begun to create the only functioning democracy in the Middle East other than Israel. Democrats opposed it all—except their phony support for war with Afghanistan, which they immediately complained about and said would be a Vietnam quagmire."[36]

As stated by Rice during her 9/11 testimony, terrorists—including al Qaeda—were at war with the United States long before September 11. The Clinton administration had eight full years to deal with the threats; when 9/11 occurred, the Bush administration had had only eight months to identify, find, and destroy a *global* terrorist cabal. Indeed, as Rice said, the very first presidential directive issued by President Bush was directed at destroying al Qaeda. But were it not for the Clinton administration's failed approach to terrorism and John Kerry's support of those failed policies— namely, that terrorism should be treated as a law enforcement problem, not a global war on democracy and American interests— perhaps Bush would have had one less worry upon which to focus.

However, in a January 2004 speech to firefighters in Oklahoma City, Kerry intimated he would return to those failed policies. Complaining that Bush "doesn't understand the war on terror," Kerry said under his administration the fight against terrorism "will involve the military now and then," but it will be "primarily an intelligence-gathering, law enforcement operation." He added, "It's a great big manhunt. [The Bush] administration has translated that legitimate threat into a completely wrongheaded kind of full-fledged military response."[37]

One of those policies had to do with a directive issued in 1995 by the former number-two person at the Clinton administration Justice Department, Jamie Gorelick, which critics say further hampered information-sharing among intelligence agencies.

According to the *Washington Times*, "Specifically, [federal 9/11] commission members need to ask her about a [March 4] 1995 directive she wrote that made it more difficult for the FBI to locate two of the September 11 hijackers who had already entered the country by the summer of 2001. . . ."

According to the four-page memo, declassified April 13, 2004, by Attorney General John Ashcroft, "Gorelick ordered [FBI Director Louis] Freeh and [Mary Jo] White [the New York-based U.S. attorney investigating the 1993 World Trade Center bombing] to follow information-sharing procedures that 'go beyond what is legally required,' in order to avoid 'any risk of creating an unwarranted appearance' that the Justice Department was using Foreign Intelligence Surveillance Act (FISA) warrants, instead of ordinary criminal investigative procedures, in an effort to undermine the civil liberties of terrorism suspects."[38]

Specifically noted, the *Times* reported, was the "oft-noted wall of separation" that prevented federal prosecutors and counterterrorism agents from communicating with each other prior to the September 11 attacks. "Information collected under special FISA warrants, which do not require a probable cause, was generally not to be shared with personnel responsible for enforcing federal criminal laws—where probable cause must be demonstrated for a warrant to be issued," the *Times* said. "[T]he practical effect of the wall was that counterintelligence information was generally kept away from law enforcement personnel who were investigating al Qaeda activities. But Ms. Gorelick's memo clearly indicated that the Clinton administration had decided as a matter of policy to go even beyond the law's already stringent requirements in order to further choke off information sharing."[39]

Under John Kerry, America will return to terrorism and homeland security policies that have already failed the nation. The American people will have to decide if that's too high a price to pay for *any* president.

7

MAN OF THE PEOPLE?

Disdain for the values of the common man

THE BEAUTY OF THE American political system is its utility. Simply speaking, our founding fathers devised a government "of the people, for the people, and by the people," which consisted of "the people" sending representatives to the nation's capital to vote on *behalf* of those who sent them. In this manner, "mob rule" democracy was meticulously avoided while still ensuring the voice of the people would be heard and, more importantly, heeded.

Granted, things have changed since the early, heady days of America in the immediate post-revolutionary period. But generally speaking, the system still operates much in the same way the founders intended—in spirit, if not in actual practice. It's true that too many of today's legislators are "professional" politicians unlike the public servants envisioned by George Washington, Benjamin Franklin, Thomas Jefferson, and Alexander Hamilton. Nevertheless, politicians still feel the need to pander to constituencies in election years to maintain their grip on power and do not totally disregard the public's opinion on many key issues of the day, because they know that—while slow to anger—the American electorate does wield its power occasionally. And when it does, professional politicians usually suffer for it. Case in point: Americans, angered by the Democrats' inaction on important policy questions, elected a huge number of Republicans to Congress during the GOP "revolution" of 1994, gaining control of the House of Representatives for the first time since 1952.

A president, meanwhile, has a much more difficult task. He (or she) must consider what is best for an entire nation—one with diverse population centers, cultures, values, mores, and opinions. Hence, a president's actions can have far greater implications if abused or used improperly. That's why it's important to gauge presidential candidates on a range of issues that face the nation—to see if the candidate has enough in common with most Americans to lead them effectively.

John Kerry does not.

THE ABORTION ISSUE

As do most Democrats, Kerry supports abortion in all its forms, at any time, and does not support measures requiring minor girls who are pregnant to give parental notification and get parental consent before obtaining an abortion.

"John Kerry believes that women have the right to control their own bodies, their own lives, and their own destinies. He believes that the Constitution protects their right to choose and to make their own decisions in consultation with their doctor, their conscience, and their God. He will defend this right as president," states his Web site.[1]

At one time, however, Kerry favored allowing states to decide the issue—as they had before the 1973 *Roe v. Wade* ruling overturned abortion bans in all fifty states. "I think the question of abortion is one that should be left for the states to decide," he said, according to the Lowell, Massachusetts, *Sun* newspaper.[2]

And while he and other Democrats have criticized Republicans and the Bush administration for any attempt—real or imagined—to apply a pro-life litmus test to potential Supreme Court justice nominees, Kerry has said openly he would apply a pro-abortion litmus test to *his* nominees.[3]

But wait—does Kerry support litmus tests for Supreme Court justices or not? At one point, he openly opposed such tests. "I don't like the idea of using litmus tests for judicial nominees. As a senator who must regularly vote on whether to confirm federal judges to lifetime appointments, I prefer to take a long, serious look at their qualifications and their judicial philosophy rather than try to determine how they might rule in hypothetical cases," he wrote in his book, *A Call to Service*.[4]

Perhaps as a matter of political convenience, Kerry's opposition—to testing judicial nominees through litmus tests—was made public when a conservative Republican was in the Oval Office, i.e. Ronald Reagan. In 1985, early in Reagan's second term, Kerry declared, "Throughout two centuries, our federal judiciary has been a model institution, one which has insisted on the highest standards of conduct by our public servants and officials, and which has survived with undiminished respect. Today, I fear that this institution is threatened in a way that we have not seen before. . . . This threat is that of the appointment of a judiciary which is not independent, but narrowly ideological, through the systematic targeting of any judicial nominee who does not meet the rigid requirements of litmus tests imposed. . . ."[5]

Now, however, as Kerry seeks the Oval Office for himself, he believes in them: "The potential retirement of Supreme Court justices makes the 2004 presidential election especially important for women, Senator John F. Kerry told a group of female Democrats yesterday, and he pledged that if elected president he would nominate to the high court only supporters of abortion rights under its *Roe v. Wade* decision," the *Boston Globe* reported in April 2003. "Any president ought to appoint people to the Supreme Court who understand the Constitution and its interpretation by the Supreme Court. In my judgment, it is and has been settled law that women,

Americans, have a defined right of privacy and that the government does not make the decision with respect to choice. Individuals do," Kerry said.[6]

Apparently, however, Kerry believes only *his* point of view on the issue is correct. In *A Call to Service*, he has pledged to block any attempt to appoint a pro-life justice to the bench. "The Supreme Court hangs in the balance and the next justices will determine whether we move forward or backward. Therefore, I will filibuster any Supreme Court nominee who would turn back the clock on the right to choose, on civil rights and individual liberties, on the laws protecting workers and the environment," Kerry wrote.[7]

Characteristically, however, Kerry doesn't see his criteria, or his vow to filibuster anti-abortion high court nominees, as a "litmus test." Rather, he views it as a means to supporting constitutional government. "Litmus tests are politically motivated tests; this is a constitutional right," he told the *Boston Globe*. "I think people who go to the Supreme Court ought to interpret the Constitution as it is interpreted, and if they have another point of view, then they're not supporting the Constitution, which is what a judge does."[8]

Regarding other issues of life (and death), Kerry has gone out of his way—literally—to protect his political position regarding support for abortion. In March 2004, he left the campaign trail for only the second time since January 2004 to return to Washington to vote with the minority against the Unborn Victims of Violence Act, a bill that makes it a separate charge to harm or kill an unborn baby during the commission of certain federal crimes. Upon voting against the bill—which passed with wide bipartisan support, 61–38, with twelve Democrats joining the majority—Kerry claimed the bill "would clearly impact a woman's right to choose to terminate her pregnancy, as that right is set forth in Roe vs. Wade." Before voting on the bill, he said he opposed "granting a fetus the same legal status in all stages of development as a human being."[9]

For his part, President Bush—who immediately said he would sign the measure—praised it as a bill that would protect mothers. "Pregnant women who have been harmed by violence, and their families, know that there are two victims—the mother and the unborn child—and both victims should be protected by Federal law," he said in a statement released by the White House.[10]

With his vote, however, Kerry made clear unborn babies don't deserve any legal protections, yet he chastised Bush in 2003 for making women less safe. "In case after case, President Bush's actions have made American women less safe and less secure—on the job and on the streets. As president, I will put American government and our legal system back on the side of women. I will stand up for their security, ensure their safety, support their rights, and guarantee their dignity."[11] With his vote, he essentially said he would protect and preserve abortion rights at any political cost, even if it meant denying extra federal protection for women who "chose" not to abort their children.

The important fact of this issue is that, on the issues of abortion and life, Kerry disagrees with much of America. While he accuses opponents of his position as being "extreme," the reality is his opinions on these issues represent extremism. Recent polls show public support for abortion wavering, if not conditional.

For example, one *ABC News*/Beliefnet poll in July 2001 found support for abortion at its lowest levels since 1995. According to the survey, a small majority—52 percent—said abortion should be legal in all or most cases, while a growing minority, 43 percent, said it should be illegal in all or most cases. "While large majorities say it should be legal in dire cases, most also have said abortions should be illegal when done solely to end an unwanted pregnancy," *ABC News* reported.[12]

In another example, an *ABC News/Washington Post* survey taken on the thirtieth anniversary of the Supreme Court's *Roe v. Wade* decision, found that a majority—57 percent—of Americans believe the procedure should be legal in all or most cases, while 42 percent want the government and the courts to make them harder to get. But the same poll also found that, while eight in ten surveyed said abortion should be legal to save a woman's life, preserve her health, or terminate a pregnancy caused by rape or incest, a much smaller majority—54 percent—said abortion should be legal to terminate the life of an impaired baby. It also found 57 percent opposed abortion just to end an unwanted pregnancy.

Regarding "partial-birth" abortion, seven in ten said they opposed that procedure.[13]

Strangely, however, Kerry said no such procedure even exists. "Just hours after President Bush signed a law banning what critics of the procedure call 'partial-birth abortion,' Senator John F. Kerry declared last night 'there is no such thing as a partial birth,' as he and the other Democratic presidential contenders sought the political support of women voters. . . . 'It is a late-term abortion. They have done a very effective job of giving people a sense of fear about it. It's part of their assault on the rights of women in America. . . . There's nothing partial about their effort to undo Roe v. Wade,'" Kerry claimed.[14]

However, public support for "late-term abortion" is not the majority opinion. A *Los Angeles Times* poll in June 2000 found that support had plunged to 43 percent, down from 56 percent in 1991.15

KERRY V. THE CATHOLIC CHURCH

There is also a religious aspect for Kerry to consider. He claims Roman Catholic faith, yet his political support for abortion-on-demand puts him at odds with the Church—so much so the Vatican has expressed concern over his beliefs. "People in Rome are becoming more and more aware that there's a problem with John Kerry, and a potential scandal with his apparent profession of his Catholic faith and some of his stances, particularly abortion," a Vatican official, who is American, told *Time* magazine. Taking that position could lead to excommunication from the Church, but Kerry dismissed those concerns. "I don't think it complicates things at all," Kerry told *Time* in the April 2004 interview, the first in which he has discussed his faith extensively. "We have a separation of church and state in this country. As John Kennedy said very clearly, I will be a president who happens to be Catholic, not a Catholic president."[16]

Other Catholic clergy, however, were not so dismissive of the Church's doctrine. And, to prove it, they have actually shunned him for not standing true to his beliefs. "If Sen. John Kerry were to stand in Archbishop Raymond L. Burke's Communion line Sunday, Burke would bless him without giving him Communion," the *St. Louis Post-Dispatch* reported in January 2004. "Kerry, a Catholic, has voted to support abortion rights, contrary to the Catholic Church's long-held teaching of opposing abortion. 'I would have to admonish him not to present himself for Communion,' said Burke."[17]

However, at one point in his political life—in another policy flip-flop—Kerry actually opposed abortion as a means of birth control. "I would say also that it's a tragic day in the lives of everybody when abortion is looked on as an alternative to birth control or as an alternative to having a child. I think that's wrong. It should be the very last thing if it has to be anything, and I say that not just because I'm opposed to abortion but because I think that's common sense," Kerry told the *Lowell Sun* in 1972.[18]

GAY RIGHTS

John Kerry splits company with many Americans on the issue of gay rights as well. According to his campaign Web site, "John Kerry believes that same-sex couples should be granted rights, including access to pensions, health insurance, family medical leave, bereavement leave, hospital visitation, survivor benefits, and other basic legal protections that all families and children need. He has supported legislation to provide domestic partners of federal employees the benefits available to spouses of federal employees."[19]

Along these lines, Kerry supports lifting the ban on gays in the military (except where it would harm unit cohesion), and he supports the creation of same-sex civil unions (but not gay marriage[20]), "so that gay couples can benefit from the health benefits, inheritance rights, or Social Security survivor benefits guaranteed for heterosexual couples."[21]

Though the issues surrounding homosexuality have been at the forefront of American politics for more than a decade, the most recent chapter in the history of homosexual activism, ironically, began in Kerry's home state of Massachusetts. In November 2003, the state supreme judicial court ruled illegal Massachusetts' ban on same-sex marriages. Justices found under the state constitution the ban was improper because it blocked "protections, benefits, and obligations of civil marriage solely because that person would marry a person of the same sex." In response, the state high court ordered Massachusetts lawmakers to write a new law that provided legal status to same-sex couples and allowed them to marry—a law which took effect in May 2004.

But according to a *Fox News*/Opinion Dynamics poll taken days after the Massachusetts court ruling, 66 percent of Americans said they oppose same-sex marriages—results *Fox News* said were "similar to those from August 2003, as well as results from 1996, when 65 percent of the public said they opposed allowing same-sex couples to marry."[22]

While a higher number of Americans said they support the concept of civil unions "that are not marriages," *Fox News* reported, the majority—48 to 41 percent—still opposed them.[23]

Months later, in March 2004, *CBS News* found that only 22 percent of those questioned said they supported the right of gays to marry legally. Forty percent opposed any legal recognition, while only a third of Americans supported civil unions.[24] An *ABC News* poll found similar results: 55 percent opposed, 37 percent favored.[25]

While a majority of Americans believe gays should be permitted to serve openly in the military, the military doesn't see it the same way—and in this case it is the Defense Department Kerry should heed on the issue, not the American public. Why? First, because most Americans have never served in the nation's military and, hence, have no basis—other than personal feelings—for their opinion. Secondly, Kerry, as commander in chief, needs the respect of the military he will command. If the Pentagon says openly gay soldiers, sailors, and airmen are bad for unit cohesion, for morale, and would serve as an unnecessary source of distraction and angst among the overwhelming majority of heterosexual troops, Kerry should put away his activist hat and listen. As a former Navy officer with combat experience, he should know how important it is to have the trust of his military. Not that presidents should abide by every Pentagon whim; after all, in America, it is the civilian leadership that controls the military, not vice-versa. But there is a body of evidence supporting the Pentagon position of not allowing gays to serve openly in the military because to do so would harm unit cohesion, and even retention. A president—and a Congress—would do well to heed the "advice."[26]

AFFIRMATIVE ACTION

Regarding the age-old issue of affirmative action, Kerry "believes in an America where we take common sense steps to ensure that our schools and workplaces reflect the full face of America," according to his Web site. "He has consistently opposed efforts in the Senate to undermine or eliminate affirmative action programs and supports programs that seek to enhance diversity, for example, by fostering the growth of minority small businesses." Some national polls indicate Americans support affirmative action generally, but in most other cases, surveys completed by varied interest groups and polling organizations suggest otherwise.

Most recently, the issue was brought to the forefront again, this time in Michigan. In the summer of 2003, the U.S. Supreme Court ruled in favor of a University of Michigan law school application process to use race as one factor in deciding who may attend. But according to the *Detroit News*, most Michigan voters—64 percent—back a ballot proposal devised in early 2004 that would ban affirmative action in government hiring and college admissions.[27]

There's even more support that shows Americans do not agree with John Kerry's platform on racial litmus tests and preferences. A 2002 survey by the Pew Research Center for the People and the Press found almost three-fourths of respondents disagreed with this statement: "We should make every possible effort to improve the position of blacks and other minorities, even if it means giving them preferential treatment."[28]

According to a January 2003 *ABC News/Washington Post* survey, most Americans agree with President Bush—that women and minorities may be in need of assistance, "but only if it doesn't do so by disadvantaging white men." (Note: The Bush administration filed legal briefs opposing the Michigan University case.) Overall, said the survey, "two-thirds of Americans oppose preferential programs—ones that 'give women, blacks, and other minorities preference over white men getting into college, getting a job, or getting a promotion.'"[29]

In another flip-flop, Kerry himself has even said he believes affirmative action is, in and of itself, a "flawed" concept, even creating racism. According to the *Boston Globe,* "Citing the Senate debate on the Civil Rights Act of 1964, Kerry argued that affirmative action was never meant to result in racial quotas. But 'not only by legislation, but by administrative decree and court order, a vast and bewildering apparatus of affirmative action rules and guidelines has been constructed. And somewhere within that vast apparatus conjured up to fight racism there exists a reality of reverse discrimination, that actually engenders racism,' he said."[30] In another instance, he called the concept "inherently limited and divisive."[31]

In his early political life, Kerry said he favored "minority hiring quotas on housing construction jobs."[32] But years later, in a June 1996 *New York Times* story, he said he had never favored quotas.[33]

FAITH-BASED INITIATIVES

As a Catholic, Kerry is already staring down the Vatican over key moral issues. But his contempt for any sort of religious faith in the public arena stretches even further.

For instance, Kerry opposes President Bush's "faith-based initiatives," a series of policy priorities that allow religious-based organizations that perform charity work to collect social-program funds from the federal government. "Sen. John F. Kerry (D-Mass.), a Catholic, said Bush sometimes mixes too much of his religion into his administration's policies," the *Washington Post* reported. "The faith-based initiative crossed that line overtly," Kerry said.[34]

To Bush and conservatives, the founding fathers' intent was made clear in the First Amendment: Washington was never to "establish" or recognize a standard singular religion (as the British did in recognizing the Church of England as the primary center of faith), nor was it to deny any American the right to worship as he pleases—in public or in private. Kerry and liberals, however, subscribe to the American Civil Liberties Union version of the First Amendment—which, many have interpreted, means virtually no displays of religion of any sort on public-owned property.

At one time Kerry backed such initiatives—perhaps when it was politically strategic. For instance, in 1989, he supported a parent's right to choose religious or secular child care: "Standards are an important issue to the child-care providers in Massachusetts. We have very high standards for our caregivers; we believe that children across the nation should have the opportunity to receive care that meets similar standards," he said on the floor of the Senate. "One of the most controversial aspects of this bill is the language on the funding of religious activities. I am well aware of arguments of the opponents of this language. But I believe that it is vitally important that parents be able to receive assistance of the type of care that they choose. I believe that the language promotes parental choice without violating constitutional principles."[35]

A decade later, Kerry joined Republicans to support faith-based charities. He "teamed up with Republican Kit Bond to bolster day care—including funding religious groups. Indeed, Kerry talks up faith-based charities with Bill Bennett-like vigor. 'No one can tell me these programs don't work,' he says."[36]

Days after President Bush was inaugurated in January 2001, he signed an executive order creating the Centers for Faith-Based and Community Initiatives in the Departments of Health and Human Services, Housing and Urban Development, Labor, Justice, and Education.[37] Of Bush's plan, Kerry said it "has the potential to be helpful . . . but the devil can be in the details."[38] A month later, in February, Kerry even claimed credit as the first lawmaker to offer faith-based initiatives. "George W. may be doing it now, but '*I was the first person to offer faith-based programs*,'" he told the *Boston Globe*.[39] But he changed directions 180 degrees when he began his presidential bid. By November 2003, Kerry was bad-mouthing Bush's initiatives, saying they impinged on the Constitution's division of church and state.

Even more confusing, Kerry has also said he supports faith-based initiatives, as long as they don't have a religious aspect.

"Democratic presidential hopeful John Kerry says the Bush administration is violating the principle of separation of church and state because it wants to give more federal money to religious organizations. Bush's plan would let more religious groups compete for government money to provide social services, as long as their services are available to anybody in need," the Associated Press reported in December 2003. "'I think George Bush and his administration has stepped over the line of separation of church and state,' Kerry said Thursday at Hopkinton High School. 'What George Bush is trying to do is allow (religious groups) funding for actually using the religious activity as a component of the service.'" AP went on to report that Kerry stood "firmly" for the Constitution's ban on establishment of religion. "All through our history we have drawn that line," Kerry said. "And I will continue to draw that line." AP continued, "The Massachusetts senator said he is for faith-based initiatives such as Catholic Charities or the Jewish Community Center that he said provide social services without blurring that line. 'There are plenty of faith-based efforts in America where they are the only intervention in helping children get food and adults get to the senior center and things like that,' Kerry said. 'And I think it's legitimate.'"[40]

More importantly, on this and other issues, Kerry is not standing with most Americans. For example, 58 percent of Americans supported government funding for Christian and Jewish religious groups which "run food kitchens, counseling centers, and other social programs, just as it is offered to secular groups," according to an *ABC News/Washington Post* poll in May 2001.

FLAG BURNING

Though he served in combat operations in the military, Kerry has not backed any congressional efforts to protect our national symbol—the American flag. On at least three separate occasions, Kerry has voted against a ban on flag-burning.[41] And he has called the pursuit of a constitutional amendment prohibiting flag burning "simply a phony, misplaced direction of our national energies."[42]

Instead, Kerry sees desecrating the American flag the way the

ACLU and the U.S. Supreme Court see it—just another form of protected speech. "Our country is defined by the rights we protect, and those of us who fought for freedom and put our lives on the line defended the right of people to do things that we disagree with," he said in January 2004. "I would not be pleased to see someone burning the flag because I love the flag, but the Constitution that I fought for preserves the right of free expression."[43]

Kerry is out of step with the American people on this issue, only 38 percent of whom agree with the senator on burning the flag, according to *ABC News*.[44] Polling groups, such as Gallup, reported similar findings.[45]

Further, all but one state legislature disagrees with Kerry. By the end of March 2000, the entire nation, except Vermont, had passed resolutions urging Congress to pass a measure banning flag-burning, according to the Citizens Flag Alliance, a group of 140 civic and veterans' groups.[46]

Because of the actions of men like John Kerry, it remains legal today to publicly desecrate the American flag, a practice most states and the people find unacceptable.

8

SHOW ME THE MONEY!

Sucking up to lobbyists, lawyers, and special interests

JOHN KERRY IS A politician who suffers delusions of grandeur. Behind his fiery populist rhetoric and blow-dried exterior lies an ordinary man with extraordinary hunger—a man who is willing to say and be virtually anything people want him to be in order to become this country's next president.

Case in point: All along the 2004 presidential campaign trail, John Kerry has criticized President Bush for his ties to big-money donors. Kerry, who has championed the issue of campaign finance reform, also has said he has not accepted money from labor and corporate PACs (political action committees), and he claimed during a February 2004 debate in Wisconsin, "The only money I've accepted is money from individual Americans."[1] Following his primary victory in New Hampshire in January 2004, Kerry told supporters that, in regards to Washington's special interests, "I have a message. I have a message for the influence peddlers, for the polluters, the HMOs, the big drug companies that get in the way, the big oil and the special interests who now call the White House their home: We're coming, you're going, and don't let the door hit you on the way out!" He has also generally criticized money in politics, saying at a restaurant in Iowa shortly before New Year's Day 2004, "There's too much money loose in the American political system."[2]

But despite this common man, anti-establishment message, Kerry is as typical a Washington "insider" as most other politicians in regards to raising big money for his campaigns. He knows the system well. While he may outwardly shun and criticize open contributions from PACs, corporations, and other typical fundraising sources, the junior senator from Massachusetts uses a variety of "insider" techniques to funnel big dollars to his campaigns. For example, he's the Senate's number one recipient of individual campaign contributions from paid lobbyists; he's taken in more money from them over the past fifteen years than any of his Senate colleagues (nearly $640,000).[3]

Kerry didn't always refuse PAC money, either. When questioned on the point early in the 2004 campaign, his aides finally admitted that he indeed took PAC money during his 1972 House bid and again in 1982, when he ran for lieutenant governor of Massachusetts. It was not until his run for the U.S. Senate in 1984 that he abandoned the practice.[4]

KERRY'S CLOSE CHUMS

One fundraising technique Kerry has used successfully is working his "big donor" contacts, and one such contact, used during his 1996 re-election campaign, was heavyweight Democratic campaign fundraiser and contributor Johnny Chung.

"John Kerry needed cash, and soon. In July 1996 the Massachusetts senator was locked in a tough re-election fight, so he was more than happy to help when he heard that a generous potential contributor wanted to visit his Capitol Hill office. The donor was Johnny Chung, a glad-handing Taiwanese-American entrepreneur," writes Michael Isikoff, in the February 9, 2004, issue of *Newsweek*.[5]

Chung, it was later learned, also brought along a "friend" to that meeting, Hong Kong businesswoman Liu Chao-ying, who, as later discovered by U.S. intelligence, was a lieutenant colonel in the Chinese People's Liberation Army and vice president of a Chinese-government-owned aerospace firm.[6]

Liu controlled a bank account of some $300,000, all of it supplied by Chinese intelligence.[7] Kerry was told Liu wanted to have her company listed on the New York Stock Exchange, and—perhaps eager to please his guest—he had his aides immediately fax a letter over to the federal Securities and Exchange Commission (SEC) regarding Liu's interest.[8] The very next day Liu and Chung were granted a private meeting with a senior SEC official, and, within weeks, Chung threw a fundraiser for Kerry at a Beverly Hills hotel, bringing in $10,000 for the senator's re-election campaign.[9]

Chung, meanwhile, visited the Clinton White House a total of forty-nine times and moved on to become a central figure in that administration's foreign money scandals, eventually pleading guilty to funneling $28,000 in illegal foreign contributions to the campaigns of Bill Clinton and John Kerry.[10] In all, Kerry took in $18,000 from Chung or Chung-arranged sources.[11]

Chung wasn't the only shady character to become involved in helping finance Kerry's campaigns. According to Federal Election Commission records, Kerry also received a $5,000 donation from Bernard Schwartz, CEO of the Loral Corporation—of Clinton administration fame.[12] In 1994, Schwartz wrote his first six-figure check to the Democratic Party, donating $100,000 to the Democratic National Committee.[13] Around that same time, Schwartz was asked to be included in a trade mission to China by then-Commerce Secretary Ron Brown, "where [Schwartz's] company hoped to win a piece of the growing telecommunications market," the *Washington Post* reported. On the trip, Brown—who was later killed in a plane crash in Dubrovnik, Croatia—arranged for a meeting between Schwartz and a "rival" industry executive with the Chinese communications minister, one that Schwartz later said "helped open doors that were not open before."[14] Still later, the Clinton administration "approved the company's request to launch a commercial telecommunications satellite aboard a Chinese rocket, choosing to side with the State Department's assessment of the launch as 'in the national interest' rather than with Justice Department concerns that approval would interfere with an ongoing criminal investigation," the *Post* reported. At the time, the Justice Department was investigating whether Loral and other companies "provided unauthorized assistance to China's ballistic missile program after an unsuccessful previous launch," the paper said.[15] Schwartz said he got nothing for his donations except good government.

The FEC also said other notables donated to Kerry: Eric E. Schmidt, president of Google.com ($5,000); Edmund F. Kelly, CEO of Liberty Mutual ($1,000); Wesley Finch, president of The Finch Group ($10,000); and William P. Lauder, president of Estee Lauder Co. ($4,500).[16]

There are still more examples of Kerry's catering to the special interests he criticizes on the campaign trail. According to *New York Times* writer David Brooks in a February 7, 2004, op-ed:

> Liu Chaoying's interest was not the only interest John Kerry took a special interest in. According to the Associated Press, Kerry took a special interest in the insurance giant American International Group. When Senator John McCain proposed legislation that would have ended a federal contracting loophole benefiting A.I.G., Kerry did not look away, as others might have done. A loophole may not seem like much to you and me, but to A.I.G. it was a very special loophole—the cuddly kind of loophole you can hold under the blankets and tell your secrets to late at night. And according to the A.P., John Kerry preserved the little loophole. And by sheer coincidence, A.I.G. donated $30,000 to help start Kerry's presidential campaign.[17]

Regarding the A.I.G. "loophole," the Associated Press reported Kerry "intervened" to keep it open—an action that served "to divert millions of federal dollars from the nation's most expensive construction project. . . ."[18] The report went on to say Kerry persuaded McCain, chairman of the Senate Commerce Committee, "to drop legislation that would have stripped $150 million from the Big Dig project and ended the insurance funding loophole. . . ." The Big Dig—a Boston-area tunnel project—"has become a symbol of government contracting gone awry, known for its huge cost overruns that now total several billion dollars, and its admissions of mismanagement," the AP report said.[19]

This is the same project for which the Transportation Department, in 1999, found it had overpaid A.I.G. $129.8 million for worker's compensation and liability insurance that was not needed.[20]

In response to Kerry's involvement in blocking the repeal of a loophole used by A.I.G., Charles Lewis of the non-partisan Center for Public Integrity, a political watchdog group, remarked, "The idea that Kerry has not helped or benefited from a specific special interest, which he has said, is utterly absurd."[21]

COMMITTEES AND SPECIAL INTERESTS

Kerry sits on several Senate committees: Commerce, Science, and Transportation; Finance; Foreign Relations; and Small Business. A variety of special interest groups encompasses each of these committees, and each group contributes mega-dollars every campaign cycle to each member—including John Kerry.

For example, as a member of the Commerce, Science, and Transportation Committee, Kerry received $341,959 from the TV/movies/music lobby; $242,325 from the insurance lobby; $92,072 from telephone utilities; $65,500 from lodging/tourism; and $62,250 from the telecom services and equipment lobby—just in the 2002 election cycle.[22] Not so ironically, this committee regulates each of the industries which contributed to Kerry's campaign.

Similarly, Kerry—as a member of the Small Business Committee—received quite a bit of money from private individuals connected to the interests the committee regulates. According to the Center for Responsive Politics, Kerry, as chairman of this committee in 2002, received more than $1.9 million from individuals representing the finance/insurance/real estate industry; $1,531,918 from lawyers and lobbyists; $920,076 from "miscellaneous business"; and $875,260 from communications/electronics donors.[23]

Early in Kerry's presidential bid, his successes in the primaries attracted even more special interest support—some of it from the very media reporting the events. In February 2004, fresh from a primary win in Maine, Kerry picked up pledges of financial support from some of the most powerful media figures in the U.S.—News Corporation's chief operating officer Peter Chernin, Viacom chief executive Sumner Redstone, and Sony chairman Howard Stringer each pledged to raise between $50,000 and $100,000 for Kerry's presidential campaign.[24] "Most of the money raised from these contributors will have to be raised through business associates, relatives and friends as individuals can only give a total of $2,000 each to presidential candidates—$2,000 during the primaries and another $2,000 during a general election," said the *Manchester Guardian*, in reporting the story.[25] The $2,000 limit for the general election will only apply if Kerry declines the nearly $75 million in federal funding available to both the Democratic and Republican nominees.

The paper reported that by the end of 2003, the Federal Election Commission showed Chernin—along with the president of the Motion Picture Association, Jack Valenti—had contributed the maximum $2,000 each to Kerry's campaign.[26] With the connections each of these entertainment and media moguls are known to have, it isn't a stretch to believe they would have little trouble raising for Kerry the funds they promised.

In all, Kerry has received more than $1.3 million from Hollywood since 1989; his 2004 presidential campaign itself has received more than $430,000 as of February, records show.[27] Other industries which have donated to Kerry since the late 1980s include the insurance industry ($554,949); oil/gas industry ($111,850); pharmaceuticals ($59,505); health products industry ($203,255); health maintenance organizations, the HMOs he so vehemently decries ($102,710); big labor ($21,381); the finance/insurance/real estate sector ($6,340,659); security and investments industry ($2,258,120); more than $1 million from the telecommunications industry; communications/electronics sector ($2,619,514); telecom services and equipment ($120,400); the health-care industry ($1,325,583); and health professionals ($531,251).[28]

Interestingly, Kerry chastised other senators in 2001 for doing the very same thing he did regarding A.I.G.—taking money from a company which had dealings with his Senate committee. According to Charles Lewis in *The Buying of the Presidency 2004*:

> In March 2001, for example, [Kerry] warned his colleagues that taking money from special interests created the perception that Congress was for sale. "When somebody sitting on a particular committee has to go out and raise money from people who have business before that committee, or when someone in the Senate has to ask for money from people who have legislative interests in front of them on which they will vote, there is almost an automatic cloud, he [Kerry] said." Kerry should know. Over the course of his Senate career, he has not been averse to taking campaign cash from companies and firms with a direct interest in his work.[29]

Along these same lines, adds *Newsweek*'s Michael Isikoff, "Over the years . . . Kerry has raised more than $30 million for his Senate campaigns. A good portion has come from industries with an interest in the committees on which Kerry has a seat—including more than $3 million from financial firms (Kerry serves on the Senate Finance Committee)."[30]

However, Kerry declares he has been careful to avoid such conflicts. "If these interests are giving money in hopes of buying influence with the senator, well, they should save their money because it won't work," Kerry presidential campaign spokeswoman Stephanie Cutter told *Newsweek*.[31]

CITIZEN SOLIDER FUND

With that denial in mind, it should be noted the senator has also used behind-the-scenes fundraising schemes, which are not visible to constituents and casual observers, but known to, and used by, career politicians, lobbyists, and favor-seekers inside the Beltway. For example, in 2001, Senator Kerry formed a fundraising organization called the Citizen Soldier Fund, which eventually raked in more than $1.2 million in unregulated soft money.[32] Interestingly, Kerry created this fund only eight months after he voted for the Senator John McCain (R-Arizona) and Senator Russ Feingold (D-Wisconsin) campaign finance reform bill that was passed, and just one week after bragging about being the only senator to be elected three times without accepting PAC money.[33]

Initially Kerry said he'd limit contributions to the fund to $10,000, but "in late 2002, just before new federal laws banning soft money took effect, Kerry quietly lifted the ceiling and took all the cash he could get," notes Isikoff.[34] "In the month before the election, the fund raised nearly $879,000—including $27,500 from wireless telecom firms such as T-Mobile, AT&T and Verizon. That same month, Kerry cosponsored a bill to overturn a judge's ruling and permit the wireless firms to bid on billions of dollars' worth of wireless airwaves. Kerry aide Cutter says it's a 'stretch' to draw any connection between the two events."[35]

According to one report, Kerry "created a vehicle in 2002 to collect large checks directly from companies, labor unions and other special interests on the eve of his presidential bid. Kerry collected more than $470,000 directly from companies and unions in 2002 for his Citizen Soldier Fund, and spent large amounts of it sowing goodwill in key primary states just before Congress banned the use of such 'soft money' donations."[36]

A February 2004 Kerry campaign press release says, "John Kerry has not taken a dime of PAC money during his four Senate elections or during his presidential races. PACs contribute a huge chunk of the money given to politics. Corporate PACs have given $1.2 billion to campaigns and parties since 1990. Not one dime has gone to John Kerry."[37]

Others see Kerry's fundraising techniques—and subsequent denials—as hypocrisy of the truest kind. "The note of reality is, [Kerry] has been brought to you by special interests," said Lewis, of the Center for Public Integrity. "It's very hard for Kerry to utter this rhetoric without some hollowness to it."[38]

Added U.S. Senator Zell Miller, a conservative Democrat from Georgia, "[Supporters] don't know John Kerry's record. They haven't examined it. This is a very vulnerable candidate on several issues. . . . He is the Olympic gold medalist, when it comes to special interest money."[39]

WE'RE IN THE MONEY

Sometimes remaining beholden to special interests backfires on politicians, something which has also happened to Kerry. Between 1985 and 1990—Kerry's first five years in the Senate—he collected more than $120,000 in speaking fees from a diverse group of interests, including oil, liquor, tobacco, and union interests.[40] He pocketed most of the money in amounts slightly less than the maximum allowed by Senate rules at the time (though lawmakers can no longer be paid speaker's fees).[41] One company, Miami-based Metalbanc, paid Kerry $1,000 for a speech in 1987; Metalbanc was later indicted for charges of drug-money laundering.[42] Eventually those charges were dropped because the company went defunct, but Kerry also received campaign contributions from the firm's executives; he said he didn't know about the drug connection until the *Boston Globe* informed him of it in 1996.[43] To make up for it, he donated several thousand dollars to charities.[44]

The Associated Press, in quoting Kent Cooper, former public disclosure chief for the Federal Election Commission, said Kerry "followed a path taken by many new lawmakers who were not wealthy," by agreeing to so many speeches and pocketing the proceeds. "Members were often pulled almost like a magnet into a circle of lobbyists, who were very willing to pay large honoraria for them to give a brief speech or a talk to their organization or group," said Cooper. "This provided instant cash to a member and, at the same time, built a relationship with that lobbyist or organization."[45]

QUESTIONABLE SOURCES

Kerry has other dubious connections to fundraising. In February 2004, the Associated Press reported the Massachusetts senator welcomed an offer by disgraced ex-Democratic Senator Bob Torricelli of New Jersey to raise money for Kerry's presidential bid.[46]

Torricelli's political career ended when his own fundraising techniques became the subject of Senate and Justice Department criminal investigations. Though Torricelli said he wasn't looking for Kerry to put him on his presidential campaign payroll, he did say he was raising money for his Massachusetts former colleague nonetheless. "I have asked people to send in checks," Torricelli told AP in a phone interview. "I have raised some money for John."[47]

The Kerry campaign in turn acknowledged Torricelli's support and even thanked him for it. "John Kerry and Bob Torricelli served together in the Senate for many years," said Kerry spokeswoman Stephanie Cutter. "Many of Kerry's current and former Senate colleagues are supporting his bid for the presidency with the united goal of defeating George Bush."[48] Regarding Torricelli's fundraising past, Cutter was noncommittal. "Cutter declined to address whether Torricelli's role conflicted with Kerry's message on the campaign trail that he has fought the taint of special interest money throughout his political career," AP reported.[49]

But were Torricelli's contributions legal? His Senate campaign committee contributed $50,000 to a group called Americans for Jobs, Healthcare, and Progressive Values—which in turn ran anti-Dean ads.[50] But, the Associated Press reported, "Federal Election Commission spokesman Bob Biersack said it was 'fuzzy' whether Torricelli's contribution was permissible under FEC rules. Donations to such groups are not included on an FEC list of permitted uses for campaign funds."[51]

In another fundraising embarrassment for Kerry, the Massachusetts senator worked on legislation benefiting a technology firm and campaign contributor: Predictive Networks, a Cambridge, Massachusetts, tech firm co-founded by Paul Davis, a longtime Democrat who favors Kerry. (Davis is no longer involved with the company; the firm is now under new management and is called Predictive Media.)

According to *ABC News*, Predictive Media monitors what Internet and cable consumers are viewing and tailors advertising accordingly—a practice that inevitably raised issues of privacy. In 2000, the Senate took up the issue, debating whether Internet and cable companies should have the up-front opportunity to reject that kind of surveillance—in what became known as an "opt-in." It was supported by consumer groups and eventually written into legislation by Senator Fritz Hollings (D-South Carolina). On July 25, 2000, Predictive Media's CEO, David Hosea, met with Kerry and his staff; the very next day, the senator from Massachusetts "introduced a bill that would have enabled companies like Predictive Networks to automatically be allowed to monitor what consumers are viewing— placing the onus on customers to 'opt-out' of surveillance if they wanted," *ABC News* reported. Making it more difficult for consumers to "opt out" was generally seen as a benefit to the industry, since the pool of customers being monitored would be larger and, hence, potentially more lucrative.[52]

Paul Davis himself said, "It absolutely is a special interest. Make no mistake about it—we were in that business to make money, not to perform any kind of social service."[53]

Then, in February 2002, "Hosea threw a fundraiser for Kerry at a Boston restaurant, Locke-Ober. According to Davis, the implied quid pro quo—never stated by Kerry staffers but inferred by many at Predictive Networks—made some executives uncomfortable," said *ABC News*. That summer, Hosea threw another fundraiser for Kerry, this time at the posh Princeton Club in Manhattan: The legislation in question never became law.[54]

SCIENCE AND APPLIED TECHNOLOGY INC.

Kerry became caught up in another fundraising scandal, this time involving the solicitation of fellow lawmakers and officials at the Pentagon, after sending letters in support of a San Diego defense contractor, who would later plead guilty (in February 2004) to illegally funneling Kerry money.[55]

"Between 1996 and 1999, Kerry sent the letters to fellow members of Congress and officials in the Pentagon, asking that they free up funds for a missile system that was under development by Science and Applied Technology Inc., a San Diego firm run by Parthasarathi 'Bob' Majumder," the *Los Angeles Times* reported. A firm from Massachusetts—Millitech—also worked on the project. Still, "some of the money Kerry received was collected at a fundraiser in December 1998 that coincided with a Kerry visit to the contractor's Woodland Hills facility," the *Times* reported. "The money collected that year helped Kerry erase a campaign debt from his 1996 Senate race." Also, the paper said, one of the firm's security representatives, Christina Andrada, said the Kerry visit was highly unusual. "It occurred on a Saturday, a nonworking day, she said, and Kerry and one of his aides came in a car rented by the company," the paper reported.[56]

"One of the corporate guys came out on the Friday before his visit and said that Kerry would someday be president and we needed his support in defense contracting," Andrada said. "When I heard Sen. Kerry was visiting on a Saturday, I was concerned. Why was this guy here? What did he have to do with California? It was very unusual. All nonessential personnel were told to stay home."[57]

Andrada also told the *Times* a number of the company's employees were invited to a reception to be held in Kerry's honor. "Those that wanted to attend had to sign up," she said. "We knew we had to pay an entrance fee. If we had to go and write checks, Dr. Majumder would pay us back." She didn't go, however, because she said she's a Republican.[58]

In February 2004, Majumder pleaded guilty to illegally reimbursing employees, friends, and other contractors for money they gave to Kerry and four other lawmakers (prosecutors argued the lawmakers supposedly did not know the money was tainted). In a CNN interview days later, Kerry said the supporters—including the contractor Majumder—"have never, ever, ever gotten anything."[59]

Nothing? What about the twenty-eight letters of support Kerry sent on Majumder's behalf? Kerry said he was fighting for home state jobs by helping Majumder. But the *Los Angeles Times* took issue with Kerry's avoidance.[60] "Massachusetts Senator John F. Kerry said last week that he was fighting for jobs in his home state when he wrote 28 letters in support of a San Diego defense contractor and campaign contributor," the *Times* reported. "But only six jobs in Massachusetts were ever at stake, the engineer in charge of the project said Saturday. 'At its peak, there were perhaps five or six people' dedicated to a federal missile project, said Richard Chedester. 'It wasn't a huge program.'"[61]

DID HE OR DIDN'T HE?

Even the liberal press have noticed Kerry's hypocrisy regarding his supposed shunning of traditional campaign finance sources, such as PACs. For instance, the *Boston Globe* wrote in June 2003:

> As a presidential candidate, John F. Kerry has repeatedly railed against the corruptive influence of special-interest money in politics, and has proudly declared on various occasions that he is the only or first person elected to the U.S. Senate three times without taking campaign contributions from political action committees. . . . But the public record shows that Kerry was neither the first nor the only senator elected three times without money from political action committees. . . . David L. Boren appears to be the first person elected three times to the Senate without PAC money, in 1978, 1984, and 1990.[62]

In addition, Warren Rudman of New Hampshire was elected to the Senate without PAC money in 1980—four years before Kerry.[63]

Kerry's history of taking special interest money isn't recent. As far back as 1972 and into the 1980s, while running for other offices, Kerry accepted PAC money. The Associated Press reported, "Kerry spokeswoman Stephanie Cutter confirmed Kerry took . . . PAC money in 1972, and another small amount in 1982 when he ran for Massachusetts lieutenant governor, before abandoning such donations starting with his 1984 run for the Senate. 'In his first public race 32 years ago, John Kerry took money from autoworkers, teachers, electricians, and Democratic groups that account for 5 percent of the money he raised in a losing House race,' the spokeswoman said."[64]

In his unsuccessful 1972 bid for the House, Kerry collected about $20,000 from PACs, with most of it coming from labor unions. The AFL-CIO PAC gave him $3,000, while the railway clerks, autoworkers, and state, county, and municipal union workers gave $500 apiece.[65]

More recently, other groups also stumped for Kerry, though they weren't openly seen as pure PACs or other entities specifically controlled by, or funded by, Kerry. Says the *Washington Post*, advertisements by groups such as Americans for Jobs, Healthcare, and Progressive Values were generally viewed as a "shadow" political campaign for both Kerry and Missouri U.S. Rep. Dick Gephardt, who quit the race for the Democratic presidential bid January 20, 2004: "At the time the ads were running. . . . [T]he group's spokesman was Robert Gibbs, who had left the Kerry campaign shortly before. . . . A top Democratic strategist said the group was widely viewed as a shadow campaign for Gephardt and Kerry, who shared a goal then of derailing Dean."[66]

GIVE AND YOU SHALL RECEIVE

Over the course of Kerry's Senate career, a media investigation found that he made nominations three times for federal positions just before, or just after, receiving donations from the named individuals. In one instance, Kerry wrote the Federal Housing Finance Board urging the reappointment of candidate Marvin Siflinger. The very next day, the Kerry campaign committee received $1,000 from the nominee.[67]

"One has nothing to do with the other," Siflinger told the Associated Press, but the records show he donated around the time of Kerry's Oct. 1, 1996, recommendation to the federal board. Also, he contributed to Kerry's campaign committee a year before his reappointment, in 1995, according to Federal Election Commission records.[68]

Another nominee up for federal appointment, investment banker Derek Bryson Park, called his pair of $1,000 donations to Kerry's campaign the month before the senator's December 29, 1998, recommendation that Park be given a position at the Federal Home Loan Bank of New York "pure happenstance." Says Park, "I got assistance from both . . . Democrats and Republicans." One analysis of FEC records says the only donations Park made around that time were to Kerry.[69]

Yet a third federal appointee, former congressional staffer Patrick Dober, insisted "there's absolutely no relationship" between his $408 donation to Kerry's campaign nearly three months after the senator recommended him to the Federal Bank Board in an October 9, 1998, letter (Kerry's letter praised Dober for having "worked closely with my office" on "the banking crisis in the early 1990s"). But at the time, Dober was employed by Boston Capital, a real estate financing and investment firm founded by Jack Manning. Manning happened to be a supporter of Kerry. As of 2004, Manning had donated some $800,000 to Democratic causes over fourteen years, and "gave $65,000 in 2001 and 2002 to a tax-exempt political group Kerry set up," AP reported.[70]

Not surprisingly, Kerry's office insists the timing of the donations and nominations are merely coincidental. "Sen. Kerry recommends dozens of very qualified individuals each year without regard to their politics or contributions. In this case each of the individuals were highly qualified for the jobs they were appointed to and served with distinction," said Cutter.[71]

Larry Noble, a former chief lawyer for the FEC and now head of the Center for Responsive Politics, says Kerry—who has long advocated campaign finance reform—is now attempting to distance himself from the kind of special-interest money that has benefited him over the years: "Kerry is out there saying he is not being part of that game, yet he is the product of the same money system."[72]

In a June 1984 fundraising appeal to voters, Kerry wrote, "I will act as a persistent watchdog over presidential appointments to ensure that only people of integrity, ability and commitment hold positions of power in our national government."

Critics and watchdogs like Noble see such talk as so much duplicity. "This is just business as usual in Washington," says Noble. "It's like a game where you say the people who support me just want good government, but the people who support my opponent are special interests."[73]

Even Kerry himself has, at times, publicly and vocally recognized the need to raise funds—but not without more controversy. In an interview with the *Boston Globe* in 1996, Kerry acknowledged the necessity of fundraising while, at the same time, insulting residents of Texas and Iowa: "I'm not suggesting this is a virtuous process. I hate it. I detest it. I hate going to places like Austin and Dubuque to raise large sums of money. But I have to."[74]

Indeed he may, since he says he won't use any of his wife's estimated $550 million Heinz foods fortune to run. "It would be a contradiction. I said to people long ago and I held to this during my Senate campaign, I came to politics based on my own initiative and my own effort to raise money and that's the way I want to finish my life in politics," he said in a March 2003 interview. "Teresa's money is Teresa's money and I've declaratively stated that."[75]

Or will he use it? In a separate statement just a few months later, he stated using his family fortune was an option, and blamed his contradiction on President Bush. Kerry said "he retained the right to use his family's wealth . . . to fight what is expected to be a $200 million Bush barrage before Labor Day 2004," according to *Newsweek*. "I know the kind of campaign they are going to run," Kerry said, "and I am prepared to fight back."[76]

The last statement might explain this: While initially claiming he wouldn't *directly* use his wife's fortune in his campaign, Kerry could employ it *indirectly*, perhaps as a way to foster support from special interest groups. According to a February 2004 report, the League of Conservation Voters, a left-leaning environmental organization, announced it was putting "money and manpower" behind the group's endorsement of Kerry. "LCV sent field workers to New Mexico . . . and will run a television ad highlighting Kerry's environmental voting record in that state and neighboring Arizona. . . ." said *Greenwire*, an environmental policy tracking news service.[77] About a week after that story appeared, the *New York Post* reported the LCV "acknowledged getting funds from a foundation headed by his wealthy wife, Teresa—but denied that played any role." The *Post* reported "LCV political director Mark Longabaugh said the group got $57,300 from the Heinz Family Foundation—headed by Mrs. Kerry who is the widow of ketchup heir John Heinz—from 1993 to 2001, including a $2,500 personal contribution from her in 2000."[78]

A coincidence? *National Review* reported, "On January 24, before the first vote was cast in New Hampshire's Democratic primary, the League of Conservation Voters (LCV) endorsed Senator John Kerry . . . for president. Weeks earlier, in an entirely unrelated matter, the Heinz Family Foundation provided an 'unrestricted-use' grant of a quarter million dollars to a group represented on the LCV board."[79] Interestingly, the Kerry endorsement was the first offered by LCV *before* the primary season had begun. "It's the first time the group [LCV] has endorsed prior to the primary season, and officials said they would target some 36,000 registered environmental voters in New Hampshire on behalf of the Massachusetts Democrat," AP reported.[80]

CONTRIBUTIONS FROM THE KETCHUP HEIRESS

In what some believed was another end-run around campaign finance rules, the *Boston Herald* reported in February 2004 the Kerrys may have overestimated the value of their Beacon Hill townhouse in Boston in order to get a loan for the $6.4 million

Kerry needed to resuscitate his campaign. "The Kerry campaign says the elegant Louisburg Square townhouse that Kerry shares with his millionaire wife, Teresa Heinz Kerry, is worth $12.8 million—exactly double the Christmas Eve mortgage the senator got from Mellon Bank," said the paper. "But Boston's Assessing Department puts the value of the swank, five-story mansion—with six fireplaces, five bedrooms, a private elevator and roofdeck—at $6.6 million as of Jan. 1, 2003. The assessed value actually dropped from 2002's figure of $6.95 million." The true value of the home is important because federal election laws only permit Kerry to finance his campaign through his own assets, not those of his wife.[81]

"It could be a very, very big excessive contribution by his wife if, in fact, he's using more than half the real value of the house," Don Simon, a Washington-based campaign finance lawyer who is unaffiliated with any presidential campaign, told the *Herald*. Heinz, the paper added, is limited to a contribution of $2,000 to her husband's campaign.[82]

Also questioned was the propriety of the loan; Kerry's wife, "heiress to the Heinz ketchup fortune, has a long history with Mellon Bank. The bank also serves as a trustee for the T & J Louisburg Square Nominee Trust, the entity that owns the townhouse," said the *Herald*.[83] Kerry's loan was crucial because it came at a time when he was running a distant second place in the polls to initial Democrat presidential frontrunner Howard Dean, former governor of Vermont (and third in the important caucus state of Iowa).[84]

CAMPAIGN FINANCE REFORM

Kerry has practiced double standards over a variety of issues relating to the financing of his various campaigns, including his 2004 presidential bid. For one, Kerry said his administration, were he elected, would support reinstatement of a five-year ban on lobbying by government officials. "We will reinstate the five-year ban on lobbying so that government officials—like Bush's former campaign manager and FEMA director—cannot cash in by peddling influence."[85] (Joe Allbaugh was Bush's campaign manager and later FEMA director.)[86]

Also, Kerry pledged he would require "every meeting with a lobbyist or any special interest deal inserted into a bill by a lobbyist be made public."[87]

Kerry also said he supported the most far-reaching campaign finance law in recent memory, the McCain-Feingold law. "As I said before, this bill, which bans soft money, regulates sham issue ads, and provides a study for public funding systems, provides a good first start to reform, and I will therefore support it," he said from the floor of the Senate. "For too long we've known that we can't go on leaving our citizens with the impression that the only kind of influence left in American politics is the kind you wield with a checkbook. This bill reduces the power of the checkbook and I am proud to support it."[88]

Kerry has even come out in support of public funding—i.e. taxpayer financing—of federal elections. "The votes we have taken on various amendments addressing public funding make it clear that a lot of my colleagues aren't ready to embrace public funding as a way to finance our campaigns. But it is, in my opinion, the best constitutional means to the important end of limiting campaign spending and the contributions that go with it. Ultimately, I believe in the potential of a system that provides full public funding for political candidates," Kerry said on the Senate floor in 2001. "I believe that any system that reduces candidates' reliance on private money and encourages them to abide by spending limits will ultimately be the best way to truly and completely purge our system of the negative influence of corporate money."[89]

In the current presidential campaign, Kerry also tried to convince potential supporters he has shunned some forms of traditional funding, such as PAC money. "I am the only United States senator who has been elected four times voluntarily refusing to ever take in any one of my races one dime of political action committee special interest money," Kerry told an audience during a February 2004 Democratic candidate debate in Wisconsin. "The only money I've accepted is money from individual Americans, and 1 percent of it, approximately, in my entire lifetime has come from anybody who's ever lobbied for anything. . . . And when I'm president, we will put back on the table the effort to get the money out of American politics and restore the voices of average Americans to the agenda of our country."[90]

And Kerry pledged to stay within the $45 million spending limit in the primary contest "until the nomination is decided."[91]

But Kerry said he expected to raise some $25 million before the Democratic Convention in July, much of it in response to an expected television advertising blitz by President Bush.[92] Based on figures supplied by the Federal Election Commission, Kerry had raised more than $85 million in campaign funds by early March 2004.[93]

For all his hypocrisy over denying he is indebted to any number of "special interest groups," Kerry still attempts to take the heat off himself by pointing the finger at President Bush, accusing him and his fellow Republicans of remaining obliged to such groups. And in many stump speeches during the campaign season thus far, Kerry still mouths the words of a candidate independent of undue influence, which translates into a litany of half-truths, fabrications, and outright lies:

- "Tonight, I think, was a victory of people who want to stand up to powerful special interests. I've stood up against them. Nobody has ever suggested that I've done other than to take them on, those special interests."[94]

- "George Bush has chosen tax cuts for the wealthy and special favors for the special interests over jobs."[95]

- "Let me tell you something, for thirty-five years I've been standing up and fighting against those special interests. I'm the only United States senator currently serving, who has run four times, voluntarily refusing to ever take a PAC check in any one of my races. I've run only with individual Americans contributing to me. And I believe I have stood up against them again and again in a way that says, 'If I'm president, I'm taking them on.'"[96]

- "I think it's important to live by the campaign finance reform standard if we can. I'm the only person now serving in the Senate with four terms who's run for election not with special interest money, not with PAC money, not with soft money, not with independent expenditures. The only people who've elected me are individual Americans. And I think it's important to live by the campaign finance reform standard if we can."[97]

- Kerry has also accused President Bush of being wed to some of the same "special interests" that have contributed mightily to his own campaign. "We need to stand up and make it clear that we're going to say no to [Bush's] cynicism. We're going to say no [to] their abuse of power. And we are going to restore to America the vitality of our own democracy, which is threatened by the power of these special interests, most recently witnessed in the energy bill and the Medicare bill. . . . And that will be one of the first things I turn back in the first hundred days of my presidency."[98]

- "I'm going to restore our place in world leadership. And I am going to break the stranglehold in this country of special interests that have brought us an energy bill."[99]

- "And for those of you who some days, you wake up and wonder, 'Is it going to work, can I make it happen,' let me just tell you something. It's the courage of individual Americans that have always defined our country. It's the courage of individual Americans who have been able to take on special interests. And that's what we need to do today."[100]

- "[The Bush administration] has the greatest feeding frenzy in modern history with special interests. And I have a record of taking on those special interests. . . . We need a president who knows how to fight for the average worker of our country, not for special interests that shove people off of Medicare into HMOs and then wind up giving the oil industry . . . $50 billion of incredible subsidies. . . ."[101]

Kerry, while campaigning in New Hampshire, also blamed lobbyists and the Bush administration for kicking seniors off Medicare and onto the rolls of HMOs: "When it comes to the lobbyists that have been parading through the halls of Congress writing a Medicare bill that pushes seniors off of Medicare into HMOs . . . that's the mission George Bush has accomplished."[102]

The Massachusetts senator also charges Bush and his administration with "pursuing a creed of greed." He said at a campaign event in New Hampshire: "If you think I'm upset about this, I am. I have never seen, in all my years in public life, I have never seen the level of unfairness as patterned as it is today in America, as institutionalized. This president is pursuing a creed of greed. And the big guys keep getting it folks. . . . I've seen it."[103]

Interestingly, though he has chastised Bush and Republican opponents for allegedly catering to special interests—even to the point of calling them "crooked" liars[104]—Kerry not only caters to them himself but also does so to the detriment of the people he supposedly represents, according to *The Hill*, a congressional newspaper. "Last Friday in New Hampshire, [Kerry] railed against the influence of lobbyists and pledged to shine light 'on the secret deals in Washington.' But during his Senate career, Kerry has helped special interests, even against the apparent interests of his own constituents. This helped cement ties with lobbyists who donated thousands of dollars to his campaign."[105]

Kerry is the Senate's top recipient of individual campaign contributions from paid lobbyists; he's taken in more money from them over the past fifteen years than any of his Senate colleagues (nearly $640,000).[106]

John Kerry has claimed there is too much money "loose" in the political system of America today. If you hear him say this on the campaign trail, listen to him; he should know, because he's a product of that system.

9

CORPORATE CORRUPTION

Enron, Halliburton, and a jailhouse interview

JOHN KERRY AS A U.S. senator and presidential candidate doesn't practice what he preaches. During this campaign Kerry continually casts aspersions on all Republicans including President Bush and Vice President Cheney over their alleged connections to big corporations and their executives.

Take for example the collapse of energy giant Enron in 2001 and the resulting scandal. Democrats, including John Kerry, have roundly criticized the Bush administration over its energy-industry contacts, claiming the White House somehow improperly consulted—or consorted—with industry leaders like Enron's former CEO, Kenneth Lay, in formulating the administration's energy policy.

Kerry has also attacked the vice president over his former employer Halliburton, another energy company which is supplying U.S. troops in Iraq.

Campaigning in Iowa in September 2003, Kerry told an audience "seniors have had their retirements stolen by Enron and WorldCom, by financial scandal, and a marketplace where this president licenses a creed of greed."[1] And just before the Iowa caucuses in January 2004, Kerry said, "We need to end an administration that lets companies like Halliburton ship their old boss to the White House and get special treatment while they ship American jobs overseas."[2] For the record, those off-shore jobs are Americans employed in the rebuilding of Iraq.[3]

In February 2004 on CNN, Kerry lumped everyone together in his corporate criticism: "George Bush and his crowd, they are the world champions in terms of special interest giveaways—the drug companies, the oil companies, Halliburton, the Enron Scandal, the WorldCom scandal. . . ."[4]

What's hypocritical about Kerry's criticism? The old saying goes, people who live in glass houses shouldn't throw stones.

According to financial records, Senator Kerry and his wife Teresa Heinz Kerry have profited personally both from Enron and Halliburton. In a *National Review* analysis, Sam Dealy explains,

> Personal financial disclosure forms filed with the Senate show that on December 11, 1995, the marital trust held by Kerry and his wife purchased Enron stock valued anywhere from $250,001 to $500,000. (The Senate requires only rough valuations for assets and liabilities.) The stock returned between $5,000 and $15,000 in dividends in 1996, and another $5,001 to $15,000 in 1997. Capital gains realized from the sale of Enron stock that year totaled anywhere from $15,001 to $50,000. All in all, the Kerrys made between $25,003 and $80,000 off their Enron buy.[5]

The same holds true for their Halliburton stock purchase. "On May 13, 1996, the marital trust purchased between $250,001 and $500,000 of stock in the company. Just seven weeks later, the stock was sold. The trust reported earning $1,001 and $2,500 in dividends and $5,001 and $15,000 in capital gains. Add it up and the gains were anywhere from $6,002 to $17,500," *National Review* reported.[6]

Maybe that's not a lot of money to John and Teresa Heinz Kerry, but it is to most working Americans. So when it comes to whether a politician running for the highest office in the land is being honest when he criticizes a company and tries to capitalize on a scandal because his political opponent has some involvement with it, his huge profits made from those same companies are fair game. It's more Kerry hypocrisy.

And it only gets worse from here.

JOHN KERRY'S JIM MCDOUGAL

The Bank of Credit and Commerce International (BCCI) was a financial institution of Middle Eastern origins "whose employees asked few questions of their wealthy and powerful customers, making it a favorite of arms merchants, drug dealers, despots such as Noriega, and intelligence agencies," according to an analysis by the *Boston Globe*.

In 1988, Senator Kerry launched a Senate investigation as chairman of the Senate Foreign Relations Committee's subcommittee on Terrorism, Narcotics, and International Relations, on allegations of criminal activity by BCCI and its corporation executives. The bank closed three years later. Questions of hypocrisy and looking the other way for his friends would surface in this effort as well; during the probe, Kerry did not shy away from being wined and dined by BCCI's chief executive officer, as well as the main suspects under investigation.

"Unlike any ordinary bank, BCCI was from its earliest days made up of multiplying layers of entities, related to one another through an impenetrable series of holding companies, affiliates, subsidiaries, banks-within-banks, insider dealings, and nominee relationships," says the December 1992 report to the Senate Committee on Foreign Relations. "By fracturing corporate structure, record keeping, regulatory review, and audits, the complex BCCI family of entities created by [BCCI founder Agha Hasan] Abedi was able to evade ordinary legal restrictions on the movement of capital and goods as a matter of daily practice and routine."[7]

BCCI was about more than just one institution, one country, one person. In fact, the entire "scandal" involved a number of powerful people, including some American politicians—including one John Forbes Kerry.

As chairman of the Senate committee investigating BCCI, Kerry learned early on one of the central figures in the scandal was David Paul, the chief executive officer and chairman of CenTrust Savings of Miami. By 1989, the thrift was declared insolvent by federal regulators—a failure that cost American taxpayers some $2 billion.[8] In the ensuing federal investigation, Paul was convicted of securities fraud and, in November of 1994, was sentenced to serve eleven years in prison and ordered to pay restitution of $65 million and a fine of $5 million.

According to authors James Ring Adams and Douglas Frantz, before its collapse "CenTrust had the outward appearance of a healthy, even robust institution."[9] Paul "maintained opulent offices in one of the most glittering new buildings on the Miami skyline, with a $3 million marble staircase and a gold-plated bathroom sink."[10] Paul is to the 1980s what Jeff Skilling, Bernard Ebbers, and L. Dennis Kozlowski are to today—the CEOs of Enron, Worldcom, and Tyco involved in large scandals for lavish spending habits on the company dime.

Adams and Frantz said Paul, a liberal Democrat, "donated heavily to politicians and entertained them lavishly," as well as to others "who could be useful to him."[11]

"On July 20, 1988," they wrote, "[John] Kerry hosted a reception honoring Paul, one of the largest contributors to the [Democratic Senatorial Campaign Committee], and later the senator used Paul's private jet to fly to a DSCC leadership meeting." According to documents and an exclusive interview with David

Paul, Kerry was one of the elite at a private, lavish dinner thrown by Paul in Miami on December 3, 1988. "Later, Paul would boast that he had derailed Kerry's [Senate] investigation."[12]

During the 1988 election cycle, Kerry served as chairman of the DSCC.[13] In 1987, Kerry had appointed Paul financial chairman of the committee.[14] More than ten years after his 1994 conviction, with Kerry running for president, David Paul still sits in a federal prison. Paul watches as his former close friend nears capturing the White House, and, like Jim McDougal in the famed Whitewater case involving Bill Clinton, Paul has very selective memory regarding his past with John Kerry.

Believing Paul had an interesting perspective to bring regarding his ordeal and his connections to Kerry, I decided to make an attempt to speak to him. After some research I located him at the Miami Federal Prison located just southwest of downtown Miami, where he was still an inmate.

After corresponding with Paul to gain permission for a prison visit to discuss his relationship with John Kerry, I received a letter from Paul agreeing to an interview. Several weeks later I found myself in sunny Miami, driving south down U.S. Route 1 toward the prison.

I'd been to the maximum-security federal prison in Miami for an interview before, and this lower-level correctional facility wasn't nearly so ominous. Still, tall barbed wire fences and rows of razor wire were constant reminders of prison life.

Before arriving, I filled out a National Crime Information Center form, so prison authorities could perform a computer background check on me. Once cleared by security, I was escorted to the visitor's area, but there was some confusion among the prison staff on where the meeting with Paul would take place. While the prison officials discussed room assignments, Paul just wandered down the hall wearing his greenish khaki uniform shirt and pants. He was just sort of hanging out in the hallway for a few moments before he walked up and introduced himself to me.

Within a few moments prison officials got organized and led us both to a meeting room in the prison chapel. There we had a small conference room all to ourselves, though a prison official sat outside the glass door, ever vigilant.

As soon as the door closed and we were alone, the first thing David Paul said to me was, "This is the face of the vast right-wing conspiracy." That statement brought some chuckles and led me to ask if he had access to the Internet. Paul told me he "loved the Drudge Report" and thought of Drudge as a new breed of journalist. "He is just like Edward R. Murrow," Paul said.

Next we discussed Paul's relationship with John Kerry, and he told me he met Kerry through Ted Kennedy in the early 1980s. "We used to socialize together regularly. We had dinner or drinks in Miami, Washington D.C., and Ted's home in Hyannisport," said Paul.

David Paul became such an important member of Kerry's circle his name was read at the Democratic National Convention in Atlanta in 1988, when he served as Kerry's fundraising chairman of the DSCC. Paul stated he couldn't remember who read his name at the convention but added that one evening during the convention a party was thrown in his honor. He also admitted CenTrust hosted a hospitality suite for attendees of the convention and Senator Kerry attended.

"I knew John Kerry well, but I knew Ted Kennedy and [Louisiana Democratic senator] John Breaux better," Paul said. "Kennedy and Breaux were instrumental in Kerry naming me head of the Finance Committee." At times during the interview, Paul tried to act innocent and naïve, stating, "I didn't understand how big a deal being chairman of the fundraising arm of the Senatorial Committee was at the time."

Paul went on to explain that Kerry and other Democrat senators knew of his business problems. A review of Paul's schedules showed he had access to virtually all Democratic senators in the late 1980s. "Kerry and other people at the DSCC knew of my ongoing fights with banking regulators. I was lobbying senators about my problems to get help," he said.

Paul liked to host parties, very lavish parties, bringing together his closest friends, business associates, and leading Democratic politicians. Paul said he held a party for a group of friends, which included several senators—among them was Kerry—at the Super Bowl in Miami on January 22, 1989, when the San Francisco 49ers defeated the Cincinnati Bengals. "I also hosted a party at my bank building that weekend for everyone," Paul said. "I also used to hold a lot of fundraisers at my home in Miami—*a lot.*"

When I asked him about his private plane and whether Kerry had used it, he said he thought "just once." But, after reviewing documents I brought with me, he agreed that Kerry may have used his private jet as many as six times. He said he also owned a huge luxury yacht and Kerry may have gone out on it as well.

Gaith Pharon, a close friend of Paul's and a Saudi national who headed BCCI, got to meet John Kerry through his relationship with Paul. The former CenTrust CEO acknowledged visiting Pharon's home in Savannah, Georgia, two or three times and stated that, "I don't remember if John Kerry ever came there with me or not." Pharon asked Paul if he could sit next to Senator Kerry at the now-famous December 3, 1988, "French Chef's Dinner" at Paul's Miami mansion. Pharon, a main suspect in the BCCI investigation, sat next to Senator Kerry—who, let's remember, was *leading the Senate investigation into BCCI.* Paul, of course, claims he did not hear anything that they discussed and did not ask either of them about their conversation.

Paul said Kerry attended the chef's dinner using one of Paul's corporate planes. The senator's girlfriend, a society reporter from the *Miami Herald* named Jane Wooldridge, also attended. Paul said the two were very close; it was right after Kerry's divorce was finalized.[15] "Jane could have been the next Mrs. Kerry, but she didn't have enough money," Paul explained. He went on to say, "John Kerry was a red-blooded American guy. He liked the ladies—at least he wasn't gay."

Is Kerry qualified to lead the country? "I don't know if I would vote for him; I knew Kerry well, but I don't think he has the intellect of Colin Powell or Condoleezza Rice," Paul continued. "It's very hard to get to know him. He's not a warm and fuzzy guy. I know he articulates a position on an issue but whether he keeps his position is the question." Paul stated Kerry, "could change his opinion on a dime. If he were to win, who will he surround himself with? That's a good question," Paul contemplated. "For me, it's not about Kerry. I really dislike Bush."

Paul also offered information about his relationship with another U.S. senator. He said Florida Democratic Senator Bob Graham had told him he was disqualified as Al Gore's vice presidential choice in 2000 because of Graham's past relationship with Paul. "'I have to stay away from you,'" Paul quoted Graham as saying.

While the prison interview with David Paul did not uncover any smoking guns, it served to underscore one of John Kerry's chief character flaws: He's a hypocrite. On the one hand he will lambaste President Bush, Vice President Cheney, and Republicans for their close ties to big business and some individuals caught up in corruption scandals. Yet Kerry himself is guilty of the very conduct he condemns in others.

10

WELFARE, CRIME, JOBS, AND VETS

Ruining life for everyday Americans

THERE ARE MANY POLITICAL, social, and cultural issues a president, Congress, and the vast bureaucracy in Washington deal with on a daily basis. The minutiae of daily political life in the nation's capital, while often uninteresting and tedious to most, is a sport (some would call a blood sport) to the professional political practitioners who manage the nation's affairs.

Unfortunately, too many Americans don't care about what goes on in Washington. Individuals may vote periodically, but beyond that, they have lives to live, families to raise, jobs to work, groceries to buy, bills to pay, school functions to attend, and a host of other obligations and diversions. Americans squeezed for time put politics low on their list of priorities. They don't feel as though their vote and voice matters much to Washington's elite, and perhaps all too often they are proven right.

But to disengage oneself from all things political because nothing good comes of paying attention is a self-fulfilling prophecy. Many of the elite in Washington count on Americans being too busy to notice what they're doing, too busy to study congressional voting records, and too busy to find out what their representatives stand for or, too frequently, even who their representatives *are*.

This year, in 2004, Americans will be asked once again to select their next president. To do so voters need the best information available, in order to make an informed choice. One man—George W. Bush, the incumbent—has already established a performance record on which to be judged. The other man—John Kerry—has twenty years in the United States Senate, and before that two years as lieutenant governor of the state of Massachusetts. All he has to distinguish himself is his past positions on a variety of important issues; those positions, in total, are more valuable than the sum of all his campaign sound bites and rhetoric. They identify who he really is, not the fictitious figure he's reinvented himself into to win an election.

WELFARE AND WELFARE REFORM

As part of Lyndon B. Johnson's "Great Society" initiative, the entitlement of welfare—introduced in the mid-1960s as a way to eliminate poverty—has, by any reasonable estimate, been a failure, at least at its stated goal. Despite pouring tens of billions of dollars into the various welfare-related programs annually, the percentage of people living below the poverty level has remained about the same since the passage of welfare programs:

> 1969: 13.7 percent
> 1979: 12.4 percent
> 1989: 13.1 percent
> 1999: 12.4 percent.[1]

Over the course of his political career, Kerry has held varied positions on welfare and efforts to reform it. But generally speaking, he supports maintaining the status quo, even though the program has not yielded appreciable benefits.

In 1972, Kerry actually viewed the issue as an "instrument of enforced poverty," a position held by many reform advocates today who believe the program perpetuates, rather than cures, poverty. The *Boston Globe* wrote in 1996, "As early as 1972, Kerry was running for Congress with campaign literature denouncing the welfare system as 'an instrument of enforced poverty which limits rather than encourages the desire to work for those who are able.'"[2]

However, by 1988, sixteen years later, Kerry called "troublesome" a reform effort introduced by a Republican colleague that required welfare recipients to work at some job in order to receive benefits. "Kerry voted against then-Senator Bob Dole's [R-Kansas] amendment requiring at least one parent in any two-parent family on welfare to work sixteen hours a week, explaining that the provision was 'troublesome to me,'" the *Globe* reported.[3]

Additionally, in 1992, Kerry voted against a reform amendment allowing states to withhold welfare from the parents of children who did not regularly attend school.[4]

Just two years later, however—as calls for reforming welfare were beginning to get louder—Kerry claimed reform was necessary and he'd "come down hard on it." But he could not decide on what limits to set. "Kerry repeatedly addressed the eroding image of the Democratic Party as a champion of the 'work ethic' and 'personal responsibility,'" the *Globe* reported, in a separate story. "'We have to get rid of the perception that we need to do things for people and create the perception that we are willing to help people help themselves,' he said. 'We have to make people believe that we're not just taking their dollars and throwing them down a rat hole.' . . . Although he stresses the importance of improving education and job training and curbing what he called 'the incentives' that contribute to teen-age motherhood, he said he has yet to decide what limits he would set on welfare recipients, a topic expected to be central to the reform debate. 'I've got to come down hard on it, but I'm sorting through it,' he said. 'These are exactly the conversations I'm having now.'"[5]

In 1995, he agreed with the "principle of cutting off cash assistance to those who have more children," opting instead to provide government-sponsored services such as "child care and job training."[6] But that year Kerry, in the Senate, voted to gut key reform provisions from the bill under consideration and in the end voted against final passage of the entire reform package—putting him at odds with his previous position.

According to a Republican summary of an amendment Kerry supported, the provision "would perpetuate welfare as we know it. It would require states to provide welfare benefits without time limit, or without any other requirement for that matter, to care for minors. Supposedly, the benefits would only flow to the children, not their parents. Surely Senators do not believe such a division is possible. For example, if vouchers were used to pay for shelter, would the parents be allowed inside as well, or would infants get their own apartments?"[7]

Furthermore, the GOP stated, "[U]nder this amendment, anyone could remain on welfare if a state did not provide job training and job assistance. This bill does not require such assistance. A state that was not interested in ending the entitlement status of welfare could assert for any welfare recipient that appropriate training had not been provided. Second, if a state were desirous of moving people from welfare to work, and if it tried to cut someone off of welfare after providing voluminous assistance, or if it even offered a job to that welfare recipient, that recipient could take the state to court and assert that appropriate assistance had not been provided or that more assistance was needed before work could be demanded."[8]

A year later, Kerry voted against a family cap provision which banned states from increasing cash benefits for recipients who have more children while on welfare (many experts have cited the government's inability to cut off all financial rewards to parents having more children while on welfare as the ultimate incentive to do so). "Sen. John F. Kerry, whom Weld is contemplating challenging in the 1996 election, voted for the Senate welfare bill after he had helped to kill the family cap provision," the *Globe* reported.[9]

However, during one 1995 debate over welfare reform, Kerry even went so far as to introduce a pair of amendments that would have preserved assistance checks for persons "disabled" by drug and alcohol abuse. Neither amendment had any co-sponsors and neither made it to the Senate floor for a vote.[10] The amendments came back to haunt him. During a tough 1996 re-election battle with Republican Governor William Weld, his GOP challenger reminded Massachusetts voters of Kerry's intentions to reward drug and alcohol abusers. Kerry, however, said his measures were, in reality, aimed at helping addicted veterans.

At a September 17, 1996, morning press conference, Weld launched his toughest attack against Kerry, accusing him of wanting to reward drug addicts and alcoholics with government-sponsored cash benefits via the Supplemental Security Income (SSI) program—a charge the Kerry campaign denied. "Weld's dishonest campaign has reached a new low with his false claims about disability benefits," the campaign replied, in a statement. "John Kerry is proud to have fought on behalf of troubled Vietnam veterans while insisting that they be in treatment programs before receiving any such benefits." The *Boston Globe* reported that the SSI program was not limited to veterans with substance abuse problems. Nevertheless, in a debate that week, "Kerry sought to defuse the issue by arguing that the cash payments were needed to help addicted vets rebuild their lives."[11]

Interestingly, neither of the amendments mentioned veterans. The first, No. 2661, read, "To provide supplemental security income benefits to persons who are disabled by reason of drug or alcohol abuse, and for other purposes." The second, No. 2679, contained the exact same language.[12]

In other welfare-related legislation, Kerry

- Voted to eliminate provisions of a bill denying cash and non-cash benefits to naturalized citizens.

- Voted in favor of allowing federal funds to be used to bring legal challenges to welfare reform.

- Voted for extended child-care assistance.

Ultimately, Congress did pass welfare reform in 1996, and, with Bill Clinton's reluctant signature, the measure became law. It was deemed at the time to be one of the most sweeping such measures since welfare was introduced in the mid-1960s, and Kerry wound up supporting the measure. "Welfare should be about work, a temporary helping hand that leads to a job," Kerry said, in a 1996 candidate questionnaire published by the *Boston Globe*. "That's why I voted for the welfare reform law President Clinton recently signed. We must ensure that our welfare system protects children and moves parents from dependency and into work."

But he also complained about a number of the bill's provisions. He "lamented the bill's deep cuts in nutritional assistance for children and its bar against most forms of federal aid for legal immigrants," said the *Globe*.[13]

CRIME AND PUNISHMENT

Democrats traditionally poll poorly on law and order issues, and John Kerry may not get much higher marks. One reason? They are viewed as too lenient and unrealistically soft on crime. One example is a man named Willie Horton; he became the subject of one of the most hotly debated campaign ads of 1988, when Vice President George H. W. Bush was running against former Massachusetts Governor Michael Dukakis.

Before Dukakis became governor, Massachusetts passed an initiative known as the Prison Furlough Program. Under it, prison inmates who qualified became eligible for unguarded, unsupervised forty-eight-hour furloughs; it basically allowed for the release of criminals (including violent criminals and murderers) on an honor system, if they promised to stay out of trouble and return when the furlough was over.

Enter Horton. On June 6, 1986, he was released from the Northeastern Correctional Center in Concord, Massachusetts. But he never came back. Nearly a year later, on April 3, 1987, he showed up in Oxon Hill, Maryland, and attacked twenty-eight-year-old Clifford Barnes, pistol-whipping him with a gun he had acquired along the way and stabbing him twenty-two times across Barnes' midsection. Then, when Barnes' fiancée returned later that evening, Horton gagged her and savagely raped her twice. Horton then stole Barnes' car and was later captured by police after a high-speed chase and shoot-out. On October 20, 1987, Horton was sentenced to two consecutive life sentences plus eighty-five years. The Maryland court refused to return Horton to Massachusetts, noting fear he may someday be furloughed again. "This man should never draw a breath of free air again," said the court.

Now for the punch line: Kerry, as Dukakis' lieutenant governor, supported the furlough program that turned Horton loose on two more victims. "As Michael Dukakis' lieutenant governor from 1983–1985, Kerry supported a furlough program for hundreds of Massachusetts' inmates, a program that many critics deemed too lenient toward criminals," wrote John Perazzo for *FrontPage Magazine*.[14]

Would Kerry, as president and chief law enforcement officer of the nation, continue to be soft on crime and criminals? His record says yes.

Kerry, a lawyer by trade, was named an assistant district attorney in Middlesex County, Massachusetts, five months after passing the bar exam. He was given "free rein" to overhaul the office.[15] His quick appointment to the office created some animosity among colleagues, some of whom remained resentful of Kerry, mostly because he reeked of opportunism. "[Middlesex County District Attorney John] Droney veterans were stunned [by Kerry being named as first assistant district attorney]. Many of his assistants were resentful. Their reaction fit a recurring pattern during Kerry's years as a young man in a hurry, thrusting his way to the forefront and irking others who coveted that prominence."[16]

Some more experienced district attorneys had Kerry's number. They could see where his rapid ascension was leading, and it didn't have much to do necessarily with crime and punishment. "I still do not think that Kerry should have been appointed first assistant to the district attorney," said DA Guy Carbone in May 1978. "I think he is a little too recent an attorney to be first assistant district attorney, and I think you'll hear from him again in politics."[17]

The appearance that Kerry was using the DA's position as a stepping stone manifested itself in other ways. For example, he handled all media relations for the office.[18] He also served as an election analyst for a television station.[19] Two weeks after he left the position, he became a twice-weekly guest on a local political talk program.[20] Kerry was obviously trying to use his position as a stepping stone to higher ambitions, noted a 1984 Boston Globe story: "Kerry became too much [of] a star for [District Attorney John] Droney's liking and infuriated some of his colleagues. One attorney said, 'There are cops who still hate [Kerry]. They remember when WEEI [radio] would hear about a raid before they did.'"[21]

One of the highlights of his brief prosecutorial career included the release of a convicted pedophile—Robert Sedach—who later kidnapped and sexually assaulted a young boy.[22] Later, the Dukakis/Kerry administration would issue furloughs for 287 sex offenders, 82 first degree murderers, and 184 second degree murderers.[23]

PLAYING SOFTBALL

The Dukakis/Kerry administration was very forgiving of criminals, which in turn put more Massachusetts residents at risk and insulted crime victims and their families. During his tenure as lieutenant governor—from 1982 to 1984—parole rates rose from 50 percent to 58 percent.[24]

Such a forgiving attitude didn't make Massachusetts safer. During the same time span, rapes increased, rising from 1,464 a year to 1,627.[25] Also, Massachusetts became the country's car-theft capital. "The vehicle theft problem, which has nearly quadrupled nationally over the past 25 years, is particularly critical in Massachusetts. Here, the rate of larcenies per 100,000 vehicles has continued to top all other states and is more than twice the average of all 50 plus the District of Columbia," reported the *Christian Science Monitor* in November 1984. "In 1982 alone the figure was 55,005, or an average of 968 per 100,000 registered vehicles, according to the Federal Bureau of Investigation's (FBI) uniform crime report released earlier this fall. Thus, Massachusetts retains one of its least-cherished distinctions: the car-theft capital of the nation."[26]

Since his early political days, Kerry has done little to help police and law enforcement do their jobs more efficiently or with better legal reinforcements. Specifically:

- He voted against legislation earmarking funds for additional prosecutors for gang-related activities.[27]

- He voted against a law that made carjacking a federal offense.[28]

- He has voted against funding for additional federal prosecutors.[29]

- In 1995, two years after the first World Trade Center terrorist bombing, Kerry voted to slash $80 million from the

FBI's budget. That same year, he unsuccessfully proposed legislation to slash $1.5 billion—over the following five years—from our intelligence budget.[30]

Kerry also opposes the death penalty, but has flip-flopped on the issue in the past, depending on the political circumstances. "Mr. President, I have opposed the death penalty for many years—as a prosecutor, as a defense attorney, as lieutenant governor of Massachusetts, and as a U.S. senator," he said on the Senate floor in 1988.[31]

In recent years, he says he believes the death penalty is applied "unfairly."[32] And he believes it "is inequitably enforced and has been wrongfully applied."[33] During one CNN interview in 1994, Kerry called the death penalty a "joke," adding that it does little to nothing to deter future crime:

CNN's FRANK SESNO: Senator Kerry, would you say that this tough crime bill that Senator Dole talks about is what's ultimately going to come out of this conference? There are an awful lot of conservatives who feel that it's going to be a soft crime bill, if you can have such a thing?

KERRY: No, I think inevitably, first of all, the . . . death penalties are almost a joke, and I think they do a—

SESNO: Why are they a joke?

KERRY: Well, they do a disservice to the notion of crime fighting, because there are only nine people or six people in the entire United States of America who would be impacted by it, and you're clearly not going to affect the wave of youth violent crime because those are offenses occurring at the state and local level, over which the federal government does not have jurisdiction.[34]

In all, Kerry has voted against applying the death penalty for drug traffickers and kingpins, police killers, drug-related murders in Washington D.C., and even for terrorists.[35]

Yet, according to research and supporting data, the implementation of the death penalty is a crime deterrent, especially when it is applied in an expedient manner. William Tucker, writing in *Human Events* in April 2003, citing U.S. Census Bureau statistics, found that a correlation between executions and the homicide rate from 1930–2000 can be shown. His data reveals falling murder rates when the death penalty is implemented and escalating murder rates when the courts prohibited capital punishment in the early 1960s.[36]

In an assessment of Tucker's work, the National Center for Policy Analysis noted "there is no way to contravene the logic of murder . . . except through the death penalty. No amount of victims' pleading or cajoling—no promises that 'I won't tell'—will ever convince a robber or rapist that there isn't an advantage to escalating the crime to murder."[37] As Tucker found, the entire increase in murder from 1966 to the mid-1990s was an increase in felony murders—those committed during the course of another crime. Only when executions resumed in the 1990s did the murder rate drop precipitously to its 1960s level.[38]

JOBS AND INTERNATIONAL TRADE

John Kerry, on the campaign trail in March 2004, pledged to create ten million new jobs in the U.S. in four years' time. "We will renew American competitiveness, make tough budget choices, and invest in our future. My pledge—and my plan—is for ten million new jobs in the next four years," Kerry said, quoted by CNN.[39] According to the network, the Kerry campaign's "economic proposal will include tax reform and credits to encourage job creation in the United States, an education and job training program, as well as a plan to 'restore fiscal discipline and confidence in the American economy.'"[40] Naturally, the issue—and the figure he cited—drew instant attention. Especially when considering how well (or rather, *how badly*) Kerry seems to understand trade and labor.

Kerry used to concur with the conventional wisdom that global trade is the answer to the creation of jobs at home and, therefore, national prosperity. In 1993, on national cable television network CNN, Kerry declared, "*Ultimately, there is no way out except for international trade and increased markets.* There is simply no way to compete with yourself, and there is no way to compete with low wages, and we're witnessing the phenomenon of globalization and technology, which is changing the workplace."[41] A decade later, in 2003, he added, "International trade enhances economic opportunity and can serve to improve workers' rights."[42]

In another instance, Kerry said he and others supported the North American Free Trade Agreement [NAFTA], by declaring—in a 2001 letter to President Bush—"we are supporters of NAFTA and of expanding international trade and investment."[43] And, as senator, Kerry has voted at least ten times in favor of expanding fast track/trade promotion authority for the president.[44]

Besides voting in favor of NAFTA in 1993, Kerry also supported GATT, the General Agreement on Tariffs and Trade, the following year.[45] And he's voted in favor of other international trade agreements, such as legislation in favor of permanent normal trade relations with China.[46]

But as the 2004 Democratic presidential nomination race heated up, Kerry—perhaps in an effort to court votes and campaign contributions—began pandering to organized labor, traditionally viewed as a solid supporter of Democratic candidates. Organized labor is opposed to international trade agreements it feels are responsible for job losses in the United States.

In a speech to the large labor union, the AFL-CIO, in Chicago in August 2003, Kerry said, "We had trade, but we began to move towards labor and environment as part of trade. When I'm president of the United States, no trade agreement will ever be signed that has a rush to the bottom. We will have labor, environment standards, and we will fight for the rights of working people in this country to be able to do better."[47]

In the same speech, Kerry used the political cover of "environmental" and "labor" standards to claim he would vote against a Fair Trade of the Americas Area plan. "If [the Fair Trade of the Americas] were before me today, I would vote against it, because it doesn't have environmental or labor standards protections in it," he said.[48]

Ironically, though he supported NAFTA, Kerry said he's opposed to CAFTA—the Central America Free Trade Agreement. "CAFTA—you're concerned about the Free Trade of the Americas Act and the Central American Free Trade Act. I will not sign either of them in their current form. They have to be negotiated to have these other standards, otherwise it will hurt the U.S. very badly."[49]

Suddenly—as he campaigns for president on the heels of a Bush administration that came into office at the beginning of a recession and subsequent job losses—Kerry says he'll apply stricter labor standards to trade agreements. "I will monitor progress of future trade negotiations closely and fully expect to see substantial progress in several areas. In particular, the inclusion of basic worker protections, as well as strong monitoring and enforcement provisions, are necessary to meet the challenges of an inclusive and progressive trade policy," he said on the floor of the Senate in July 2003.[50]

But such "protectionist" policies will actually hurt American labor and the job market. According to Federal Reserve Chairman Alan Greenspan, in February 2004, "The protectionist cures being advanced to address [current job and fiscal] hardships will make matters worse rather than better." He added that "protectionism will do little to create jobs and if foreigners retaliate, we will surely lose jobs." Rather than protect U.S. markets unreasonably, Greenspan said the best remedy to joblessness is for workers "to be

THE MANY FACES OF JOHN KERRY

equipped with the skills to compete effectively for the new jobs that our economy will create."[51]

Some traditionally liberal media pundits inveighed against the kind of protectionism advanced by Kerry. Said David Ignatius in the *Washington Post*, "This anti-trade talk is dangerous nonsense, and the Democrats should be embarrassed by it. It suggests to U.S. workers that there is an alternative to change and adaptation . . . That's wrong, most of all because it misleads people about their real options."[52]

Curiously, a decade ago, in 1993, Kerry warned against the U.S. invoking the kind of trade protectionism he espouses now in his 2004 presidential campaign. According to the *Toronto Star*, "'There will be some intensification in some industries and areas for measures' to stop the hemorrhaging of jobs to foreign countries 'if new job creation doesn't replace it,' [Kerry] warned. 'And that is something we all need to be worried about, because it is a danger that can create its own political momentum and the president may be trapped by it.'"[53]

Six years later, in 1999, Kerry and his Massachusetts colleague, Senator Edward Kennedy, also voiced concern about trade protectionism. "John Kerry and Edward Kennedy chose the right course in favor of free trade in one of this session's critical roll calls last week. Kerry issued a warning that ought to be heeded by future administrations and Congresses as they seek to maintain U.S. prosperity in an interdependent world. . . . Kerry is right to worry that 'if the economy goes down, you'll have a backlash of protectionism' across a range of industries."[54]

But as he progressed along this year's presidential campaign trail, Kerry waivered, proclaiming NAFTA should be fixed. "*I don't want to nix NAFTA, I want to fix NAFTA*. . . . It does need fixing, but it ought to be fixed. We got more trade into Mexico [than] Mexico got into the United States under NAFTA," Kerry said.[55]

At one point Kerry said the trade agreement was not to blame.

"NAFTA is not the problem," Kerry said at a November 1993 news conference in his Boston office. "Job loss is taking place without NAFTA. The hard reality is that as a nation we can't put our heads in the sand like ostriches."[56]

More recently, however, Kerry has tried to distance himself from his past support for NAFTA—in order to please his labor union allies—but in reality the jobs situation since NAFTA was implemented is, overall, much better. Says the Cato Institute's Center for Policy Studies:

> Civilian employment in the U.S. economy grew from 120.3 million in 1993 to 135.1 million in 2001, an increase of almost 2 million jobs per year. The unemployment rate fell steadily after the enactment of NAFTA, from an average of 6.9 percent in 1993 to under 4 percent in 2000. The unemployment rate jumped to 6 percent in 2002, but that was because of the recent and relatively mild recession of 2001—a recession brought on not by NAFTA but by rising interest rates and energy prices and a falling stock market.[57]

The same institution found that, contrary to the rhetoric in some quarters, the loss of manufacturing jobs has not been linked to NAFTA:

> [I]n the first eight years of NAFTA, manufacturing output in the United States rose at an annual average rate of 3.7 percent, 50 percent faster than during the eight years before enactment of NAFTA. . . . Manufacturing employment has fallen in the past few years, but that cannot in any plausible way be blamed on NAFTA. . . . The decline in manufacturing jobs since 1998 has not occurred because those jobs have gone to Mexico; it has occurred because of (1) collapsing demand for our exports due to the East Asian financial meltdown in 1997–98, (2) our own domestic slowdown in demand due to the 2001 recession, and (3)

the ongoing dramatic improvement in manufacturing productiv-
ity-fueled by information technology and increased global com-
petition that has allowed American factories to produce more and
better widgets with fewer workers.[58]

Kerry has proposed a "ten million new jobs" campaign,
which is necessary because he alleges the Bush administration's
economic policies have led to outsourcing of American jobs to
cheaper labor environments abroad. And he has blamed the Bush
White House for the loss of nearly three million jobs since taking
office.

The Bush campaign says Kerry's charges are "factually false
and deeply cynical." And Steve Schmidt, a Bush campaign
spokesman, said Kerry himself has been quoted as saying that his
plan won't stop outsourcing and won't create jobs.[59] That may just
be campaign rhetoric, but a study of outsourcing by the Organization for International Investment found an inverse to the phenomenon: "Insourcing."

"The debate about outsourcing is essentially about globalization," Todd Malan, executive director of the Organization for
International Investment, said in a February 2004 press release by
the group. "The media has focused on one facet of globalization:
outsourcing. But the flip side of 'outsourcing' jobs abroad is
'insourcing' jobs to the U.S. from companies based abroad."[60]

In 2001, some 6.4 million U.S. jobs were supported by insourcing, says a *Wall Street Journal* report on Malan's study. "According
to Mr. Malan's organization, U.S. units of foreign companies
employed 6.4 million so-called insourced jobs in 2001, up from 5.1
million in 1996 and 4.9 million in 1991," the paper said.[61]

On trade, perhaps one of America's most important partners as
the world entered the twenty-first century was China—a huge and
burgeoning market of nearly 1.4 billion people, which economists,
Congress, and trade experts have said repeatedly it is in America's

best interest to find ways to tap. It's a nearly limitless market. Kerry once thought the same things, but now, as he campaigns for the presidency, Kerry has flip-flopped on this issue, too.

As far back as 1987, Kerry introduced amendments in the Senate to improve and promote trade with China.[62] "This bill represents a major export opportunity for Massachusetts, small- and medium-sized businesses," he told *Business Wire*. "Increased trade with China will mean increased economic development and jobs for Massachusetts."[63]

Then, throughout the 1990s Kerry supported measures granting China most-favored nation trade status, even at times by breaking ranks with fellow Democrats.[64] In 2000, Kerry voted to make normal trade ties with China permanent; prior to that time, they had to be reauthorized annually by Congress.[65] But that vote hurt him with labor unions. They repeatedly called his offices to complain and ran negative ads against him in Massachusetts for his vote.[66]

Now, in 2004, Kerry suddenly believes the U.S. should be "tough" on China. And as president, he claims he'll review all trade agreements, including the one with Beijing.[67] "We have to be tough on some things. China understands that," Kerry said, quoted by the *San Jose Mercury News*. "It's a way of life out there to get away with what you can until you are called on it. The violations of intellectual property are disgraceful and unacceptable. We need to be tough on currency manipulation."[68] But his answer isn't one born of an American solution. John Kerry, ever the internationalist, wants the World Trade Organization—not the American people, via Congress and the office of the presidency— to address the issue.[69]

U.S. issues—trade or otherwise—are not issues to be decided by a global entity that does not have Americans' best interests in mind. An American president working with the people's representatives in Congress is the only plausible way to solve our problems. John Kerry doesn't seem to agree.

MILITARY VETERANS

John Kerry is a Vietnam veteran, was in the U.S. Navy from 1966 to 1970, and served in combat for four months in late 1968 and early 1969. He deserves credit for that portion of service to his country. But what he has done with his life since then is certainly fair game for scrutiny, and that includes his anti-war activities following his discharge from the Navy. His record of treatment of fellow veterans since becoming a U.S. senator is not only fair game but worth a serious look, if nothing else for what it reveals about a man many believe is driven by political opportunism.

Among veteran's issues, on the campaign trail Kerry has said he'll "end the game of playing politics" with veterans, especially over funding of their health care. He says he'll streamline the Department of Veterans Affairs (VA) to better serve their clients and customers. He claims he'll support social programs that in turn support struggling veterans. And he says he'll increase benefits for active duty service personnel.[70]

If only he meant what he says.

For starters, Kerry—perhaps in an effort to hide his own dismal record of support for veterans—has accused the Bush administration of withholding veterans' benefits and funding. "[Bush] is breaking faith with veterans all across the country. They've cut the VA budget by $1.8 billion. There are forty thousand veterans waiting months to see a doctor for the first time. Whole categories have been eliminated from application to the VA," he charged during a Democratic presidential debate in Manchester, New Hampshire, in January 2004.[71]

In reality, the Bush White House has *increased* funding and benefits for veterans and vet-related programs. The University of Pennsylvania's Annenberg Center stated in a FactCheck, "[F]unding for veterans is going up twice as fast under Bush as it did under Clinton. And the number of veterans getting health benefits is going up 25 percent under Bush's budgets. That's hardly a cut." FactCheck.org twice contacted the Kerry campaign when it published those figures, around February 2004, asking how Kerry justified his claim that the VA budget is being cut, but received no response.[72]

Also, the number of veterans registered to receive health benefits increased by about 18 percent under Bush and is expected to increase by almost 26 percent by October 2004. Says FactCheck.org, "According to the VA, the number of veterans signed up to get health benefits increased by 1.1 million, or 18%, during the first two fiscal years for which Bush signed the VA appropriations bills. And the numbers continue to grow. By the end of the current fiscal year on Sept. 30, the VA estimates that the total increase under Bush's budgets will reach nearly 1.6 million veterans, an increase of 25.6 percent."[73] All of this, no thanks to Kerry.

In 1997, Senate colleague and fellow Navy Vietnam War vet John McCain (R-Arizona) offered an amendment which he claimed would make "distribution of veterans benefits fair." A Republican policy statement on the McCain amendment stated, "The VA is using an antiquated formula for the distribution of VA benefits that does not take into account population shifts. As a result, areas with growing numbers of veteran retirees are receiving too little in funding. The amendment would make the Veterans Affairs Department correct the problem."[74] For three previous years, the amendment never made it out of conference in the Democrat-controlled Senate. So Republicans sought to have the measure put before the entire chamber via a roll call vote, "to show that a strong majority of senators favor making the distribution of veterans benefits fair." In the end there were only eighteen senators voting against the measure, and John Kerry was one of them.[75]

Senator Kerry has since voted against measures that would add funding to veterans' benefit programs, especially health care—a campaign issue he says he specifically wants to support. In 1999 and 2001 he voted against measures that would have provided increased veterans' health funding.[76] And in December 2003, he completely skipped the vote that funded the VA for Fiscal Year 2004.[77] Interestingly, according to congressional records, most VA spending bills pass with near-unanimous support.

If American politics is about anything, it is about *people*. Our founding fathers realized early on that in order to be truly free, the people had to have a voice in government. John Kerry may represent the liberal thinking of some of his Massachusetts constituency, but as president he will have to represent the general will of the whole of the American people. His voting record in the Senate, as well as his previous political machinations, suggests he may be out of step with mainstream America.

11

GAS, OIL, AND HOT AIR

Hugging trees and lawyers

Besides dealing with issues that directly affect the American people, a president is also tasked—along with Congress—in crafting responsible policies that deal with people in an indirect manner. Such issues—those involving the environment, energy, tort reform, for instance—are equally important because despite the general public's lack of interest in them, they are issues that affect our lives.

In the case of John Kerry, he is a liberal extremist on all of these issues. If elected president, his past voting record indicates he can be expected to approve or veto legislation that fits into a specific agenda that puts other concerns ahead of those of most Americans. In the end such decisions will cost Americans money and jobs and could conceivably affect ancillary issues such as health care, insurance affordability, and a family's ability to make ends meet.

MINDING MOTHER EARTH

Solidly perceived in the domain of Democrats is the issue of supporting the environment. But while many Americans who aren't Democrats don't intentionally harm or want to harm the environment, they clamor for more sensible environmental regulations and policies that preserve and protect without costing jobs, affecting necessary development, and worsening the economy.

On his campaign Web site, Kerry hints he will take conservation to a new height. He says he "will enter into a *'Conservation Covenant'* with the American people to tread lightly on the public lands and protect and restore our nation's parks and other treasures for the benefit of future generations. . . . Kerry will implement the Endangered Species Act in a cooperative manner that extends the benefits of wildlife and habitat protection to public and private lands. *He will put new teeth* into *requirements* that private companies who lease public lands return the land to its original state."[1]

In addition, Kerry says he'll "lead a 'Restoring America's Waters' Campaign to clean up our nation's waters, protect communities' fresh water supplies, and help communities reclaim their riverfronts and lake-fronts as new centers of economic growth."[2]

But the centerpiece of his policies is subjugation of America's environmental policy to international standards. "John Kerry understands that some of our most serious environmental challenges—and opportunities—are taking place *on an international stage* and that they require American leadership in *the international community*. . . . When John Kerry is president, the U.S. will re-engage in the development of an *international climate change* strategy to address *global warming*, and identify workable responses that provide opportunities for American technology and know-how. And a Kerry administration will meet new challenges associated with the *global exploitation* of marine resources and the *global crisis* of access to fresh water supplies," says his campaign.[3]

Kerry believes the federal government is the best source to solve *local* growth problems. He "recognizes that local communities are struggling with how to address issues of traffic congestion and sprawl," says his campaign. "A Kerry administration will work with states and communities to ensure they have the tools and resources they need to tackle these difficult problems. Kerry will ensure that we have 'Clean and Green Communities' throughout America by coordinating *federal* transportation policies, *federal* housing incentives, *federal* employment opportunities, and the use of *federal* dollars to acquire parks and open space."[4]

But the federal government is rarely the best arbiter of what is environmentally sound policy. Take for instance management of the nation's vast forest land. Over the years, government bureaucrats have taken many of their cues from liberal environmental groups who oppose virtually *any* productive use of federal lands, such as logging. As a result, many federal lands became so overgrown with unnecessary underbrush and old growth trees that, during record dry seasons, the lands burned like matchsticks when they caught fire.

In the summer of 2003, during one of the worst fire seasons in recent U.S. history, President Bush signed the "Healthy Forests Initiative," which focused "on reducing the risk of catastrophic fire by thinning dense undergrowth and brush in priority locations that are on a collaborative basis with selected federal, state, tribal, and local officials and communities."[5] The legislation was a direct result of a rash of fires that—by way of more than 147,000 fires in 2002 and 2003—had burned nearly 11 million acres, killed 51 firefighters, destroyed nearly 6,800 structures, and cost more than $250 million to fight.[6]

John Kerry opposed the legislation.

"When it comes to poor environmental protection records, George W. Bush is without peers," Kerry said in a press release. "We must modernize our nation's forest fire policy and reduce fire risk in the 'red zone'—areas where the fire risk to people and homes is the greatest. That means targeting federal resources and logging activities where the danger is greatest. I am also outraged that one of the first actions by the new administrator of the Bush Environmental Protection Agency will be to gut regulations that reduce mercury emissions and other toxic pollutants; a move that will pollute our air and reward the coal industry at the expense of the health of children and pregnant women. . . . We need a president that will go to bat for the environment to protect the health of all Americans, not one that turns a double play for special interests and leaves the rest of us down and out."[7]

As Bush talks about reducing undergrowth to reduce the amount of fuel an out-of-control fire uses to continue on its destructive, deadly path, John Kerry talks abstractly about "mercury emissions" and other alleged "toxic pollutants." Such political sniping doesn't go far to instill confidence in the vast number of Americans who found President Bush's initiative not only sensible, but necessary.

TILTING AT WINDMILLS

As they had repeatedly since 2001, gasoline prices were again edging upward to near-record levels by April 2004, just as the presidential contenders were gearing up for a hot summer of campaigning.[8]

Economically, there is much tied to the price of energy—which means oil, mostly—and when energy prices rise, so too do the prices of nearly every consumable product used by Americans. At a time when the Bush White House began to get some decent economic news (unemployment dropping, job creation strong, etc.), the rising price of energy threatened to stall the administration's economic growth—a phenomenon that without question benefited John Kerry and Democrats.

Some pundits opined that Saudi Arabia, the Mideast's largest oil supplier, likes Bush personally but wants to see him lose the election because he's been tough on Islamic fanatics that many Saudis help to fund.[9] Whether or not that's true, it does seem odd that the Organization of Petroleum Exporting Countries (OPEC), which is dominated by Mideast oil producers, decided in early 2004 to cut production a) when U.S. supplies were already tight; b) just before the traditional heavy summer driving season in America; and c) in the run-up to the U.S. election.

But perhaps the more important issue regarding energy policy is why America continues to be so reliant on foreign oil and petroleum producers for what could be its largest commodity import. To answer that, it may be easier to look at the positions and voting records of Democrat politicians like John Kerry.

If you believe his campaign rhetoric, Kerry says he supports efforts to harvest and develop domestic energy sources—but only on his terms. "John Kerry has outlined a comprehensive energy plan that will tap America's initiative and ingenuity to strengthen our national security, grow our economy, and protect our environment. Kerry's plan will increase and enhance domestic energy sources and provide incentives to *help Americans use energy more cleanly and efficiently*," says his campaign Web site.[10]

However, Kerry has an extreme record of voting for measures that reduce Americans' choices of what they want and can afford to drive. For instance, he has regularly supported measures to force automakers to build cars with unreasonably high federal gas mileage standards.[11] But if Congress had imposed the fuel standards he proposed, U.S. sales would have plummeted, which in turn would have led to massive lay-offs and job losses in the industry. "[P]assage of the Kerry proposal would reduce annual profits at General Motors by $3.824 billion, at Ford $3.423 billion, and at Chrysler $1.959 billion. Total losses to U.S. automakers would amount to $9.206 billion," said the Competitive Enterprise Institute, in a 2002 study. "In contrast, foreign manufacturers would see an increase in profits of $4.434 billion. If these standard levels were to be enacted, consumer surplus would decline $17.603 billion. Employment in automobile industries, including both manufacturers and parts suppliers, would decline by approximately 104,000 jobs."[12]

Another unintended consequence—higher gas mileage standards on Americans is, in many ways, hazardous to health. According to a *USA Today* study, higher standards are killing people. "Federal 'corporate average fuel economy (CAFE) standards' effectively forced people into less-safe smaller cars, and 46,000 have died as a result, according to a *USA Today* analysis. . . . Looked at another way, 7,700 people have died for each mile-per-gallon boost in over-all fuel economy," the paper reported in 1999.[13]

As in many of his positions, there is a fair amount of hypocrisy in Kerry's demand for higher fuel standards. Specifically, he demands more for everyone but himself. Writes Henry Payne in an op-ed for *National Review Online*:

> A look at Kerry's cars . . . suggests the senator leaves his green principles on the Senate floor. "Well, we have a couple of Chrysler minivans," begins Kerry the seasoned politician, who long ago learned to buy American brands only. "We have a Jeep . . . and a PT Cruiser up in Boston . . . and we have some SUVs . . . and an old Dodge 600 that I keep in the Senate . . . and. . . ." And suddenly, Kerry the Average American Buyer is Kerry the Blueblood with more cars than he can count. And that's not his only political faux pas. His PT Cruiser is built in Mexico. Oops. When prodded about whether he buys anything other than Chrysler products, Kerry is quick to add: "Oh yes, I also have a Chevy. A big Suburban." Stop the presses! The King of CAFE owns the most notorious gas-guzzler in the U.S. fleet, GM's super-sized 13-mpg SUV! The moral high ground is lost.[14]

In reality, the issue of energy dependence or independence boils down to this: How much of America's natural oil resources are politicians like Kerry willing to develop? A perfect opportunity for Kerry to answer this question developed early on in the Bush administration.

As part of his energy plan, Bush proposed—among other things—to explore a tiny uninhabitable sliver of the Arctic National

Wildlife Refuge (ANWR) in Alaska. Geologists and industry analysts said they believed the area was ripe with oil and, while it wouldn't solve America's dependency problem, that field and others would eventually decrease and remove America's foreign oil dependency (along with the ability of OPEC and other supplier nations like Mexico and Venezuela to blackmail U.S. leaders and the American people into accepting proposals and policies unfavorable to the U.S.).

"Our national security situation continues to demonstrate that we need to have American oil available to us," said Interior Secretary Gale Norton, in January 2003.[15]

Kerry says he backs such domestic energy harvesting but has vehemently opposed the Bush administration's ANWR plan.

"The Bush administration thinks we can drill our way out of our energy problems. And their solution is to drill in one of our precious national treasures—the Arctic National Wildlife Refuge. That's not an energy policy, that's simply the needless pursuit of profit," he told an audience in Boston in February 2003.[16]

"[I]n seeking energy independence, we have to do more than find a little more oil by drilling in and despoiling the Arctic National Wildlife Refuge. It does far more harm than good, and it is wrong for our future," Kerry said in comments in Iowa a few months later.[17]

Is his decision to oppose ANWR simply a political move, because it was offered by a Republican administration? Perhaps.

According to Kerry's campaign Web site, he supports drilling for natural gas in Mexico—as well as *Alaska's* northern slope. "There are 35 trillion cubic feet of known natural gas reserves on the North Slope of Alaska that have no way to get to markets in the lower 48 states. *John Kerry believes that we must build the Alaska pipeline to expand natural gas as a resource* and provide important jobs for American workers. . . . John Kerry would bring together . . . interested parties to make this a domestic priority, including providing appropriate regulatory streamlining to get this project built. . . ."[18]

Regarding power and electricity, Kerry also stubbornly resists efforts to improve the national infrastructure. While he says he wants to see 20 percent of all power generated in the United States made from renewable sources by 2020—wind and solar power, biomass, geothermal, and hydrogen sources, an admirable goal—he doesn't support today's technology to make power more plentiful and cheaper for consumers. And at times, his voting record shows he's not really serious about his reform ideas.

In one example, in late 2003 an energy bill that would have included tax credits for wind power developers came up in the Senate. "If we weren't in the bill, the credit that is the foundation of our industry was going to expire and with it our industry would expire. . . . If the energy bill dies, extension of the wind production tax credit will also die for any time in the foreseeable future," said American Wind Energy Association President Randall Swisher, in an interview with National Public Radio.[19]

But Kerry was campaigning and was absent during a vote for cloture, which helped to defeat the bill altogether.[20] So not only did the tax credit die, but several jobs were lost too. "Vestas Group, the world's leading maker of wind turbines, had planned a new plant in Oregon with a thousand employees. Now that may not happen. Wind farms proposed for Minnesota and Iowa are stalled, and Swisher says layoffs are coming," National Public Radio reported in December 2003.[21]

Then there is the issue of the Cape Wind project—a plan to build a wind farm near one of Kerry's homes in Massachusetts. Though it might seem a perfect opportunity for Kerry to highlight his desire to find cheaper alternative sources of energy, the senator has been strangely silent about Cape Wind—in a not-in-my-back-yard sort of way. "I don't think it is appropriate for me (to weigh in)," he told the *Telegraph* of Nashua, New Hampshire, in April 2003. "I think the most appropriate thing to do is listen to the people on the Cape, listen to the people who have concerns, weigh

the arguments."[22] He went on to say he's discussed with partici-
pants "whether or not there aren't alternative sites."[23]

Observers and even some supporters quickly got the message:
Kerry wasn't as serious about his energy policies as he made out to
be, at least when it came to building a project within sight of his own
property. Noted an April 2003 *Providence Journal-Bulletin* editorial:

> Hot-wind power in Massachusetts Sen. John Kerry's office:
> "Senator Kerry recognizes that wind power and other renewable
> sources of energy are imperative if this nation is to lessen its
> dependence on heavily polluting and unreliable energy sources
> while still nurturing its economy. This [Cape Wind's Nantucket
> Sound windmill project] is the first project of its kind in the U.S.,
> so there are a lot of questions that need to be answered before a
> final decision can be made. . . . To that end, the Senator is wait-
> ing for completion of the Environmental Impact Statement, so we
> have a better understanding of the impacts. All of the issues must
> be considered as this nation moves toward greater investment in
> renewable-energy sources and for the good of Massachusetts."
> Sounds about as clear as his stance on Iraq.[24]

Even environmental advocacy group Greenpeace, usually a
Kerry ally, criticized his flip-flopping stance regarding the Cape
Wind project. "Kerry is the one who really needs to be called out
on this stuff," Kert Davies, research director of Greenpeace, told
The Hill, a newspaper that covers Congress. "He's been pretty
mum so far. We don't know where he stands. He's obviously very
pro-renewable energy; he knows the climate better than almost
anyone in the Senate. And by that logic, he should be in favor of
this project being implemented."[25]

The Competitive Enterprise Institute seemed to also have
Kerry's number. In a letter to "selected" senators (including Kerry),
CEI wrote, "If renewable energy is going to be required by federal

mandate, then people on Cape Cod or Martha's Vineyard or Nantucket, as in South Dakota or Iowa or Minnesota, are just going to have to get used to it. Merely living in a very nice spot with high real estate values should not exempt anyone from sharing the renewable burden. . . ."[26]

The 2003 energy bill that Kerry missed containing wind power tax credits also contained tax breaks for solar panel development. "Glenn Hammer of the Solar Energy Industries Association . . . says the bill would expand the use of solar with a $2,000 credit for home solar heaters and a plan to put solar panels on federal buildings. Hammer says that's key because solar products' costs go down by about 20 percent every time the use of the technology doubles," said National Public Radio.[27]

No oil or gas drilling unless it's on Kerry's terms. Missed votes for key energy industry funding and development. Job losses due to lost energy development opportunities. Small cars for your family, big ones for his family. These are Kerry's primary energy policy "ideas."

Meanwhile, gas prices continue to rise as America remains hostage to other nations (mostly in the Middle East) for more than half its oil.[28] Development technology sits idle as American energy dependence grows. No new energy-related jobs are being created. Power outages in places like California continue to plague Americans while costs rise.

If Kerry expended as much energy solving America's energy problems as he is expending trying to win the White House, maybe most Americans wouldn't be paying so much at the gas pump.

TORT REFORM

In the months before launching his presidential bid, and in the months since, John Kerry—an attorney and one-time local prosecutor in Massachusetts—has said little about the issue of tort reform and how the pursuit of high damage awards could be harming the nation's legal system, as well as the targeted industries. That in and of itself may not seem so significant, considering Kerry is one lawyer-legislator in a governing body dominated by lawyer-legislators.

But although they shun President Bush the Republican, trial lawyers contribute heavily to Democratic causes and politicians.[29] And they have also contributed heavily to Kerry; since 1989, the Massachusetts Democrat has received more than $6.3 million from lawyers.[30] His presidential campaign has received nearly $3.5 million from the same industry.[31] Over the last fifteen years, Kerry has received the second-highest amount of money from trial lawyers of all U.S. senators.[32] These figures could explain his lack of enthusiasm for so-called tort reform.

According to the American Tort Reform Association (ATRA) president Sherman Joyce, "Some astonishing decisions come out of the courts these days. Hundreds of millions in punitive damages piled on top of relatively minor actual damages. Meritless cases settled because defendants fear the outcome of an emotion-filled jury trial or a lawless court."[33] Other civil justice reformers feel the same way, which is why they'd like to see the tort system in the U.S. reformed.

How bad is the system? Some of the cases monitored by ATRA include:

- A West Bend, Indiana, man claims he became addicted to cable TV, which also caused his wife to be overweight and his kids to be lazy; he wants $5,000 or three computers and a lifetime supply of free Internet service.

- A two-year-old child model and actor is seeking unspecified lost wages and other compensation from the city of Stamford, Connecticut, because he cut his head at a playground—he ran into a green railing which, claims his mother, blends into the background at the park and, hence, makes it difficult to see.

- The City of Chicago settled a case brought by three thousand panhandlers, paying each of them $450 after they claimed arrest by Chicago police for begging on sidewalks.

- The post office in Fulton, Missouri, removed a tape dispenser that had long been available for customers for sealing packages because a customer who had hurt himself using it had filed a claim against the U.S. Postal Service.

- A man in jail near San Diego, California, and awaiting trial for raping an underage girl, filed a lawsuit against the jail facility because of the mental stress and anguish caused by finding a fly in his mashed potatoes.

- A woman filed a lawsuit against the transit system in Juneau, Alaska, because a driver's attempt to enforce the well-known no-eating rule on a bus caused her, she says, at least $50,000 worth of emotional distress; she was trying to eat a Snickers bar.

These are the kinds of cases tort reform advocates want to see given the boot—not only because they are, to the average American, ridiculous and senseless, but because if successful, they cost consumers and taxpayers untold amounts of revenue they would otherwise not have to pay, if the cases had been (thankfully) dismissed by courts.

But don't expect to see much action from John Kerry regarding tort reform. Not only is there little information about his position regarding tort reform on his campaign Web site, he has continued to accept large sums of money from the same trial lawyers who profit from the kind of ridiculous lawsuits the ATRA has highlighted. In fact, as recently as May 2003, trial lawyers in Miami hosted a breakfast for Kerry.[34]

In the past, Kerry has been accused of catering to trial lawyers. In 1999, he was accused by Democratic Senator Ron Wyden of

Oregon of sponsoring legislation Wyden said would create more inconsequential lawsuits. The *San Francisco Chronicle* reported:

> Silicon Valley scored a sweet political victory yesterday, knocking back a Senate filibuster on a bill to protect companies from lawsuits over the Y2K computer glitch and closing in on enough votes to defeat a promised White House veto. . . . [Senator Fritz] Hollings charged that Silicon Valley is demanding an unprecedented legal shield, comparing it to General Motors making a car that turns left when the driver steers it right, and then asking Congress to prevent anyone from suing. But a powerful alliance of Democrats from states with strong technology sectors, including Feinstein, Oregon's Ron Wyden and Connecticut's Chris Dodd, accused Hollings and Massachusetts Democrat John Kerry—who has drafted a weaker alternative that has White House backing—of catering to trial lawyers. "The Kerry amendment is a lightning rod for additional frivolous lawsuits," Wyden charged. "Some of the language is so vague it's going to ignite a litigation derby." Kerry's amendment went down to defeat . . . on a 57-to-41 vote.[35]

Elizabeth Austin and Jim Day, writing for *Chicago Lawyer* in November 2003, describe Kerry as a longtime opponent of damage caps and product liability reform.[36] While Kerry says he supports sanctions against persons making meritless legal claims and supports the creation of judicial panels to screen out frivolous lawsuits against doctors, he has opposed or blocked—at least ten times in the past decade—legislation seeking medical liability reforms.[37]

His so-called support for tort reform, like many of his other positions, can be considered duplicitous, however. While cheering for reform, he's opposed capping attorney's fees for tobacco-related lawsuits, as well as product liability punitive damages for small businesses and a "loser pays" system for securities fraud lawsuits.[38] He is against capping attorney's contingency fees for non-economic damages, and he opposed a bill that would establish nationwide standards on how victims should be compensated, provide incentives to settle lawsuits, and establish alternatives to litigation.[39]

As this book went to press, Kerry had not yet announced his running mate. Some political and media pundits have speculated it could be Senator John Edwards (D-North Carolina), though Edwards has ruled out the possibility. That may be a benefit to Kerry since Edwards—a once-successful trial lawyer before running for office—is decidedly against tort reform.

"Senator Edwards' campaign has been funded by personal injury lawyers who would drive a pro-litigation, anti-civil justice reform agenda," said ATRA President Sherman Joyce in a press release in March 2003. "Kerry should be wary of aligning himself with someone who is beholden to these 'Learjet lawyers.'"[40] The tort reform group released an analysis which showed Edwards received more than 63 percent of his campaign financing from personal injury lawyers, their employees, and their children.[41]

One common thread between the two men: both like to use lawyers for a source of campaign funding. Kerry and Edwards spoke at an Association of Trial Lawyers of America function in July 2003.[42] They spoke to "M Club" ATLA members—those who contribute more than $1,000 to the organization's political action committee.[43]

While a good number of Americans aren't in favor of disassembling the entire legal system, many do favor reforming the system of damage awards—not simply because many such cases are foolish and defy common sense, but because their cost is driving up the cost of the industries affected by astronomical damage awards, like medicine.

A bumper sticker in the Farm Belt of the Midwest says, "If you're going to badmouth farmers, don't talk with your mouth full." Maybe as a lawyer himself and a recipient of so many campaign contributions of lawyers and lawyers' groups, John Kerry has taken this axiom to heart.

Not every political issue is important to every voter. But clearly there are issues which, while largely dealt with out of the public's eye, have a great affect on millions of Americans.

John Kerry has a proven record of increasing government regulation and the philosophy that the federal government knows best. In a Kerry administration Americans can count on more government interference and regulation.

12

KERRY ON GUNS

Eliminating rights for law-abiding Americans

T HE SECOND AMENDMENT to the United States Constitution, which was ratified as one of the nation's first ten amendments and embodied in the Bill of Rights in 1791 states, "A well regulated militia, being necessary to the security of a free state, the right of the people to keep and bear arms, shall not be infringed."

Considered by our founders to be as important as freedom of speech, freedom of religion, the right of assembly, and the right to be secure in our homes from unreasonable searches, "the right of the people to keep and bear arms" has been considered, by some, as the one inalienable right that acts as a protector of all the others. Noah Webster, the Revolutionary-era colonial who created the first American dictionary and was credited with Americanizing the English language, wrote in 1787:

Before a standing army can rule, the people must be disarmed; as they are in almost every kingdom in Europe. The supreme power in America cannot enforce unjust laws by the sword; because the whole body of the people are armed, and constitute a force superior to any band of regular troops that can be, on any pretence, raised in the United States. A military force, at the command of

Congress, can execute no laws, but such as the people perceive to be just and constitutional; for they will possess the power, and jealousy will instantly inspire the inclination, to resist the execution of a law which appears to them unjust and oppressive.[1]

Firearms, the early Americans believed, were essential not only to the establishment of liberty and freedom, but to the ability to keep both. As Thomas Jefferson once wrote, "No freeman shall ever be debarred the use of arms."[2] Yet many of today's politicians, including John Kerry, neither understand nor appreciate the founders' vision—and the Constitution's explicit language—regarding the right to keep and bear firearms.

In Kerry's case, he views firearms in the way most liberal politicians and potential tyrants view them—an inherent right during election cycles, but one that should be regulated and limited after the elections are over.

On the issue of gun control, Kerry opposes granting gun makers protection from lawsuits designed to drain them financially. He supports subjecting gun show firearm buyers to background checks. And he wants to renew the so-called "assault weapons" ban, a law which penalizes certain semi-automatic rifles because they happen to look like their military "assault weapon" cousins.[3]

But he doesn't mind appearing as though he supports gun rights or, perhaps more appropriately, *hunting* rights. The flip-flopping double-standard was summed up in November 2003 by the *New York Times*:

> John Kerry blasted away at Howard Dean . . . accusing him of currying favor with the National Rifle Association and opposing an assault-weapons ban that Mr. Kerry and other supporters of gun control fought for in the 1990's. Then Mr. Kerry took his 12-gauge shotgun and blew two pheasants out of the sky in two shots.[4]

The paper went on to report that Kerry disagreed with Dean who, in 1992, told the NRA in a signed questionnaire Dean opposed any restrictions on the ownership of the military-weapon look-alikes. "So it was that Mr. Kerry spoke out for gun control one minute and then led photographers on a classic hunter's photo opportunity the next," the *Times* said.[5]

"It's not a mixed message," he told reporters, who were following him on his mini hunting trip. "I'm just being where I've been all my life. I believe in the Second Amendment in this country. But I don't believe that assault weapons ought to be sold in the streets of America. Never believed it, don't believe it now."[6]

But to millions of American gun owners—Democrats, Republicans, and Independents—it *is* a mixed message. It's mixed because John Kerry is applying a different constitutional standard to the Second Amendment than he is applying to other, equally clear and important, amendments in the Constitution. "I want to prove to people that you can be responsible about guns, and you're not anti-Second Amendment, but you can still vote for common sense in this country," Kerry said during his pheasant hunt.[7] But other experts who criticize the senator's stance would argue a "responsible" reading of the Second Amendment is not that it simply allows Americans to own a gun for hunting.

"The current debate concerning whether a particular gun is better suited for a hunting or sporting purpose completely misses the aim of the Second Amendment," says Thomas M. Moncure Jr., writing in the *Howard Law Journal*. "The Second Amendment recognized a common law and natural law right, taken for granted as inalienable, to keep and bear arms. Additionally, the Second Amendment was directed at maintaining an armed citizenry for mutual defense, and perhaps most significantly, to protect against the tyranny of our own government."[8]

That position was seconded, so to speak, by *Washington Post* syndicated columnist George Will, who identified the underlying theory as one which "says that, free individuals must be independent from coercion, and such independence depends in part on freedom from the ménage of standing armies and government monopoly on the means of force."[9]

UNARMING AMERICA

Kerry is obviously trying to woo a great many of the nation's gun owners, which some estimates put at about ninety million people.[10] But if that's his goal, his voting record in the Senate puts him out of step with gun owners and gun rights supporters. As a lawmaker, Kerry has voted 51 of 55 times against gun owners.[11] Writes Wayne LaPierre, executive director of the National Rifle Association, in May 2004:

> For all we've read lately about how enemies of the Second Amendment are shying away from the "gun control" issue in this election year, a series of votes in the U.S. Senate in March changed all that, with Kerry eagerly taking center stage. In working to sabotage S.1805—the NRA-backed legislation to stop the endless series of predatory lawsuits aimed at strangling the law-abiding firearms industry—Kerry voted to extend the Clinton gun ban on semi-autos, to make now-legal private gun sales at gun shows criminal acts, and voted to support [fellow Massachusetts Senator] Ted Kennedy's ammunition ban, which would have prohibited most centerfire hunting rounds. . . .[12]

Even Kerry's supposed "guns for hunting" campaign comes up short. The Humane Society of the United States and the Fund for Animals, both groups that abhor hunting, gave Kerry a 100 percent rating for the first session of the current 108th Congress.[13] In the case of the Humane Society, Kerry received special recognition for not only introducing legislation favored by the organization, but speaking in favor of it on the floor of the Senate.[14]

FIREARMS FAKE-OUT

Senator Kerry, as one of the most anti-gun voices in the Senate, will have to hide his viewpoints from the gun-owning public. But he may have found a way to do that—and it's somewhat more stealthy than simply staging a pheasant hunt.

After the 2000 presidential election, one statistic "that just leapt off the page was the finding that 48 percent of voters lived in households with guns," said the *New Dem Daily*, a publication of the Democratic Leadership Council. Of that figure, "voters went for George W. Bush by nearly a two-to-one margin."[15]

That figure led to the development of a strategy by analysts with Americans for Gun Safety, an organization that ostensibly pushes for "sensible gun reforms."

"Jonathan Cowan and Jim Kessler of Americans for Gun Safety argue persuasively that the old, stale debate between pro-gun absolutists and anti-gun advocates of gun control unnecessarily polarizes the population, plays into the hands of the NRA, and ignores a 'third way' position that actually commands strong majority support among Americans, whether or not they own guns," says the *New Dem Daily*. "This 'third way,' they suggest, involves a 'gun policy that treats gun ownership as neither an absolute right nor an absolute wrong and that calls for a balance between gun rights and gun responsibilities.' That means making 'gun owners partners in developing policies that help keep guns out of the hands of criminals and make guns safer in the home.'"[16]

Enter John Kerry. Many of his answers in a 2004 candidate's questionnaire by Americans for Gun Safety (AGS) sound eerily familiar to the "third way" gun strategy outlined by the same organization:

AGS: Do you believe that the Second Amendment to the Constitution confers an individual right to bear arms or a collective right that allows for state militias to be armed?

KERRY: I believe that the Constitution, our laws, and our customs protect law-abiding American citizens' right to own firearms.

AGS: If you believe that the Second Amendment confers an individual right to own a gun, what types of restrictions (if any) do you believe are permissible on that right?

KERRY: I believe that the right of gun ownership comes with responsibilities. . . . I've carried a rifle for my country in Vietnam, and my rifle saved my life and that of my crew. I believe in the Second Amendment. But I believe with gun ownership comes rights and responsibilities—responsibilities to make sure that criminals and children don't get them.

In the Senate on March 4, Kerry—speaking in opposition to S.1805—mouthed similar "third way" rhetoric. He said, "I believe strongly in the Second Amendment. I believe in the right to bear arms *as it has been interpreted in our country.*" The italicized portion of that statement is a vital qualifier, which comes from a man who, as president, would most likely be nominating federal judges and Supreme Court justices to interpret gun rights as subject to these "reasonable" limitations.[17]

NO LIMITATIONS ON OTHER RIGHTS

But Kerry, like many liberal Democrats, is hypocritical in the interpretation of the Constitution's supposedly inalienable rights. While he supports "responsible" restrictions on gun rights, he doesn't feel the same about many other guarantees in the Constitution.

Kerry obviously believes in the First Amendment's guarantee of free speech and the right to redress grievances to the government (his famous anti-Vietnam War speech before the Senate in the early 1970s is a prime example). He believes a mother has a "right" to murder her unborn child.[18] He believes gays, lesbians, bisexuals, and transvestites deserve special protection and rights.[19] He believes women deserve "expanded" opportunities to go to college.[20] But he thinks gun rights should be subjected to "reasonable" restrictions imposed by the government.

In the days of the American Revolution, colonists and states-men debated the contents of the Bill of Rights and the ensuing Constitution which would embody them, but they did so with images of war fresh in their minds. George Mason, who was attending the Virginia constitutional ratification convention, said, "When the resolution of enslaving America was formed in Great Britain, the British Parliament was advised by an artful man, who was governor of Pennsylvania, to disarm the people; that it was the best and most effectual way to enslave them; but that they should not do it openly, but weaken them, and let them sink gradually. . . ." Added Zacharia Johnson: "[T]he people are not to be disarmed of their weapons. They are left in full possession of them."[21]

Obviously these were men of vision; they could see power-hungry elitists like John Kerry on the horizon.

13

BAD MEDICINE

A return to Hillary's socialized health scheme

AMERICA HAS SOME OF the best health care available in the
entire world. Our medical schools turn out highly competent
doctors. Skill and the latest medical technology enable American
physicians in every specialty to perform medical miracles daily.
America continues to be a world leader in medical advancement
through ongoing research and development.

If there is a problem with this kind of system, it is cost: Every year
health insurance coverage becomes more expensive for the average
working family. While many insurance plans raise rates annually,
they offer less in return for higher premiums. Doctors and hospitals,
meanwhile, have to continually charge more—often just to keep up
with inflation—as unemployment and cost factors contribute to the
growing number of uninsured, which includes millions of children.
According to 2002 figures from the U.S. Census Bureau (the most
recent year available), 43.6 million Americans remain uninsured.[1]

Even so, according to the same report, 242.4 million
Americans—or 84.8 percent—*did* have health insurance coverage,
a figure which rose by 1.5 million people between 2001 and 2002.[2]
(What the government figures don't show is the number of people
who purposely elect to forego health insurance coverage.)

"The good news is that the bad news about the uninsured,

upon examination, isn't that awful," writes Sally C. Pipes for *Investor's Business Daily* in January 2004. "The uninsured aren't universally poor. One in three uninsured live in households with income greater than $50,000, and one in seven live in households that earn more than $75,000 a year. Nor are all deprived of access to employer-subsidized insurance. One in five workers who are uninsured and offered group health insurance actually decline it."[3]

Politicians like John Kerry either don't know these facts or worse, choose to spin "misery" messages to voters. In Kerry's case, it may never have occurred to him some people don't have insurance because they don't want it. As far as he's concerned, everybody *should* have it, regardless of cost, whether they want it or not, and American taxpayers will have to foot the bill.

According to his campaign Web site, Kerry would begin to overhaul the health-care system by providing nearly every American access to the same health plan as members of Congress and federal employees. "Nine million federal employees get health care through the Federal Employees Health Care Benefits program (FEHBP), which offers a wide range of plans with good benefits," says his campaign. "The Kerry plan will allow every American access to this system. With tax-based incentives to employers and tax credits to individuals and the self-employed, the Kerry plan will ensure that this coverage is affordable."[4]

Further, he pledges to insure every child via "a new compact with the states," in which "the federal government will pick up the cost of Medicaid coverage for children in exchange for automatic enrollment of all school children eligible for the Children's Health Insurance Program." The plan includes extending eligibility for coverage "to 300 percent of poverty-level incomes for children," then extending it further "to the six million single and childless adults who are uninsured and live below the poverty line." The campaign says "independent experts estimate that the Kerry plan will cover 99 percent of America's children."[5]

Kerry also pledges to extend coverage to small businesses. "By joining the new Congressional Health Plan under Kerry's plan, small businesses will be able to provide more affordable coverage. Kerry is also proposing refundable tax credits up to 50 percent of coverage to small businesses and their employees to help subsidize the cost of health insurance," says his campaign. And he wants to implement a "75 percent tax credit to assure workers can keep their health insurance between jobs." And he says he'll extend the Congressional health coverage to retirees and individuals age fifty-five to sixty-four.[6]

DEVIL IN THE DETAILS

Kerry claims a health-care plan offered by President Bush will do little to lower health-care costs, won't cover additional uninsured people, and is not affordable for people who can't save money. "His plan does nothing to lower costs. His plan is only available to people who have the ability to save some money. If you can't save some money, you can't afford George Bush's healthcare plan," Kerry said in a February 2004 interview with *ABC News.*[7]

"What is this administration's offer on health care, ladies and gentlemen? Nothing. They don't talk about forty-one million Americans who don't have health care and how we're going to provide it. They don't talk about how we're going to reduce the cost of health care for all Americans," the senator said at a town hall-style meeting in New Hampshire.[8]

Kerry has also attacked Bush for pandering to special health-care industry interests, such as insurance companies and health maintenance organizations (HMOs). "George Bush promised us action on health care when he ran for president. But . . . this president hasn't lifted a finger to help. Who's he been fighting for instead? The big insurance companies and HMOs that line his campaign coffers—the same ones that have caused so much of the hurt in the first place," Kerry said at a hospital in Iowa in December 2003.[9]

In reality, there are several problems with Kerry's health-care plan, not the least of which is cost. If John Kerry is elected president, Americans will spend hundreds of billions more in the form of taxes and other costs to fund his health-care plan. In fact, a study by Kenneth Thorpe, a health-care economics professor at Emory University and former Clinton administration official, found Kerry's plans would cost a whopping $895 billion over ten years—and still would not cover all currently uninsured people. "Federal costs under the Kerry plans would be $895 billion over ten years to extend insurance to 26.7 million uninsured [of 43.6 million total uninsured]," he wrote. "This includes approximately $230 billion in federal spending for the reinsurance pool that targets those with health insurance and $665 billion for programs targeting the uninsured."[10]

Even though it agreed with Thorpe's first estimate, the Kerry campaign asked him to take another look at the Massachusetts senator's plan and revise his numbers to include savings, which Thorpe did. "Thorpe said he could not account for savings in his original analysis last year because Kerry's proposals lacked details that have since been given to him," the Associated Press reported. "'They wanted me to look at the savings,' he said of the Kerry campaign. 'They were concerned it wasn't the full picture.'"[11]

Thorpe's revised analysis found a total cost of about $940 billion starting in 2006, but he then factored in about $290 billion worth of savings, according to the Kerry campaign's plan. That lowered the overall cost to about $653 billion, but oftentimes cost estimates and savings are wrong, so the plan could still wind up costing billions more.[12]

Nevertheless, in a PBS interview Kerry himself has acknowledged his program would be expensive:

KERRY: [I]f you look at $75 billion a year, the president
has just passed a tax cut, 54 percent of which went to
1 percent of Americans, which was about $352 billion.
. . . That's the choice of this race.
PBS's MARGARET WARNER: But your plan totaled,
as scored by an independent authority, $900 billion over
ten years.
KERRY: Yes.[13]

Others noticed the problematic price tag as well. Ronald
Brownstein of the *Los Angeles Times* wrote in February 2004,
Kerry's "plan to increase access to health care is more expensive
than any single idea [Democratic presidential nominee Al] Gore
advanced in 2000."[14]

POLITICKING MEDICARE

One example of just how expensive Kerry's health plan could be is
to compare it to Medicare. Kerry's plan does not call for a government health-care takeover, but still the example is appropriate
because Medicare has far outstripped its initial cost projections
when the program was first implemented.

"When Medicare was debated in 1965 (the year it was signed
into law), taxpayer groups were concerned that program expenditures might grow out of control," says the Institute for Health
Freedom, in a 2000 cost analysis. "They argued that taxpayers
shouldn't have to foot the bill for wealthy seniors who could afford
to pay for their own health insurance [Author's note: Does that
sound familiar?]. However, politicians assured taxpayers that all
seniors could easily be covered under Medicare with only a small
increase in workers' payroll taxes." The analysis went on to note
the hospital portion of Medicare would "grow to only $9 billion by

1990," but in fact "it ended up costing more than $66 billion that year." Says the institute, "Even after adjusting for inflation and other factors, the cost of Medicare Part A (in constant dollars) was 165 percent higher than the official government estimate, according to the actuary who produced them."[15]

Liberal Democrats, including John Kerry, have been pushing for many years to expand government-run health-care programs. One such expansion—providing prescription drug benefits for Medicare recipients—originated as a Democratic program but was actually implemented by President Bush and Republicans. Known as the Medicare Prescription Drug Improvement and Modernization Act, the bill was signed into law by President Bush December 8, 2003, during a ceremony at Constitution Hall in Washington D.C. According to a White House summary, the law provides prescription drug benefits under Medicare, gives older Americans more health-care choices, makes Medicare more efficient by "providing screenings that will enable doctors and patients to diagnose and treat health problems early," and creates health-care savings accounts.[16]

The Bush administration added some elements of the free market in its Medicare prescription program, but Kerry—who still says he supports Medicare drug coverage—doesn't like that plan. "John Kerry supports adding a strong affordable prescription drug benefit to Medicare. However, he believes that the prescription drug benefit should not rely on HMOs or undermine retiree coverage that exists today," his campaign said. "In addition, the Kerry plan will reduce drug costs for everyone by using *the federal government's purchasing power* to induce giant drug wholesalers to pass along to consumers the rebates they get from the drug manufacturers; getting more affordable generic drugs to the market, giving states the flexibility to negotiate better deals, and allowing people to buy quality drugs through Canada."[17]

It isn't as though Kerry and other advocates of government-supported (read *taxpayer-supported*) health-care programs don't know how expensive and inefficient they can be. As early as 1968, studies indicated Medicare costs had far outpaced forecasts, even noting health-care financing was beginning to shift to Washington. The *New York Times* reported on a Tax Foundation study which concluded three years after Medicare's creation, "To date, the major demonstrable effect of the 1965 federal legislation creating Medicare and Medicaid has been a shift in financing medical care from the private to the public sector."[18]

"Consequently," the Institute for Health Freedom noted, "Medicare payroll taxes and general taxes have been raised over the years to pay for skyrocketing health-care costs." Before an out-patient prescription drug benefit, "Medicare [represented] 12 percent of federal spending [in 2000], and it is the largest payer of health care in the world, spending $212 billion in 1999."[19]

Not surprisingly, there is also a fair amount of hypocrisy from the Kerry campaign regarding Medicare, and in particular the issue of adding prescription drug coverage. When it came time to provide it—as he had promised for more than thirty years—Kerry instead chose to play politics.

Back in 1972, during a bid for the U.S. House, Kerry said Washington "can also aid the elderly in many other ways . . . by instituting out-of-hospital drug prescription services which now are not covered by Medicare."[20] He has mentioned such coverage numerous times since, but the real moment of truth came shortly after George W. Bush came to office. In 2001—at a time when Democrats had control of the Senate—Kerry promised to deliver prescription drug coverage. "With a Democratic Senate, no family will go bankrupt buying life-saving medicine—no elderly American will freeze in an apartment all winter just to have enough money to pay for prescriptions—because our party will provide prescription drug coverage for all our senior citizens," he pledged in June 2001 to the Massachusetts Democratic Party State Issues Convention.

"The Republicans failed to do these things for our fellow citizens. They had the chance and they didn't lead—we have the chance now and I promise you we will."[21]

But less than two years later, when the opportunity finally came (under the auspices of a GOP-controlled House, Senate, and White House), Kerry balked. In November 2003, he joined with some other Democrats in an effort to kill an otherwise bipartisan Medicare drug bill.[22] He pledged to join with fellow Massachusetts liberal Senator Edward (Ted) Kennedy to filibuster the legislation. According to an Associated Press report, "Kerry announced that he'd be returning to Washington to help his Senate colleagues filibuster the Medicare bill. . . . Kerry called the legislation 'a boondoggle for the pharmaceutical industry and a raw deal' for the nation's elderly. 'That is why I am going to join Senator Ted Kennedy to lead the filibuster of this legislation,' said Kerry."[23]

There's more. When the bill was in the Senate Finance Committee, before it ever reached the full Senate, he voted against it.[24] Then later, sensing some political gain from his actions, Kerry claimed he "led the fight" against the measure but was almost entirely AWOL when the votes came up. "There is a special interest feeding frenzy going on in Washington. A $130 billion dollar giveaway to the drug companies. John Kerry led in the fight against it," said a Kerry campaign ad in December 2003.[25] In reality, however, Kerry did not bother to show up for 36 of 38 votes on Medicare reform and the prescription drug bill, including the final passage of the bill.[26] In fact, Kerry was only one of two senators in the entire U.S. Senate to miss the final landmark vote. (The other was fellow Democratic presidential candidate Joe Lieberman.[27])

Kerry's fight-to-the-end image on Medicare took another hit when he admitted he didn't show for the final vote because he saw no point in it. As AP reported, "The two Democratic candidates said there was no point in staying in Washington after losing the critical vote to halt the bill's progress by invoking arcane budget rules. 'There was no question about the passage,' said Kerry, who was stumping in Iowa. . . . 'The vote was not going to make a difference in the outcome.'"[28]

Kerry proved even more hypocritical in June 2003, when he *sponsored* a Senate amendment to the chamber's prescription drug bill, claiming "seniors need prescription drug relief and they need it now," and "millions of seniors can benefit" from it.[29] But he didn't even show up to vote for it; on June 26, 2003, Kerry's amendment was withdrawn by unanimous consent while he was in Los Angeles attending a League of Conservation Voters forum.[30]

Kerry also misled seniors about several aspects of the Medicare drug bill. First, he accused Republicans of "holding [the] prescription drug benefit hostage to a scheme to privatize Medicare."[31] In reality, though, the law—which was approved on a bipartisan vote—provided significant savings for all forty million seniors and disabled persons on Medicare. "For the first time in Medicare's history, a prescription drug benefit will be offered to all 40 million seniors and disabled Americans in Medicare to help them afford the cost of their medicines," said a White House fact sheet.[32] Lending credence to the White House statement was the fact that more than sixty health-care and senior's organizations, including the thirty-five million-member American Association of Retired Persons (AARP), the American Hospital Association, and the American Medical Association pledged their support for the plan.[33]

Kerry also said the Medicare law would push seniors into HMOs—a baseless charge. "Kerry flatly accused President Bush of 'pushing seniors off of Medicare into HMOs,'" reported the Associated Press. Yet, "Nothing in the law forces seniors off of Medicare. Kerry's assertion was shorthand for an argument that Medicare could eventually become so expensive under the program that the elderly will be effectively coerced into private plans."[34]

Rhetorical licenses aside, Kerry's accusation was false. "If a person is hearing this and says, 'I'm going to be forced out,' they've been misled," according to the Annenberg Public Policy Center's Kathleen Hall Jamieson.[35]

Kerry also went so far as to accuse other Democrats who sided with Republicans in approving the Medicare law of voting to destroy it, during one Democratic presidential debate:

NBC's TOM BROKAW: Senator, Hillary Clinton has already issued a press release saying that this is a Trojan horse that is designed to bring about the demise of Medicare. Do you honestly think that the AARP, that Senator Dianne Feinstein of California, for example, or Senator Dorgan of North Dakota, are determined to bring about the demise of Medicare? Because they've indicated that they support this.

KERRY: I think that will be the impact. I agree with Hillary Clinton.[36]

One final hypocrisy: as Kerry bashed President Bush mercilessly for allegedly writing a Medicare prescription drug bill that benefited drug companies, he accepted thousands of dollars in pharmaceutical company campaign contributions.

"This bill is really about President Bush passing the buck on prescription drug coverage and passing the bucks from seniors to the pharmaceutical industry," Kerry said, according to a *Boston Herald* editorial.[37] Then, Kerry accused Republicans of doing the same thing he did: accepting campaign contributions from pharmaceutical companies, "We learned that in their incredible cave-in to the powerful interests of the drug companies of America, they dunned the taxpayers of our nation $139 billion extra so they can line the pockets of people who contributed to their campaign."[38]

Yet, since 1989, Kerry personally has received $59,505 from

pharmaceutical manufacturing industry employees (his presidential campaign, as of February 2004, had received nearly $19,000 in pharmaceutical manufacturing industry employee contributions), as well as an additional $203,155 from pharmaceutical/health products industry employees.[39]

Incredibly, even after Republicans introduced Medicare prescription drug coverage—and pushed the issue through committees to votes on the floors of the House and Senate—Kerry still tried to convince the American people the GOP was against the measure. "I can tell you that we have been fighting to get prescription drug coverage. I want a Medicare prescription drug coverage. The Republicans are fighting us. They don't want it," he told *Fox News*.[40]

He also criticized some senior groups that supported the measure, such as AARP: "I wish AARP had chosen to oppose this bill, and I wish AARP was spending its $7 million to help tell Americans what is wrong. This bill is the indication of what is wrong in America today," he said at a Democratic presidential candidate debate in New Hampshire—sponsored by the AARP.[41]

In the end, said the *Wall Street Journal*, Kerry only criticized Republican plans to add the benefit to Medicare—without coming up with his own solution.[42]

Also worth noting, Kerry—the so-called champion of Medicare—has voted at least six times during his Senate career to cut billions from the program.[43] For example, in 1997 Kerry voted to cut $115 billion from Medicare in order to balance the federal budget.[44] A year earlier, he voted to cut Medicare by $118 billion.[45] In 1995, according to the Congressional Record, Kerry voted for $156 billion in Medicare cuts. Also, in 1993, Kerry backed nearly $56 billion in Medicare cuts; the Fiscal 1994 Budget Reconciliation included $55.8 billion reduction in Medicare funding, as part of $255 billion in spending cuts and $241 billion in additional taxes.[46]

Fast forward to his current run for the presidency. Now, Kerry shuns such cuts: "Other candidates have supported major cuts that cause premium increases and cutbacks in benefits. John Kerry won't," says his campaign Web site.[47]

Can you be sure?

KERRY MATH

The cost of Kerry's health-care plans is also a major point of contention. He says he will finance his health-care plans—plus other programs and deficit reduction—by only rolling back President Bush's tax cuts on "wealthy" Americans. "[W]e can balance the budget and be fiscally responsible in America. . . . I have enough money for my health care, for education by rolling back the high end, the wealthy tax cut of people $200,000 and more," he said at a Democratic presidential debate in November 2003.[48]

But since making that claim, a number of analysts—some even from liberal think tanks—have publicly debunked them, noting the finances just don't add up.

In the PBS interview, when Kerry acknowledged Thorpe's $900 billion health-care plan cost estimate, he also denied he would have to roll back Bush tax cuts on middle- and lower-class Americans:

> PBS's MARGARET WARNER: But your [health] plan totaled, as scored by an independent authority, $900 billion over ten years. Now the president's tax cuts, at least on paper, the two of them add up to $1.6 [billion]. Surely, you'll have to roll back the tax cuts for more than just the wealthiest. . . .
>
> KERRY: For the wealthiest.
>
> WARNER: But only the wealthy?

KERRY: Yes, it works for the wealthy and the inheritance tax. . . . I don't want to roll back the marriage penalty, I don't want to roll back the child-care credit, I don't want to punish people who got a $300 break at the 10 percent and 15 percent, so I don't take that back.[49]

A tax expert from the Brookings Institute, a liberal think tank, Peter Orszag, calculated that Kerry's tax cut repeal wouldn't fund health care, let alone his other initiatives. The *Los Angeles Times* reported Orszag "said [Kerry's tax-cut repeal] proposals would save about $80 billion to $90 billion a year by 2013," adding, "That wouldn't be enough to pay for Kerry's health-care plan, much less the other initiatives he is considering."[50]

Americans voiced concerns about giving up their tax cuts to fund health care. "For people who are nervous and [are] independents, it's not about whether they want a big health-care plan, but they may not be sure they want to see tax cuts rolled back," Robert Blendon, professor of health policy and political analysis at Harvard's School of Public Health, told the *National Journal*.[51]

Although Kerry has said his tax roll-back plan would not only fund health care but would also finance the deficit, at another point during his campaign he said the health plan would make the deficit worse. "Kerry conceded that his plan would deepen federal budget deficits, but he said it would ultimately help eliminate them by stimulating the economy through corporate and consumer assistance," the *Boston Globe* reported in May 2003.[52]

When the numbers are finally added, it's clear Kerry's health plan would worsen the deficit. According to a Cato Institute review of it, the plan's "expected cost in 2013—$157 billion—is more than twice that of the new [2003] Medicare prescription drug benefit." Just to fund Kerry's plan, Cato estimated "Medicaid and [State Children's Health Insurance Program] expansions would cost the federal government an estimated $502.7 billion from 2005 to

2013—123 percent of the cost of the Medicare prescription drug benefit—including $17.4 billion in 2013."[53]

Kerry's plan would also add a further large burden on an over-burdened system of federal entitlements, say estimates. "Government spending on [health-care] proposals would compound the enormous budgetary pressures of existing federal entitlements. . . . Under current law (again before adding the cost of the new Medicare benefit), Social Security, Medicare, and Medicaid will consume nearly 80 percent of federal spending by 2040. *In addition to placing new duties on taxpayers, the candidate's health proposals would make existing obligations greater by subjecting Medicare and Medicaid to greater medical inflation,*" Cato noted.[54]

SPINNING PRESCRIPTION DRUGS

Since the Medicare prescription drug benefit debate, a number of partisan Democrats have stumped for approval for seniors to be able to order drugs from Canada because they are cheaper. John Kerry has also entered this debate, but his contention that the Medicare law forbids reimportation is incorrect.

"I will repeal the ban on reimportation of drugs from Canada so people can actually have a marketplace that works and is competitive," Kerry told a New Hampshire newspaper.[55] Only, it's not illegal to import such drugs. The 2003 Medicare law "allows consumers, pharmacists and wholesalers to reimport from Canada drugs approved by the Food and Drug Administration," says an analysis by *Congressional Quarterly.*[56]

Regarding the limitation on Canadian prescription drug reimportation, Kerry blames the law on Bush. "George Bush has served the powerful interests of this country. How else could you take a Medicare bill . . . and turn it into a windfall profit of $139 billion for . . . the drug companies . . . prohibiting seniors from importing drugs from Canada or other countries? The only reason for doing that is to line the pockets of your friends," Kerry said during an interview on CBS.[57] In reality, the government has such restrictions in place because it cannot guarantee the safety of drugs from other nations—even Canada. "The FDA says it cannot guarantee the drugs' safety, or even that imported drugs come from Canada as claimed instead of originating in other countries like Thailand. The government has intercepted pills made of sugar as well as drugs that require refrigeration shipped hot," the Associated Press reported in January 2004.[58]

Some pundits speculate that Kerry's overall plan is to impose price restrictions on the health-care industry—a draconian, if not socialistic, approach. "Kerry wants to, in effect, impose price controls on drugs by allowing the government to 'negotiate' with drug companies on behalf of the Medicare and Medicaid program and by legalizing mass importation of drugs from Canada," writes Morton Kondracke of Capitol Hill newspaper *Roll Call*. "However, Medicare does not 'negotiate' with providers such as doctors and hospitals on reimbursement levels. It imposes them, and Congress often gets into the act of changing formulas. And, the reason that drugs are cheaper in Canada and Europe is that governments there fix prices based on the production cost of new drugs, escaping participation in the astronomical cost of drug development."[59] Even the traditionally liberal *Washington Post*, in an editorial, warned against medical price controls, noting the federal government isn't very good at it. "[B]efore the call for price controls gains too much momentum lawmakers should make sure they've looked at all the options. Governments are notoriously bad at setting prices, and the U.S. government is notoriously bad at setting prices in the medical realm."[60]

To do so—to control the price of medications—would most likely lead politicians (and presidents) like Kerry to lower them so much as to remove all incentive for drug companies to continue research and development on new medications, new treatments, and, ultimately, new cures for diseases, say analysts. "It's tempting to say in these circumstances, 'Hey, we can mandate lower prices for Medicare, treating American retirees the way we treat AIDS sufferers in Africa, because drug companies will keep making and selling drugs even at a much lower price as long as it's higher than current manufacturing costs.' That's right, and the price of drug company stocks will crash instantly, and no more capital will be available to research new products," wrote Holman W. Jenkins Jr. in the *Wall Street Journal*.[61]

Kerry says he will instruct the government to negotiate lower prices, but the non-partisan Congressional Budget Office (CBO) in a study said that idea won't lower costs any more than private plans would: "CBO has examined the effect of striking the 'non-interference' provision . . . of the Social Security Act," which "bars the Secretary of Health and Human Services from interfering with the negotiations between drug manufacturers and pharmacies and sponsors of prescription drug plans. . . . We estimate that striking that provision would have a negligible effect on federal spending because CBO estimates that substantial savings will be obtained by the private plans and that the Secretary would not be able to negotiate prices that further reduce federal spending to a significant degree."[62]

VICTIMS OF TRIAL LAWYERS

Perhaps one of the most important issues for doctors and other medical providers—as well as the companies that insure them—is the issue of medical tort reform. Litigation costs in the medical and health industry have skyrocketed over the past few decades, though during the same amount of time medical training and technology have improved dramatically. Some industry analysts say the legal industry is driving the litigation trend, encouraging lawsuits for non-malpractice related cases and winning huge damage awards on behalf of trial lawyers and victims alike.

One idea is to limit the amount of damages that can be awarded in medical malpractice cases, with the idea being if insurance company liability to insure doctors and medical providers is reduced, so too will the cost of doing business with medical providers. Hence, malpractice insurance rates for practitioners will fall and with it the overall price of health care to patients.

The concept has been validated before. In 1975, the state of California passed the Medical Injury Compensation Reform Act, now considered the model tort reform legislation for the rest of the nation. Before the law was passed, medical malpractice losses were approaching catastrophic. Some companies "that specialized in medical liability were insolvent and taken over by the Insurance Commissioner," writes William K. Scheuber and Bradford P. Cohn, MD. "Some were unable to pay claims, and their liabilities fell upon the doctors they insured. The largest liability premium increases were as much as 485 percent. Some refused to insure at any price or refused to insure high-risk specialties and canceled selected individuals. Some insured for only 90 days, with premium increases and cancellations at each renewal. They renounced agreements with medical societies to disclose underwriting, claims handling and actuarial and financial experience."[63]

The experiment worked; California's law caps non-economic malpractice awards at $250,000 and also caps attorney's fees on a sliding scale. As malpractice awards dropped, so too did insurance companies' rates to physicians for coverage. That has helped keep medical costs in California lower than what they otherwise would have been. "[Tort reform] has worked in California; no one questions it has worked in California," said Senator John Ensign (R-Nevada) in May 2002.[64]

Kerry, however, opposes such medical liability reform efforts. According to his Senate record, he's voted at least ten times from 1995 to 2004 to block medical liability reform efforts.[65] In July 2003 and again in February 2004, he failed to cast votes in medical liability reform legislation before the Senate.[66] And though

Kerry is touting the implementation of a so-called "Patients Bill of Rights" in his 2004 presidential campaign, he voted against just such a measure in 2001 because it included a provision capping medical non-economic damages.[67]

The Massachusetts candidate says he opposes such limits and tort reform because they don't actually work to lower insurance premiums or other health-care costs. "Kerry . . . strongly opposes capping damages in medical malpractice lawsuits," says his campaign Web site. "Capping damages will neither reduce premium costs for doctors, nor lower the cost of health care for Americans. Experience in states that have capped damages demonstrates that reality conclusively."[68]

But besides the California experience—which has proven that caps *do* work to keep costs and premiums in check—the CBO has estimated such costs would drop by an average of 25 to 30 percent under federal medical liability reform passed by the House of Representatives in March 2003. "The CBO also notes that about one-third of the states would see reductions in premiums 'substantially larger than the overall average,'" said the agency in its study. The agency went on to say pointedly the House bill would "lead to lower charges for health-care services and procedures and, ultimately, to a decrease in rates for health insurance premiums."[69]

A separate study by the Department of Health and Human Services found almost the same results: "States with limits of $250,000 or $350,000 on non-economic damages have average combined highest premium increases of 12–15 percent, compared to 44 percent in states without caps on non-economic damages. . . ."[70]

Does John Kerry believe capping medical liability claims does *not* lead to cheaper insurance premiums and a reduction in overall health-care costs? Only if he ignores the evidence.

Or is it because in 2002 the top donors to Kerry's "Citizen Soldier Fund" political action committee were lawyers and law firms—the industry most strongly opposed to caps on medical malpractice awards?[71]

VETERANS' HEALTH

As a veteran, many Americans might suspect John Kerry would be one of the most sympathetic ears in Congress—especially in terms of veterans' health issues. After all, he's made a lot of political hay trading off his military record over the years. But, shockingly, Kerry's record on providing health care for veterans does not match his campaign rhetoric.

In his 2003 book, *A Call to Service*, Kerry claimed he has "fought" for veterans' health care: "About 400,000 qualified veterans are denied access to Veterans Administration health care and more than 235,000 veterans already in the system have to wait six months or more for their first doctor's visit. . . . That makes me angry. And it makes me even angrier that the Bush administration is fighting to cut veterans' health benefits. . . . I have already fought this injustice and as president will fight it even more passionately."[72]

In August 2003, Kerry accused the Bush administration of "not keeping faith" with military reservists who have no health insurance. While claiming some 20 percent of reservists lacked coverage, Kerry stated, "I regret to say that even as we are creating a new generation of veterans . . . this country and this administration is not keeping faith with those who serve."[73]

But in May and November 2003, Kerry failed to vote on measures extending military health coverage to National Guard reservists and their families, if called to active duty.[74] Also, Kerry voted against a supplemental defense funding bill in October 2003 that contained, among other things, an extra $1.3 billion in funding specifically for veterans' health care.[75] He also skipped a vote that funded the Veterans Administration with $28.6 billion for Fiscal Year 2004—a measure which included $1 billion to expedite processing of VA benefits claims.[76]

There are more examples:

- In 2001, Kerry voted against an amendment that would have increased funding for veterans' medical care by $650 million.[77]

- In 1999, he voted to kill an amendment that would have reallocated $210 million for veterans' medical benefits, and $10 million for construction of veterans' extended-care facilities.[78]

- In 1996, he voted against an amendment offered by Sen. John McCain (R-Arizona) to require equal access to health care for all vets—Kerry was one of only eighteen senators to vote against the measure.[79]

As much as Kerry claims in his campaign rhetoric to be "angry" about America's health-care system, including prescription drug coverage and veteran health benefits, he actually fought against corrective legislation in order to make a political statement. Just as bad, he missed important votes on crucial legislation for the issues about which he claims to care so deeply.

Senator Kerry has failed to put policy ahead of politics again and again.

14

DUMBING DOWN EDUCATION

Trapping children, scrapping school choice

WITHOUT QUESTION, education is a very important part of our nation's fabric. Without it, there is no way to ensure future generations will be able to achieve personal or professional success. If they fail, so does the nation.

However, various "education" lobbies are trying to push their own agenda on our children. It is an agenda that preaches a "blame America first" attitude—one that seeks to desecrate the memory of our founding fathers, our history, and our success. In using the public school system of the nation's capital as his example, educator, columnist, and author Walter Williams sums up the pitiful state of education in general by pointing out that education is rarely what animates the so-called "education establishment" in America.

Williams, in citing earlier information, "looked at the disastrous state of education in the nation's capital, where at only one of the city's 19 high schools do as many as 50 percent of its students test as proficient in reading. At no school are 50 percent of the students proficient in math. At 12 of 19 high schools, more than 50 percent of the students test below basic in reading, and at some of those schools it's almost 80 percent. At 15 high schools, over 50 percent test below basic in math. In 12 of them, 70 percent to 99 percent do so," he wrote.[1] He went on to say results are similar in many other predominantly black schools around the nation, but the poor academic performances don't seem to interest black civil rights leaders and politicians. Rather, Williams writes, what concerns them most is "what Sen. Trent Lott has said and whether the Confederate Flag is publicly displayed."[2]

This education establishment—which consists of a consortium of politicians, education unions, advocacy/civil rights groups, and government agencies—has been accused of promoting certain politically correct agendas on children. At the same time, critics say much about what made the U.S. system so good early on has now disappeared, replaced by police with drug-sniffing dogs, metal detectors, and violence. Despite the critical importance of education and what it means to the future of our nation, John Kerry has a history of allowing these lobbies to dictate what is in *their* best interests, not those of our children.

Unlike the nationally regulated and financed public education systems of other industrialized nations, the system of compulsory education in the United States has ties to the federal government, but is primarily operated by individual states and local school districts.[3] Developed in the nineteenth century, it differed from other nations in three fundamental respects, according to one description: "First, Americans were more inclined to regard education as a solution to various social problems. Second, because they had this confidence in the power of education, Americans provided more years of schooling for a larger percentage of the population than other countries. Third, educational institutions were primarily governed by local authorities rather than by federal ones." After the American Revolution, our founders argued "that education was essential for the prosperity and survival of the new nation." Subsequent national leaders took that argument to heart; in terms of real numbers, by the year 2002, 86 percent of adults between twenty-five and twenty-nine had graduated high school.[4]

Early education reformers Horace Mann of Massachusetts and Henry Barnard of Connecticut are credited with developing the American school system in the 1830s and 1840s. They had these goals and beliefs in mind as they shaped the nation's school system:

- They believed a common education could transform all youth into virtuous, literate citizens.
- They believed widespread education and literacy would help America compete with other educated nations in the world.
- They believed common schooling could create a common bond among citizens, regardless of their ethnicity, religious, or social background.
- They believed universal education would alleviate crime and poverty, thereby preserving social stability.
- They believed common elementary (primary) education should be free, available to all children, should be financed by the public, and accountable to local school boards as well as the state.
- They argued for compulsory education laws for children of elementary age.[5]

By the end of the nineteenth century, the reformers and their followers had largely achieved these goals. By 1918, all states had passed laws requiring children to attend at least elementary school.[6] Some opposed the common-public school concept, such as the Roman Catholic Church, and, after U.S. courts agreed, children were permitted to attend privately run and financed schools as well.

Over the years, private schools grew in number and size, mostly because of disappointment in the performance of public education. According to J. H. Snider, a research fellow for the New America Foundation, writing in the *Washington Post* in September 2003,

"The result of the increase in private school enrollments is that public schools are being turned into a welfare service for the disadvantaged. . . . In the long-term, the transformation of the public schools into a welfare service is a disaster for the United States."[7]

Another alternative—home-schooling of children—has also begun to catch on; by 2002, it was estimated that between 1.75 and 2.1 million of the nation's children are schooled at home.[8]

While it is difficult to argue with the contention that compulsory primary education is a large part of the glue that bonds a successful society, it can also be said that the same system of national education can be—and has been—exploited by political interests seeking specific outcomes.

In 2000, Texas Governor George W. Bush, while campaigning for the White House, alluded to this phenomenon when he said he wanted to put more accountability and order back in the system of education, to ensure children learned the basics that led to the creation of a great and educated society, such as reading, writing, and arithmetic. In order to protect the education system from further deterioration and abuse, Bush proposed the "No Child Left Behind" act, which was finally passed into law January 2002. It mandates higher performance standards by both teachers and students, adds accountability requirements, and offers repetitive poor performers additional assistance and resources while offering more options for parents so their children are not trapped in a failing school. In short, the law attempts to heed Thomas Jefferson's warning: *"If a nation expects to be ignorant and free, in a state of civilization, it expects what never was and never will be."*[9]

John Kerry, as you might imagine, has a different view.

MORE PUBLIC FINANCING

"Kerry believes that we need to consider indicators of school performance other than simply test scores," says his presidential campaign Web site. "Kerry will revise the accountability standards in No Child Left Behind to include ways of assessing student performance in addition to testing. . . . Possible indicators include graduation rates, teacher attendance, parental satisfaction, and student attendance."[10]

The Massachusetts senator is also wedded to the public school concept—so much so that, in fact, he opposes any efforts to provide alternatives or choices to parents who want the best possible primary education for their children. "John Kerry opposes private school vouchers. . . . Instead, he supports efforts to increase resources to public schools to ensure all students have quality teachers, high standards, smaller classes, and safe, modern schools. Kerry also would expand public school choice programs and support for pilot schools to empower parents and students and provide more options to fill specific needs without draining funds from public education," says the Kerry Web site.[11]

Unlike the nation's modern education system founders, Kerry wants to force the public to also finance secondary and higher education. According to his campaign, he would force taxpayers to finance billions in government-sponsored college- and university-level education:

> Kerry will help students prepare for college by creating new pathways to college and with new "I Have A Dream Scholarships." The scholarships provide an additional $1,000 for students to participate in . . . early intervention programs that help prepare students for college. Kerry will help students pay for college with new "College Opportunity Tax Credit" and "Service For College" program. He will provide a credit for each and every year of college on the first $4,000 paid in tuition—the typical tuition and fees for public college tuition. The credit will provide 100 percent of the first $1000 and 50 percent on the rest. Kerry's "Service for College" plan will provide the

cost of four years at a public college to young people in exchange for serving their communities and country in national service.[12]

Some aspects of his education platform include more *manda-tory* spending. "John Kerry is proposing an Education Trust Fund that makes sure—with mandatory funding—that we meet the promises in the No Child Left Behind Act and the Individuals with Disabilities Education Act. He has fought for mandatory funding for special education for years and as president he will ensure that we get it for all elementary and secondary education. This will enable schools to fund more after school programs, hire more teachers, and improve quality."[13]

Kerry is advocating more mandatory funding of more programs and higher levels of education—more than ever envisioned by the founders of America's modern compulsory system—but, as results have proven, more money is not a bona fide prescription for success. Worse, Kerry wants to fund education alright, but only as long as parents accept his vision of what is right for their children and do not insist he provide them with a choice in the matter.

MORE IS BETTER?

Spending more money on education—primary, secondary, or otherwise—is not the way to guarantee a *better* education. But nevertheless, Senator John Kerry thinks that is the solution, though many others who are actually education experts do not. And the latter have the data to back up their claims.

"Among more than 25 industrialized nations, no country spends more public and private money to educate each student than the United States, according to an annual review by the Paris-based Organization for Economic Cooperation and Development [OECD]," the Associated Press reported in September 2003. In summary, AP said, "given its investment in education, the United

States isn't getting the return it expects when compared with the performance of other nations."[14]

According to the OECD's report, the U.S. in 2000 spent an average of $10,240 per student between elementary school through college. That compares with a global industrialized nation average of just $6,361. In all, America spent 7 percent of its gross domestic product—the combined value of all goods and services—on education in 2000, the second-highest among the twenty-five countries.[15]

"Lack of money is not the problem. Increased funding has not led to increased achievement," says the Heritage Foundation. "Over the past three decades, per-pupil education spending has doubled, but test scores have remained stagnant."[16]

"Federal education spending is up 36 percent since 2001. In fact, federal education funding is increasing faster than states can spend it. . . . $84 million in state education funds was recently returned to the U.S. Treasury because states had not used it for more than three years," Heritage adds. "As House Education and Workforce Committee Chairman John Boehner (R-Ohio) has said, further funding would be like putting more gas in a flooded engine. . . . The real problem is a broken education system that prevents resources from getting to teachers and students. We need to fix that by making sure more dollars reach the classroom, by streamlining federal education programs, and by giving parents more education choices. As much as forty cents on the dollar may be lost between Washington and the classroom."[17]

Throughout his career, Kerry has advocated for more spending—but not always for the accountability that should accompany any federal funding increases. In 1996, in a debate over school vouchers for children in Washington D.C., Kerry said the best way for Congress to help was to provide more money. The *Boston Globe* reported, "Kerry agrees that children should be able to choose among public schools, but opposed the D.C. voucher plan because it would subsidize students who transfer to private schools as well. He said the best way Congress can help children in depressed areas is with money for public education—for computers, remedial education, subsidized lunches. He even suggested a tax credit for parents who buy phonics programs to help their children learn to read."[18]

He seemed to alter his stance somewhat just a few years later, in 1998, by appearing to call for reform *and* funding. "[W]e can't just finance more failure. . . . If we are to have a debate about true education reform, we must search out the truth. . . . Let us begin by acknowledging that the answer is not just new spending or private schools, but new ideas and new commitment for the public schools," he said in remarks at Boston's Northeastern University.[19]

But the change didn't last long. Now, as the 2004 election approaches, Kerry is back to stumping for more spending. At a Democratic presidential candidate debate in Baltimore, Maryland, he said, "I believe that we deserve a president that recognizes until you have equality of education in America, until the federal government is prepared to make up the difference in funding, we do not have a prayer at making real the full promise of our country. That means 21st century learning centers have to be funded. After-school programs have to be funded. We have to fully fund special needs education, we have to fully fund the capacity of teachers to teach in the most difficult areas. We have to raise the salaries, and we have to fully fund title one. . . ."[20]

In other speeches touting his education plans, he continues the same theme of *spend more, not less.* "Kerry said teachers' pay needs to be raised. Kerry has pledged that if elected president . . .[he would] fully fund special education, rebuild crumbling schools and provide early education for all. Kerry said an increased federal contribution to education in his administration would come from rolling back some of the Bush tax cuts," the *Patriot Ledger* of Quincy, Massachusetts, reported in July 2003.[21]

If these pledges to spend more aren't enough, Kerry—if elected—would also seek to create a new "Education Trust Fund," which he says "will finally guarantee we fully fund our schools."[22]

"With the National Education Trust Fund, never again will teachers and parents and students have to worry about the whims of politicians in Washington. The funds our students need will be there—year in and year out," he said during a speech at Thomas Jefferson High School in Council Bluffs, Iowa, in November 2003.[23]

Regarding the Bush No Child Left Behind Act, Kerry wants to "reform" it by throwing more money at the law. "My first priority as president will be to live up to the funding commitments made in the No Child Left Behind Act and fully fund the law," he said in response to a question about the act from the American Federation of Teachers. "Where the Bush administration sought to cut funding for school reform and issued restrictive guidelines, I will fund the law and ensure states have the flexibility to meet the goals of the law."[24]

Kerry also wants to extend federal government reach and financing beyond the primary school level to the college level. In remarks to an audience in Iowa early in the campaign season, Kerry claimed, "If we're going to be a country where our economy is on the move we need to make sure our young people can make the move to college. And we need the courage to stand up and say it is high time we made four years of college as universal and as afford-able as a high school education is today."[25]

Along these lines, he wants to implement a host of new feder-ally funded programs ostensibly aimed at "preparing" students for college, specifically "a new 'Ready For College' initiative." Kerry says "early intervention can reduce the large number of college stu-dents who drop-out of college or who need remedial courses," and he "supports high school reform including: encouraging more states to allow eleventh or twelfth graders to take college courses; ensuring that Advanced Placement programs are available in all schools; strengthening math, science, and writing instruction; and expanding early intervention efforts like the GEAR-UP and TRIO programs for students who are at risk of dropping out of school."[26] (The TRIO programs are funded under Title IV of the Higher Education Act of 1965—initially just three programs—which were designed to help students overcome class, social, and cultural barriers to higher education.)

In addition, Kerry says he wants to increase federal funding for states for higher education. He would help students stay in and complete college, and "provide fiscal relief to states to help stop rising tuitions, encourage colleges and universities to make higher education system more efficient, without sacrificing quality, by streamlining services and reducing duplication, and help institutions provide better counseling and support services to keep students in college," according to remarks made in Iowa City, Iowa, in October 2003.[27]

Another way Kerry would increase taxpayer funding of education would be to increase federal money available for Pell grants. "I strongly support increased funding for existing federal programs that help people afford college. I have consistently supported increases in the maximum Pell grant award as well as loan forgiveness programs, and the HOPE and Lifetime Learning Scholarship programs," he told the American Federation of Teachers.[28]

ANTI-CHOICE

John Kerry has never been an advocate for allowing parents to choose the type and kind of schools their children attend. In other words, Kerry supports the compulsory education system founded by education pioneers in the 1830s, but he doesn't support the right of parents to choose which system they want their kids attending. All compulsion, no compassion.

In 1996 alone, for example, Kerry voted four times to deny the parents of poor children in Washington D.C. a school choice option.[29]

And while Kerry and other Democrats often argue low-income families should have the same education options as middle-class and wealthy families, those positions are often suppressed by the powerful National Education Association (NEA) lobby—which routinely opposes school choice initiatives. John Leo of *U.S. News & World Report* summed up the opposition by Kerry and other Democrats:

> Democrats are not famous for stiffing the D.C. government, for opposing "choice" in any form or even for defending Senate talkathons as a method of frustrating majorities. When it comes to essential services, Democrats routinely argue that the poor should have the same options as the middle class and the rich, even if it takes public funds to provide them. But all these normal party instincts are suppressed when the subject is schools and the lobby applying pressure is the major teachers' union, the National Educational Association.[30]

Leo continues, saying Democrats were exposed to pressure from the NEA that was "so intense," they caved on school choice— nearly on cue:

> "[T]he pressure was so intense that the Democrats preferred 'a looming crisis of Congress's own making' as the *Washington Post* put it, rather than keep alive the possibility that some poor Washington children might be able to attend nonpublic schools," he wrote. "[T]he NEA did not want District voters to decide for themselves, and it didn't want Congress on record as favoring choice in any way, even for parents confronted with the worst public-school system in America. Unionized teachers, like beneficiaries of monopolies everywhere, can always be counted on to suppress competition. So as expected, the White House and the Senate Democrats caved in on schedule."[31]

In a 1998 speech, perhaps because vouchers were popular in the polls, Kerry stopped short of an outright rejection of them, expressing sympathy for parents who want to use them to exercise education choice for their kids, and said it was right for schools to "compete" for the chance to educate the nation's children. "Shame on us also for not realizing that there are parents in this country who care little about politics or party, who today support vouchers. . . . [Parents] want alternatives—and seeing none in our rigid system, they are willing and some even desperate to look elsewhere," he said, in a speech at Boston's Northeastern University. "Intuitively, it makes sense that parents ought to have the freedom as consumers to choose the public schools that fit their children's needs. It makes sense that schools ought to compete for the chance to educate our children."[32]

Kerry's implied approval of school choice for parents, via the voucher system—which would apply to private schools—could not be believed. Before 1998's brief foray into supporting school choice—and after—Kerry was often heard stumping against school choice, if not voting for measures that banned or limited school choice initiatives. By 2001, he was back to opposing choice, calling the concept of allowing parents to choose a school for their children a "back-door voucher" program. "The prospect of using federal dollars—in the form of sacrificed tax revenues—to subsidize private education is still divisive among Democrats. Senators John Kerry and Edward Kennedy, both Massachusetts Democrats, have opposed the broader application, calling it a 'back-door voucher,'" reported *CBS MarketWatch*.[33]

Also that year, Kerry openly boasted that a voucher provision in President Bush's No Child Left Behind legislation would not survive negotiations. "Kerry said he is 'quite hopeful' about passage of a plan close to Bush's, which has 'common ground' with his own proposals. Bush's voucher ideas, Kerry said, 'are ripe for bargaining away, and I'm confident they will be'. . . . Kerry, along with Sen.

Gordon H. Smith (R-Ore.), will . . . suggest plans to expand char-
ter schools significantly as an alternative to vouchers. 'People have
the same concepts,' Kerry said. 'To some degree, it's at the fringes
where the differences exist.'"³⁴

In revealing his own education plan during the debate over
Bush's bill, Kerry's lacked a "choice" provision. "Centrist Democrats,
including Sen. John F. Kerry (D-Mass.) and Sen. Joseph Lieberman
(D-Conn.) unveiled their education bill, which while somewhat
similar to the Bush plan, does not include a voucher provision," the
Boston Herald reported.³⁵

And in 2004, as he geared up in earnest for his presidential bid,
Kerry vehemently argued against any sort of school choice as an
education option for parents. He said the issue should not become
a moral argument, because choice would abandon students in public schools. "[W]e have to guarantee that vouchers are not made
into an argument that somehow there's a morality in taking care of
kids, fifty of them, and abandoning four thousand in the school
behind them. I refuse to accept that," he said at a Congressional
Black Caucus-sponsored debate.³⁶

He claims vouchers and choice will somehow destroy the public school system in America, especially in inner cities, thereby
leaving "more children behind." While campaigning in Iowa in
November 2003, he said, "We need a president who will tell the
truth about vouchers—that they weaken public education, make
it harder to build good citizens, and hurt those most in need.
Don't cry crocodile tears for inner city kids while trying in effect
to destroy inner city schools. Vouchers aren't choice; they're a
bad choice that would leave even more children behind." Kerry
was resolute: "I have never supported vouchers. I will never support them. And if it ever comes to my desk, I'll veto vouchers or
voucher-like programs the day that bill arrives," he said in Iowa
in November 2003.³⁷

Surely that's a statement of principle by the Massachusetts

Democrat. Surely it doesn't have anything to do with the more than $610,000 he's received from various education lobbies between January and April 2004.[38]

NO SCHOOL PRAYER

One issue important to millions of Americans is the right of their children to voluntarily pray in school if they wish. Kerry, a Catholic, disagrees. His anti-school choice attitudes extend to this issue as well.

As far back as 1985, during his first year as a U.S. senator, Kerry made known his disdain for voluntary school prayer. In a speech on the Senate floor in opposition to a bill for voluntary school prayer, Kerry, as do many liberals, labeled supporters "far right" extremists—instead of advocates of the First Amendment's freedom of speech and religious expression protections:

> Today, the far right seeks to tear down the wall of separation and to attack the principles which Thomas Jefferson espoused. They seek to extend governmental intrusion into the most private and sensitive areas of our lives, by forcing so-called voluntary school prayer into the public school classrooms of our children. Mr. President, I support prayer and the constitutional right of every American to private prayer. But support [of] the bill is not the way to address private prayer. Sometimes the proponents of this legislation are carried away with personal belief that America is a Christian nation. They would like to do what is expressly forbidden by the establishment clause of the U.S. Constitution—that is, to establish an official religion in this country. This so-called voluntary school prayer amendment is only a first step in that direction. Mr. President, I hope the legislation before us today, or measures like it, may never become law.[39]

DUMBING DOWN EDUCATION

Interestingly, a decade later, in February 1994, Kerry voted in a sort of reversal to deny federal money to state or local school agencies who prohibit constitutionally protected voluntary school prayer.[40] But only five months later, Kerry voted against virtually the same amendment—one offered by Senator Jesse Helms (R-South Carolina).[41] Instead, Kerry voted for one offered by Senator Nancy Kassebaum that withheld funds from schools violating a court order on school prayer.[42] The Senate Republican Policy Committee noted:

> We sympathize with the underlying intent of the Helms Amendment. Children do have a constitutional right to pray voluntarily in public schools, and we are as upset as our colleagues are at some of the restrictions that schools have placed on that constitutional right. However, we part from our colleagues in our view of how easy it is to differentiate between what is constitutional and what is not. The courts have not been that consistent on the issues. . . . The Kassebaum Amendment, unlike the Helms Amendment, does not place any onus on a school for making a wrong decision in this difficult area. Instead, whichever way it decides, whether to restrict prayer or not to restrict prayer, it is only punished if it refuses to change its policy after it has been ruled to be wrong. . . .[43]

NO ABSTINENCE EDUCATION

To round out his education stance, it should be noted that Kerry also voted against using federal education funds for abstinence education—despite proof such programs work. One 1998 study managed by New York's Columbia University's School of Public Health, which taught the benefit of abstinence to sixth graders (the goal being that fewer kids would have sex as they grew older), "reduced the pregnancy rate for very young adolescents by one-third and also encouraged one-fifth of sexually active students to practice abstinence."[44]

According to research by the Heritage Foundation, "Abstinence education programs encourage a delay in sexual activity. Abstinence is widely popular, and many evaluations show that abstinence education programs can substantially reduce teen sexual activity."[45]

Besides reducing unwanted pregnancies, abstinence also reduces the number of teens who contract sexually transmitted diseases—some of which, like HIV, could eventually lead to death while others, like herpes, have no known cure. Still, John Kerry has a history of opposing abstinence education. In July 1996, he voted against a provision of the Budget Act to use $75 million of the Maternal and Child Health Block Grant Program to teach kids the benefits of sexual abstinence.[46]

In all, John Kerry—led by political correctness and controlled by teachers' unions and other entities whose agendas are demonstrably bad for our children—has a record of backing the education establishment instead of the founding principles of education that worked well for decades. As president—and as a Democrat—there is nothing to indicate he's learned anything new.

AFTERWORD

The cost of a Kerry presidency

IN MAKING HIS RUN FOR THE WHITE HOUSE, John Kerry has hit the pinnacle of his professional career. By any measure, he has arrived at a place he has been trying to reach his entire life, but it is the way in which he has arrived that should worry Americans. While the motivation to seek elected office differs from person to person, it is obvious Kerry's lifelong ambition has been to climb the ladder of politics. He has reinvented himself so many times, as demonstrated by his numerous flip-flops documented in this book, it's impossible to tell who is the real John Kerry. And he has said and done whatever he had to in order to get ahead of the game.

His "anything to get elected" style began around 1960. At one time Kerry suggested he worked extensively on the John F. Kennedy campaign, even going so far as to claim he helped register black voters in the South. "[E]very person here believes very deeply that we have an obligation that's unfulfilled in this country," Kerry told a largely African-American audience in Des Moines, Iowa, in January 2004. "[Senator] Joe [Lieberman, D-Connecticut] and I became involved in that a long time ago in the Mississippi voter registration drive."[1]

But, as the Boston Globe pointed out earlier, Kerry embellished his roles, both in Kennedy's campaign and his so-called black voter registration effort. In a June 2003 story, the paper quoted a Kerry campaign flyer that said, "Ever since I worked as a young volunteer in John Kennedy's presidential campaign, I have been deeply committed to participation in politics and political issues. . . . Back then, I joined the struggle for voting rights in the South."[2]

Not quite. According to the Globe, "Kerry's involvement with the JFK campaign of 1960 was minimal. Today, he acknowledges he may only have participated in a single literature drop in Concord, New Hampshire, while boarding at St. Paul's School. Moreover, his role in the struggle to register black voters in Mississippi was confined to the Yale campus in New Haven, Connecticut."[3]

John Kerry is not the only politician who has ever been accused of being an opportunist, but clearly he is one of the most vivid modern examples. From his anti-war beginnings in the early 1970s onward, Kerry has used every issue he could find—no matter how distasteful—for his own benefit. Kerry, much like Bill Clinton, wants to be all things to all people, a chameleon who adapts his stripes to win the next battle.

Consider the scandal of the abuse of Iraqi detainees by a few U.S. military personnel, which was first reported in mid-April 2004. Images of the abuse were used by the Kerry campaign to raise money a month later. Kerry campaign manager Mary Beth Cahill "made fundraising pitches over the weekend urging Kerry supporters to send money to the campaign as a way of showing support for Kerry's demand that Defense Secretary Donald Rumsfeld resign," the Cybercast News Service reported.[4]

Like many politicians, Senator Kerry is quick to point out the inequities and failures of his political competitors. For example, in early May 2004, Kerry launched a campaign criticizing President Bush for escalating health insurance premiums and treatment costs—a problem that began to get worse years before Bush was elected.

"Our health-care system is badly broken," Kerry told an audience at Pennsylvania's Edinboro University May 10. "Today, regular checkups are emptying family checkbooks. Waiting for a doctor's bill is causing as much anxiety as waiting for a diagnosis. And cutting through endless red tape and paperwork is wasting millions that could be spent on better care."[5] But what has Senator Kerry done to help fix health-care problems as a lawmaker? Very little, as noted during a Democratic presidential debate in Greenville, South Carolina. Former Vermont Governor Howard Dean had Kerry's number—literally—on the occasions he attempted to pass health-care reform legislation. "[I]n nineteen years in the Senate, Senator Kerry sponsored eleven bills that had anything to do with health care," said Dean. "Not one of them passed."[6]

Republicans, meanwhile—led by President Bush—managed to pass a Medicare prescription drug benefit as a way to reduce health-care costs for older Americans. The issue was one championed by Kerry, but it took the GOP to actually get the job done.

Kerry's political career is laden with such examples. He criticizes but doesn't deliver; he complains about issues but doesn't solve them; he condemns others whose solutions may or may not work but fails to offer his own. In short, he is a great politician. He knows the game of politics and how to manipulate it to his advantage, but that doesn't make him a good leader. Far from it.

Warren Bennis, PhD., distinguished professor of business administration at the University of Southern California, founding chairman of USC's Leadership Institute, and author of eighteen books (many on the subject of leadership), wrote, "Managers are people who do things right, while leaders are people who do the right thing." As a longtime senator, Kerry has learned how to swim in the political waters. And while he can be counted on to do the right thing for his own political interests and career, that is not the same as doing the right thing for the country.

"I'm John Kerry, and I approve of this message," the Democrat from Massachusetts intones in his television and radio campaign ads. But as he has so often demonstrated, his far-left liberal ideology is held by a minority of Americans. On Election Day 2004, a majority of voters will have an opportunity, once and for all, to show their disapproval of Senator Kerry's message.

NOTES

INTRODUCTION
1. Steve Turnham, "Good Cops, Bad Cops," CNN.com, 10 May 2004.

CHAPTER 1—THE EVERREADY BUNNY
1. Todd S. Purdum, "Storied Past, Golden Resume, But Mixed Reviews For Kerry," *New York Times*, 30 November 2003.
2. Charles Laurence, "The Secret Society That Ties Bush And Kerry," [London] *Sunday Telegraph*, 1 February 2004.
3. Laurence, "The Secret Society That Ties Bush And Kerry."
4. Betsy Rothstein, "With Hefty Political War Chest Well In Hand, Kerry Ponders Making Presidential Bid In '04," *The Hill*, 17 April 2002.
5. Michael Kranish, "With Antiwar Role, High Visibility," *Boston Globe*, 17 June 2003.
6. Brian C. Mooney, "First Campaign Ends In Defeat," *Boston Globe*, 18 June 2003.
7. Franz Scholz, "Kerry Poised For The Run-If," [Lowell, MA] *Sun*, 19 March 1972.
8. Frank Phillips, "Kerry Had Everything Going For Him . . . But," *Lowell Sun*, 12 November 1972.
9. Mooney, "Taking One Prize, Then A Bigger One," *Boston Globe*, 19 June 2003.
10. Mooney, "Taking One Prize, Then A Bigger One."
11. Johnson, "Democrats On The Stump Plot Their War Rhetoric," *Boston Globe*, 11 March 2003.
12. Johnson, "Kerry Says U.S. Needs Its Own 'Regime Change,'" *Boston Globe*, 3 April 2003.
13. Johnson, "Democrats On The Stump Plot Their War Rhetoric," *Boston Globe*.
14. H.J. Res. 114, CQ Vote #237: Passed 77–23: R 48–1; D 29–21; I 0–1, 11 October 2002, Kerry voted yea.
15. *ABC News*, Democrat Presidential Candidate Debate, Columbia, SC, 4 May 2003.
16. MSNBC, *Hardball*, 6 January 2004.
17. MSNBC, *News Live*, 31 July 2003.

18. Fox News, *Special Report*, 23 October 2003.
19. S. 1415, CQ Vote #154: Rejected 48–50: R 5–49; D 43–1, 10 June 1998, Kerry voted yea.
20. H.R. 3162, CQ Vote #313: Passed 98–1: R 49–0; D 48–1; I 1–0, 25 October 2001, Kerry voted yea.
21. John Kerry, remarks at town hall meeting, Manchester, NH, 6 August 2003.
22. Kerry, remarks at Iowa State University, 1 December 2003.
23. 1996 Massachusetts Senate Debate, 16 September 1996.
24. Timothy J. Connolly, "The 'Snoozer' Had Some Life," [Worcester, MA] *Telegram & Gazette*, 3 July 1996.
25. NBC, *Meet the Press*, 1 December 2002.
26. S.J. Res. 2, CQ Vote #2: Passed 52–47: R 42–2; D 10–45, 12 January 1991, Kerry voted nay.
27. John Aloysius Farrell, "At The Center Of Power, Seeking The Summit, *Boston Globe*, 21 June 2003.
28. Farrell, "At The Center Of Power, Seeking The Summit."
29. Jake Tapper, "Stealth Negativity?" ABCNews.com, 17 January 2004.
30. Tapper, "Stealth Negativity?"
31. Nedra Pickler, "Dean Says He's Closing Fast On Kerry, Accuses Rivals Of Dirty Tricks," Associated Press, 26 January 2004.
32. Pickler, "Dean Says He's Closing Fast On Kerry, Accuses Rivals Of Dirty Tricks."
33. Kranish, "A Privileged Youth, A Taste For Risk," *Boston Globe*, 15 June 2003.
34. Charles M. Sennott, "The Making of the Candidates: John Forbes Kerry," *Boston Globe*, 6 October 1996.
35. Joe Klein, "The Long War Of John Kerry," *New Yorker*, 2 December 2002.
36. Franklin Foer, "John Kerry: Outsider; Teen Wasteland," *New Republic*, 12 April 2004.

CHAPTER 2—LET THEM EAT CAKE!

1. Kerry, remarks in Davenport, IA, 17 January 2004.
2. Rich Lowry, "John Kerry And Benedict Arnold," *King Features Syndicate*, 1 April 2004.
3. Lowry, "John Kerry And Benedict Arnold."
4. Jim VandeHei, "Kerry Donors Include 'Benedict Arnolds;' Candidate Decries Tax-Haven Firms While Accepting Executives' Aid," *Washington Post*, 26 February 2004.
5. "Heinz Lays Off 100 Workers, Many In Pittsburgh," Associated Press, 26 April 2001.
6. Stuart Silverstein, "Jobless Rate Dips As State Shrugs Off Negative Trends," *Los Angeles Times*, 17 March 2001.
7. "Kodak, Heinz Plan Hundreds Of Layoffs," *Bloomberg News*, 11 November 1998.

8. "Business Notes," *Daily News of Los Angeles*, 2 May 1997.
9. Steven Oberbeck, "Heinz To Close Clearfield Plant," *Salt Lake Tribune*, 24 July 1996.
10. Sherri Buri, "Panel Says High-Tech Wages May Be On Rise," *Eugene Register-Guard*, 1 August 1995.
11. Cape Argus, "South Africa," *Africa News*, 22 September 2003.
12. "Heinz Bakery Jobs To Be Moved," *Calgary Herald*, 18 July 1997.
13. John Murray Brown, "Efforts Focus On The Consumer," *Financial Times*, 21 May 1997.
14. "Business Heinz Means Big Beans For Sunny Bay," *New Zealand Herald*, 7 October 2000.
15. Geoff Percival, "Business This Week," *Business And Finance*, 11 May 2000.
16. Steven Theobald, "Heinz Bakery Sweet On Trenton," *Toronto Star*, 18 July 1997.
17. Steve Schultze, "Kerry Campaign Fires Phone Service," *Milwaukee Journal Sentinel*, 11 February 2004.
18. Kerry, remarks in Des Moines, IA, 5 January 2004.
19. CNN, *Late Edition*, 25 February 2001.
20. Kerry, remarks in Davenport, IA, 14 January 2004.
21. Kerry for President, "John Kerry's Plan To Fight For America's Economic Future," Press Release, 28 August 2003.
22. Dan Balz and Paul Farhi, "Kerry, Edwards Attack Bush On Workers' Woes," *Washington Post*, 26 February 2004.
23. MSNBC, *Hardball*, 10 February 2004, emphasis added.
24. Jennifer Peter, "Presidential Contender Confronts 'Massachusetts Liberal' Label," Associated Press, 21 December 2002.
25. Scott A. Hodge and J. Scott Moody, "The Growing Class Of Americans Who Pay No Federal Income Taxes," Fiscal Facts, The Tax Foundation, 14 April 2004.
26. Stephan Dinan, "Bush's Tax Cuts Add Up To Zero," *Washington Times*, 19 June 2003.
27. Dinan, "Bush's Tax Cuts Add Up To Zero."
28. Christopher Frenze, Congressional Joint Economic Committee, U.S. House of Representatives, available online: http://www.house.gov/jec/fiscal/ tx-grwth/ reagtxct/reagtxct.htm, April 1996.
29. Federal Reserve Chairman Alan Greenspan, remarks to the Senate Budget Committee, 25 January 2001.
30. U.S. Senate Republican Policy Committee, Sen. Larry Craig, Chairman, "Is The Bush Tax Cut Too Large? No!" Available online: http://rpc.senate.gov/ ~rpc/releases/1999/tx021501.htm, 15 February 2001.
31. ABC, *Good Morning America*, 2 September, 2003.
32. John Maggs, et al, "A Kerry Top 10," *National Journal*, 30 January 2004.
33. "Kerry: Those Who Question Me Are 'Crooked Liars,'" NewsMax.com, 10 March, 2004.

34. David R. Guarino and Andrew Miga, "None Of Your Business: Teresa Won't Give Up Tax Records," *Boston Herald*, 16 April 2004.

35. Thomas B. Edsall, "Kerry Mortgages Home To Keep Campaign Afloat," *Washington Post*, 19 December 2003.

36. Guarino and Miga, "None Of Your Business: Teresa Won't Give Up Tax Records," *Boston Herald*.

37. H.J. Res. 1, CQ Vote #67: Motion agreed to 66–32: R 49–3; D 17–29, 14 February 1995, Kerry voted nay.

38. Figures and statistics culled from Sen. John Kerry's legislative voting record since 1985.

39. S. 1689, CQ Vote #373: Motion agreed to 57–42: R 50–1; D 7–40; I 0–1, 2 October 2003, Kerry voted nay; Senate Republican Policy Committee, "Security Supplemental/Small Business Tax Hike To Pay For The Bill," 2 October 2003.

40. S. Con. Res. 23, CQ Vote # 97: Rejected 43–56: R 1–50; D 41–6, I 1–0, 25 March 2003, Kerry voted yea.

41. S. Con. Res. 20, CQ Vote #76: Motion rejected 54–44: R 12–41; D 42–3, 25 March 1999, Kerry voted yea.

42. Senate Republican Policy Committee, "Tobacco Bill/Strike $755 Billion Payments," 20 May 1998.

43. S. Con. Res. 86, CQ Vote #82: Motion rejected 47–51: R 4–50; D 43–1, 2 April 1998.

44. S. Con. Res. 86, CQ Vote #67: Motion agreed to 55–44: R 44–10; D 11–34; 2 April 1998, Kerry voted nay.

45. S. 1033, CQ Vote #198: Motion agreed to 52–48: R 40–15; D 12–33, 23 July 1997, Kerry voted nay.

46. S. Con. Res. 27, CQ Vote #89: Adopted 51–49: R 51–4; D 0–45, 23 May 1997, Kerry voted nay.

47. S. Con. Res. 57, CQ Vote #136: Motion agreed to 61–39: R 51–2; D 10–37, 22 May 1996, Kerry voted nay.

48. S. Con. Res. 13, CQ Vote #226: Adopted 45–55: R 2–52; D 43–3, 25 May 1995, Kerry voted yea.

49. H. Con. Res. 64, CQ Vote #83: Adopted 54–45; R 0–43; D 54–2, 25 March 1993, Kerry voted yea.

50. Figures and statistics culled from Sen. John Kerry's legislative voting record since 1985.

51. Figures and statistics culled from Sen. John Kerry's legislative voting record since 1985.

52. Fox News, *Special Report*, 23 October 2003.

53. S. 1415, CQ Vote #154, 10 June 1998.

54. "Double Taxation Of Dividends Hypocrisy," *American Shareholder's Association* press release, 8 May 2003, accessed online at: http://www.atr.org/pressreleases/2003/050803pr.html.

55. Kerry, remarks at the City Club of Cleveland, 3 December 2002.

56. Kranish, "GOP Sees Momentum For Gas Tax Cut," *Boston Globe*, 4 May 1996.

57. John H. Cushman Jr., "The Budget Struggle," *New York Times*, 8 August 1993.
58. Kerry, Fox News/CBC, Democrat Presidential Candidates Debate, Detroit, MI., 26 October 2003.
59. "Remarks By The President In Tax Cut Bill Signing Ceremony," White House, accessed online at http://www.whitehouse.gov/news/releases/2001/06/20010607.html on 7 June 2001.
60. CNN, Arizona Democrat Party, Democrat Presidential Candidates Debate, Phoenix, AZ, 9 October 2003.
61. Eric Pianin and Albert B. Crenshaw,"GOP Fight Bares Schism On Taxes," *Washington Post*, 22 January 2000.
62. Gov. George W. Bush, remarks at Republican National Convention, Philadelphia, PA, 3 August 2000.
63. James W. Pindell, "Kerry And Lieberman Talk Jobs In Latest New Hampshire Visits," PoliticsNH.com, accessed 1 August 2003.
64. Nell Henderson, "Economists Say Recession Started In 2000," *Washington Post*, 22 January 2004.
65. Kerry for President Web site, "Restoring Jobs And Rebuilding Our Economy," www.johnkerry.com, accessed 23 January 2004.
66. Kerry for President Web site, "John Kerry's Plan To Fight For America's Economic Future," www.johnkerry.com, accessed 28 August 2003.
67. Kerry, remarks in Manchester, NH, 27 December 2003.
68. Howie Carr, "Liveshot's Golden Tax Rule: Raise Unto Others, But Not Me," *Boston Herald*, 27 February 2004, emphasis added.
69. Carr, Op-Ed, "Liveshot's Golden Tax Rule: Raise Unto Others, But Not Me," *Boston Herald*.
70. NBC, *Today Show*, 2 September 2003.
71. Kerry, *A Call to Service*, 2003, p. 73.
72. Kerry, CNBC/*Wall Street Journal*, Democrat Presidential Candidate Debate, New York, NY, 25 September 2003.
73. Kerry, Congressional Record, 23 May 2001, p. S5507.
74. S. Con. Res. 23, CQ Vote #100: Rejected 37–62: R 1–50; D 35–12; I 1–0, 25 March 2003, Kerry voted yea.
75. H. Con. Res. 83, CQ Vote #69: Adopted 53–47: R 4–46; D 49–1, 4 April 2001, Kerry voted yea.
76. H. Con. Res. 83, CQ Vote #71: Rejected 47–52: R 1–49; D 46–3, 4 April 2001, Kerry voted yea.
77. Kerry, remarks in Manchester, NH.
78. "Kerry: 'Worst Jobs Record' Since Hoover," *Washington Post*, 11 July 2003.
79. Kerry, remarks in Davenport, IA.
80. "Last U.S. Recession Began With Clinton, Panel May Say ," *Bloomberg News Service*, 22 January 2004.
81. CBS, *Face the Nation*, 9 September 2001.
82. CNN, *Money*, "U.S. Economic Growth Revised Up," 25 November 2003.

83. Editorial, "'G' In G. W. Bush Stands For Growth," *Lancaster New Era*, 31 December 2003.
84. Editorial, "Some Notable Successes To Celebrate In 2003," *Home News Tribune* [East Brunswick, NJ], 1 January 2004.
85. James J. Cramer, Op-Ed, "Bush's Rising Stock," *Wall Street Journal*, 15 January 2004.
86. Kerry, remarks at the Council on Foreign Relations, New York, NY, 3 December 2003.
87. "Economy Adds 308,000 Jobs In March," *Reuters*, 4 April 2004.
88. Larry Kudlow, Op-Ed, "Bush's Inflation-Free Boom," *National Review Online*, 18 December 2003.
89. Kerry, *A Call to Service*, p. 67.
90. Kerry, *A Call to Service*, p. 68.
91. Kerry, *A Call to Service*, p. 75.
92. GAO: Cheney Hindered Probe," Associated Press, 26 August 2003.
93. "In Their Own Words, Candidates Talk About The Issues," Associated Press, 25 January 2004.
94. VandeHei, "Democrats Will Try A Hybrid Of Old, New Policies," *Washington Post*, 15 February 2004.
95. David E. Rosenbaum, "Pin The Label On Tax Policy, " *New York Times*, 15 February 2004.
96. Maggs, et al, "A Kerry Top 10," *National Journal*.
97. Stephan Moore, "Kerry Taxes Will Sock It To Middle Class Families," *Human Events*, 9 April 2004.
98. Kerry, remarks at the City Club of Cleveland.
99. Kerry, NPR Democrat Presidential Candidates Debate, Des Moines, IA.
100. CNBC, *Capitol Report*, 8 January 2004.
101. Kerry, NPR Democrat Presidential Candidates Debate, Des Moines, IA.
102. Kerry, Op-Ed, "Give America A Payroll Tax Cut," *Boston Globe*, 26 December 2002.
103. ABC, *This Week with George Stephanopoulos*, 22 February 2004.
104. "Democrat Hopefuls Urge Repeal, Freeze Of Tax Cuts," *Record*, 19 January 2003.
105. Holly Ramer, "Kerry Touts Manufacturing Plan, Takes Swipe At Dean, Gephardt," Associated Press, 21 October 2003.
106. Joan Vennochi, "In Search Of A Simple Tax Message," *Boston Globe*, 7 October 2003.
107. Kerry, "Kerry Offers Budget Amendment That Promotes Fiscal Responsibility," Press Release, 25 March 1999.
108. Dukakis For Governor Committee, "Economic Prosperity And Jobs For Our People," Campaign Literature, 1982.
109. Dukakis For Governor Committee, "Economic Prosperity And Jobs For Our People," Campaign Literature.
110. Moore, "Kerry Taxes Will Sock It To Middle Class Families," *Human Events*.

CHAPTER 3—THIRTY-YEARS WAR

1. George Lardner Jr. and Lois Romano, "At Height Of Vietnam, Bush Picks Guard," *Washington Post*, 28 July, 1999.
2. William Campenni, Colonel (Ret.), U.S. Air Force/Air National Guard, Letter to the Editor, *Washington Times*, 11 February 2004.
3. John DiStaso, "Kerry Puts Emphasis On His War Record," [Manchester] *Union-Leader*, 14 August 2003.
4. DiStaso, "Kerry Puts Emphasis On His War Record," [Manchester] *Union-Leader*.
5. DiStaso, "Kerry Puts Emphasis On His War Record."
6. Kerry, Letter to President Bush, 21 February 2004; available on the Internet: http://www.johnkerry.com/pressroom/releases/pr_2004_0221d.html.
7. Kerry statement, 21 February 2004; available on the Internet: http://www.johnkerry.com/pressroom/releases/pr_2004_0221d.html.
8. Noelle Straub, "Kerry Presents Himself As GOP's Worst Nightmare," *Boston Herald*, 3 February 2004.
9. Nick Anderson, "Buoyant Kerry Embraces Role Of Frontrunner," *Los Angeles Times*, 4 February 2004.
10. CNN, *War In Iraq*, "Forces: U.S. & Coalition/Army, Army National Guard," *Special Report* Web site, http://www.cnn.com/SPECIALS/2003/iraq/forces/coalition/deployment/army/army.national.guard.html, accessed 25 February 2004.
11. Ron Martz, "Guard, Reserve Dying In Iraq," *Cox News Service*, 17 January 2004.
12. Matt Kelley, "Air National Guard, Reserve Forces A Big Part Of War In Afghanistan," Associated Press, 20 April 2002.
13. Air National Guard Web site, www.ang.af.mil, accessed 4 February 2004.
14. Sennott, "The Making Of The Candidates: John Forbes Kerry." *Boston Globe*.
15. Meg Kinnard, "Kerry Showcases Vietnam Experience," NationalJournal.com, 10 September 2003.
16. Don Bendell, "Another SF Nam Vet Looks At Kerry," *Soldier of Fortune*, p. 6, June 2004.
17. Bendell, "Another SF Nam Vet Looks At Kerry," *Soldier of Fortune*, pp. 6, 81.
18. Kranish, "With Antiwar Role, High Visibility."
19. Kranish, "With Antiwar Role, High Visibility."
20. Kranish, "With Antiwar Role, High Visibility."
21. Vietnam Veterans Against the War, accessed online at http://www.vvaw.org on 18 April 2004.
22. Kranish, "With Antiwar Role, High Visibility."
23. Sennott, "The Making Of The Candidates: John Forbes Kerry."
24. *ABC News/Union-Leader*, Democrat Presidential Candidate Debate, Manchester, NH, 22 January 2004.

25. U.S. military chronology/Vietnam War records.
26. Kranish, "With Antiwar Role, High Visibility."
27. Kerry, Senate Committee On Foreign Relations, 22 April 1971, emphasis added.
28. Phillips, "Kerry Calls Pro-Nixon Veterans Blind To Acts," *Lowell Sun*, 3 June 1971.
29. Kerry, Senate Committee On Foreign Relations.
30. Mackubin Thomas Owens, "Vetting The Vet Record," *National Review Online*, 27 January 2004, emphasis added.
31. Kranish, "With Antiwar Role, High Visibility."
32. Douglas Brinkley, *Tour Of Duty: John Kerry And Vietnam War*, 2004, p. 372.
33. John Hassell, "Kerry's Life, Philosophy Shaped By War Years," [New Orleans] *Times-Picayune*, 21 December 2003.
34. Sawyer, "Kerry's War Record Plays Well Now, But . . ." *St. Louis Post-Dispatch*, 8 February 2004.
35. Kranish, "With Antiwar Role, High Visibility."
36. Carl Limbacher, NewsMax staff, "Kerry Photo Shocker: Candidate Teamed Up With 'Hanoi' Jane Fonda," Newsmax.com, 9 February 2004, accessed online at http://www.newsmax.com/archives/ic/2004/2/9/134218.shtml.
37. David M. Halbfinger, "To Kerry, FBI Scrutiny of Him In 1970s Was 'Surreal,'" *New York Times*, 23 March, 2004.
38. Laura Blumenfeld and Dan Balz, "FBI Tracked Kerry In Vietnam Vets Group," *Washington Post*, 23 March, 2004.
39. Mark Barringer, "The Anti-War Movement In The United States," *Oxford Companion to American Military History*, © 1999, accessed online at http://www.english.uiuc.edu/maps/vietnam/antiwar.html.
40. Barringer, "The Anti-War Movement In The United States," *Oxford Companion to American Military History*.
41. Scott Canon, "Kerry Hedges On '71 KC Meeting," *Kansas City Star*, 20 March 2004.
42. Canon, "Kerry Hedges On '71 KC Meeting," *Kansas City Star*.
43. Scott Stanley Jr., "FBI Verifies Kerry At 'Assassination Summit,'" *Insight on News*, available online 24 March 2004 at http://www.wnd.com/news/article.asp?ARTICLE_ID=37706.
44. David Thorne, interviewed on Fox News' *Hannity & Colmes*, 8 February 2004.
45. Dinan, "Photo Of Kerry With Fonda Enrages Vietnam Veterans," *Washington Times*, 11 February 2004.
46. Brinkley, *Tour of Duty*, pp. 343–345.
47. Brinkley, *Tour of Duty*, p. 356.
48. David Jackson, "Veteran Politician," *Chicago Tribune*, 4 December 2003.
49. Jeannie Williams, "Aspen's Hills Were Alive With Holidaying Celebs," *USA Today*, 4 January 1989.

50. CNN, Wolf Blitzer, "Kerry Confronts Image From Anti-Vietnam War Era," 11 February 2004.
51. Limbacher and staff, "Gen. Giap: Kerry's Group Helped Vietnam Defeat U.S.," Newsmax.com, 10 February 2004.
52. Limbacher and staff, "McCain: Hanoi Hilton Guards Taunted POWs With Kerry's Testimony," Newsmax.com, 17 February 2004.
53. Limbacher, "McCain: Hanoi Hilton Guards Taunted POWs With Kerry's Testimony," Newsmax.com.

CHAPTER 4—INTERNATIONALIST MAN OF MYSTERY

1. Kerry, Speech Before The Council On Foreign Relations, www.cfr.org/publication.php?id=6576, New York, NY, 3 December 2003.
2. Kerry for President, "Kerry Statement On President's News Conference," Press Release, 13 April 2004.
3. Kerry for President, "Kerry Statement On President's News Conference."
4. Linda Greenhouse, "The War On Terrorism, From Tripoli To Belfast," *New York Times*, 30 April 1986.
5. Richard Clarke, press briefing, August 2002, reprinted 26 March 2004, *Washington Times*. http://washingtontimes.com/op-ed/20040325-091451-8041r.htm.
6. Kerry Agreeing That Sen. Patrick Moynihan's Concerns Be Addressed, Congressional Record, 1 May 1997, p. S3891.
7. Kerry, *New War*, 1997, p. 97.
8. Phillip Morris, "Top Analysis Of Global Crime Lacks Solutions," [Cleveland] *Plain Dealer*, 20 July 1997.
9. Michael Crowley, "Kerry's Odd Book On Terrorism," *New Republic*, 9 February 2004.
10. ABC, 20/20. President George W. Bush's interview with Barbara Walters, 13 December 2002.
11. Kerry, "Kerry Reaction To U.S. Air Strikes In Afghanistan And Sudan," Press Release, 21 August 1998.
12. Kerry, Committee On Armed Services And Committee On Foreign Relations, U.S. Senate, Joint Hearing, 3 September 1998.
13. CNN, *Late Edition*, 12 December 1999.
14. Kerry, Democrat Presidential Candidates Debate, Greenville, SC, 29 January 2004.
15. Kerry, Senate voting records; S.1163, Introduced 24 June 1993; S. 1826, Introduced 3 February 1994; S. Amdt. 1452, Introduced 9 February 1994; H.R. 2076, CQ Vote #480: Adopted 49–41: R 9–40; D 40–1, 29 September 1995, Kerry voted yea; S. 1290, Introduced 29 September 1995; S. Con. Res. 13, CQ Vote #181: Rejected 28–71: R 2–51; D 26–20, 24 May 1995, Kerry voted yea.
16. "World War III strikes Spain," *New York Daily News* editorial, 12 March 2004.
17. Kerry, Committee On Banking, Housing And Urban Affairs, U.S. Senate, Hearing, 26 September 2001.

18. CNBC, *Hardball*, 21 May 2002.
19. Christopher Scott, "Lawmakers: 'Congress Has The Right To Ask Questions' About 9–11 Warnings," Lowell [MA] *Sun*, 22 May 2002, emphasis added.
20. Seth Gitell, "Clash Of The Titans," *Boston Phoenix*, 13 June 2002.
21. NBC, *Meet the Press*, 23 June 2002.
22. "In His Words: John Kerry," *New York Times*, 6 March 2004.
23. CNN, *Late Edition*, 12 December 1999.
24. "Patterns of Global Terrorism 2002: The Year in Review," U.S. Department of State, accessed online at http://www.state.gov/s/ct/rls/pgtrpt/2002/html/19980.htm on 16 April 2004.
25. Kerry, Democrat Presidential Candidates Debate, Greenville, SC.
26. E.J. Kessler, "Dem Hopeful; Bush Fiddled In Iraq While Qaeda Rebuilt," *Forward*, 23 May 2003.
27. Kerry, Press Conference, 23 February 1998.
28. Pickler, "Kerry Discusses Issues In Town Hall Meeting," Associated Press, 14 December 2003.
29. Fox News, *Special Report*, 15 December 2003.
30. *Des Moines Register*/Iowa Public Television, Democrat Presidential Candidate Debate, Des Moines, IA, 4 January 2004.
31. Kerry for President Web site, www.johnkerry.com/issues/iraq, accessed 21 February 2004.
32. Kerry for President Web site, www.johnkerry.com/issues/iraq.
33. "In His Words: John Kerry," *New York Times*.
34. Glenn Kessler, "Engagement Is A Constant In Kerry's Foreign Policy," *Washington Post*, 21 March 2004.
35. Kessler, "Engagement Is A Constant In Kerry's Foreign Policy," *Washington Post*.
36. Kessler, "Engagement Is A Constant In Kerry's Foreign Policy," *Washington Post*.
37. "Kerry Calls Al-Sadr Voice 'Legitimate,'" 7am.com, 7 April, 2004.
38. Kessler, "Engagement Is A Constant In Kerry's Foreign Policy," *Washington Post*.
39. Kessler, "Engagement Is A Constant In Kerry's Foreign Policy," *Washington Post*.
40. Kerry, *A Call to Service*, p. 48–49; Peace Action Web site, "Where Do The Candidates Stand On Foreign Policy?"http://www.peace-action.org/2004/Kerry.html, accessed 26 February 2004.
41. Fox News, "Kerry's 'Regime Change' Comments Draw Fire," 3 April 2003.
42. Johnson, "Kerry Says U.S. Needs Its Own 'Regime Change.'"
43. Tom Raum, "Democrats Thwart China-Policy Votes," *Austin American-Statesman*, 24 June 1998.
44. Kerry, Press Conference, 16 December 1998.
45. David S. Broder, "U.S. Internal Debate Over Gulf Crisis Is Healthy For Democracy," [Bergen County] *Record*, 18 December 1990.

46. CBS, *CBS Evening News*, 16 October 1993.

47. NPR's, *Morning Edition*, 17 May 1994.

48. Kerry, Op/Ed, "Make Haiti's Thugs Tremble," *New York Times*, 16 May 1994.

49. H.R. 2330, CQ Vote #280: Passed [Thus Cleared For The President] 94–1: R 49–1; D 44–0; I 1–0, 16 July 2003, Kerry missed vote.

50. Kerry, Press Conference, 16 December 1998.

51. Kerry, Press Conference, 16 December 1998.

52. Mark Magnier and Barbara Demick, "N. Korea May Be In 'Anybody But Bush' Camp," *Los Angeles Times*, 25 February 2004.

53. Andrew Ward Seoul and James Harding, "North Korea Warms To Kerry Presidency Bid," *Financial Times*, 4 March 2004.

54. Seoul and Harding, "North Korea Warms To Kerry Presidency Bid," *Financial Times*.

CHAPTER 5—KERRY'S DEFENSE-LESS RECORD

1. Kerry, remarks at Drake University, Des Moines, IA, 16 December 2003.

2. CNN, *Inside Politics*, 21 January 2004.

3. Massachusetts Political Action For Peace/ Citizens For Participation Politics, Candidate Questionnaire, 1972, emphasis added.

4. Samuel Z. Goldhaber, "John Kerry: A Navy Dove Runs For Congress," *Harvard Crimson*, 18 February 1970.

5. Goldhaber, "John Kerry: A Navy Dove Runs For Congress," *Harvard Crimson*.

6. "Candidates For Congress Capture Campus In Andover," *Lawrence* [MA] *Eagle-Tribune*, 21 April 1972.

7. "State Primary Candidates," *Bedford Minute-Man*, 14 September 1972.

8. Dukakis-Kerry Campaign Flyer, 1982.

9. Dukakis For Governor Committee, "Economic Prosperity And Jobs For Our People," Campaign Literature, 1982.

10. Patrick Garrity, "Reagan and the Cold War," Ashbrook Center for Public Affairs, research paper, December 2002.

11. Lt. Gov. John Kerry, Letter To Constituent, April 1983.

12. Senate Candidate Questionnaire," Massachusetts Freeze Voter '84, 25 May 1984.

13. Senate Candidate Questionnaire," Massachusetts Freeze Voter '84.

14. Senate Candidate Questionnaire," Massachusetts Freeze Voter '84.

15. Mass. Senate Candidates Quizzed On Women's Issues," *GenderWatch*, 30 June 1984.

16. "John Kerry On The Defense Budget," Campaign Position Paper, John Kerry For U.S. Senate, 1984.

17. Chris Black, "Kerry Asks Cuts In Defense Outlay," *Boston Globe*, 30 May 1984.

18. Kerry, Letter To U.S. Senate Campaign Supporters, June 1984.

19. "John Kerry On The Defense Budget," Campaign Position Paper, John Kerry For U.S. Senate.

20. "Senate Candidates' Positions," *Boston Globe*, 8 July 1984.
21. "Kerry Asks $54 Billion Cut In Reagan Defense Budget," *Berkshire Eagle*, 30 May 1984.
22. Senate Candidate Questionnaire, Massachusetts Freeze Voter '84.
23. Senate Candidate Questionnaire, Massachusetts Freeze Voter '84.
24. Black, "Democratic Senate Hopefuls Clash On Arms," *Boston Globe*, 16 June 1984.
25. Senate Candidate Questionnaire.
26. Black, "Kerry Asks Cuts In Defense Outlay," *Boston Globe*.
27. "Kerry Asks $54 Billion Cut In Reagan Defense Budget," *Berkshire Eagle*.
28. Senate Candidate Questionnaire.
29. "Poseidon," *Encyclopedia Astronautica*, accessed online at http://www.astronautix.com/lvs/poseidon.htm on 30 March 2004.
30. Senate Candidate Questionnaire.
31. "John F. Kerry," 1984 State Primary Newspaper Supplement, *Cape Codder*, 11 September 1984.
32. "John Kerry On The Defense Budget," Campaign Position Paper.
33. "Kerry Asks $54 Billion Cut In Reagan Defense Budget."
34. Senate Candidate Questionnaire.
35. "Kerry On Anti-Satellite Weapons," Campaign Position Paper, John Kerry For U.S. Senate, 1984.
36. "Kerry On Anti-Satellite Weapons," Campaign Position Paper, John Kerry For U.S. Senate.
37. Kerry, remarks to Citizens for Participation in Political Action Convention, 19 January 1985.
38. Johnson, "Kerry Admits To An Error In Boast About 1st Speech," *Boston Globe*, 1 May 2003.
39. Michael E. Knell, "Kerry: Arms Cuts May Spell Economic Boom," *Middlesex News*, 15 March 1989.
40. Kerry, Congressional Record.
41. Mooney, "Taking One Prize, Then A Bigger One."
42. "Kuwait Seeks 40 F-18 Fighter-Bombers," *Baltimore Sun*, 13 May 1988.
43. S. 1163, Introduced 24 June 1993.
44. Kerry, Congressional Record, 15 May 1996, p. S5061.
45. Kerry, Congressional Record.
46. S. Con. Res. 18, CQ Vote #50: Motion agreed to 58–41: R 6–37; D 52–4, 23 March 1993, Kerry voted yea.
47. S. 1298, CQ Vote #251: Adopted 50–48: R 6–36; D 44–12, 9 September 1993, Kerry voted yea.
48. S. Con. Res. 63, CQ Vote #64: Rejected 40–59: R 2–42; D 38–17, 22 March 1994, Kerry voted yea.
49. S. Con. Res. 13, CQ Vote #181: Rejected 28–71: R 2–51; D 26–20, 24 May 1995, Kerry voted yea.
50. Kerry voted nay; "Military Construction Up $2.4 Billion," *CQ Almanac*, 1995, pp. 11–68.

51. S. 2182, CQ Vote #179: Rejected 45–55: R 8–36; D 37–19, 1 July 1994, Kerry voted yea.
52. S. 1087, CQ Vote #384: Rejected 45–54: R 5–49; D 40–5, 10 August 1995, Kerry voted yea.
53. S. 1077, CQ Vote #224: Motion agreed to 77–22: R 48–0; D 29–21; I 0–1, 10 July 2001, Kerry voted nay.
54. Fred Kaplan, "John Kerry's Defense Defense: Setting His Voting Record Straight," Slate.com, 25 February 2004.
55. George H. W. Bush, "Address Before A Joint Session Of Congress On The State Of The Union," 28 January 1992.
56. Vice President Dick Cheney, in testimony before the Senate Armed Services Committee, 31 January 1992.
57. John Solomon, "Kerry's 1994 Effort To Cut Defense Eyed," Associated Press, 19 March 2004.
58. Solomon, "Kerry's 1994 Effort To Cut Defense Eyed," Associated Press.
59. Solomon, "Kerry's 1994 Effort To Cut Defense Eyed."
60. Solomon, "Kerry's 1994 Effort To Cut Defense Eyed."
61. Solomon, "Kerry's 1994 Effort To Cut Defense Eyed."
62. Solomon, "Kerry's 1994 Effort To Cut Defense Eyed."
63. Sen. Daniel Inouye, Congressional Record, 10 February 1994, pp. S1330–S1332.
64. Inouye, Congressional Record, 10 February 1994.
65. Sen. Dennis DeConcini, Congressional Record, 10 February 1994, p. S1360.
66. Solomon, "Kerry's 1994 Effort To Cut Defense Eyed."

Chapter 6—Homeland Insecurity

1. Senate Candidate Questionnaire.
2. Senate Candidate Questionnaire.
3. Gov. Michael Dukakis, Executive Order No. 242, The Commonwealth Of Massachusetts, 28 June 1984.
4. Tanya N. Ballard, "Bush Seeks Employee Support For Homeland Security Reorganization," *Government Executive Magazine*, 10 July 2002.
5. H.R. 5005, CQ Vote #218: Motion rejected 50–49: R 0–48; D 49–1; I 1–0, 19 September 2002, Kerry voted yea; H.R. 5005, CQ Vote #225: Motion rejected 49–49: R 1–47; D 47–2; I 1–0, 25 September 2002, Kerry voted yea; H.R. 5005, CQ Vote #226: Motion rejected 50–49: R 1–48; D 48–1; I 1–0, 26 September 2002, Kerry voted yea; H.R. 5005, CQ Vote #227: Motion rejected 44–53: R 1–46; D 42–7; I 1–0, 26 September 2002, Kerry voted yea; H.R. 5005, CQ Vote #228: Motion rejected 45–52: R 2–46; D 42–6; I 1–0, 1 October 2002, Kerry voted yea; H.R. 5005, CQ Vote #241: Motion agreed to 50–47: R 48–0; D 1–46; I 1–1, 13 November 2002, Kerry voted nay.
6. H.R. 5005, Received In The Senate 30 July 2002; H.R. 5005, CQ Vote #249: Passed 90–9: R 48–0; D 41–8; I 1–1, 19 November 2002, Kerry voted yea.

7. H.R. 2555, CQ Vote #306: Passed 93–1: R 50–0; D 42–1; I 1–0, 24 July 2003, Kerry did not vote.

8. See Jon E. Dougherty's *Illegals: Imminent Threat Posed by Our Unsecured U.S.-Mexico Border* (Nashville: WND Books, 2004).

9. S. 1200, CQ Vote #179: Rejected 26–65: R 0–46; D 26–19, 13 September 1985, Kerry voted yea.

10. S. 1394, CQ Vote #311: Motion agreed to 55–45: R 31–15; D 24–30, 7 October 1987, Kerry voted nay.

11. "Arabic Diary Found Near Border," WorldNetDaily.com, 13 February 2003.

12. DeConcini, Congressional Record, p. 1360.

13. DeConcini, Congressional Record.

14. Inouye, Congressional Record, pp. S1330–S1332.

15. Amdt. To H.R. 3759, CQ Vote # 39: Rejected 20–75; Kerry voted yea.

16. Mike Glover, "Kerry Rips Bush On National Security Issues," Associated Press, 19 July 2003.

17. Bryan Bender, "Kerry Blasts Bush Over War On Terror," *Boston Globe*, 19 May 2003.

18. Council On Foreign Relations Web site, "Senator John Kerry's Statement In Response To The President's Speech To The Nation," www.cfr.org, 18 March 2003.

19. Kerry, remarks at International Association of Firefighters Legislative Conference, Washington D.C., 18 March 2003.

20. Kerry for President Web site, "Defending The American Homeland," www.johnkerry.com, accessed 21 February 2004.

21. Kerry for President Web site, "Plan To Make America Stronger And Safer," www.johnkerry.com.

22. Kerry for President Web site, "Plan To Make America Stronger And Safer."

23. H.R. 3162, CQ Vote #313, 25 October 2001.

24. MSNBC, *Hardball*, 24 September 2001.

25. David Goldstein, "Ashcroft Focus Of Campaign Rhetoric," *Kansas City Star*, 27 May 2003.

26. Kerry, remarks at Iowa State University, 1 December 2003.

27. "President Rallies First Responders In Georgia," remarks by the President to Georgia first responders, 27 March, 2002, accessed on the White House Web site at http://www.whitehouse.gov/news/releases/2002/03/20020327-7.html.

28. Chris Strohm, "Homeland Security Inspectors Analyze Grant Spending Delays," *Government Executive Magazine*, 9 April 2004.

29. Gavin McCormack, "Wise Gives $31.1M For Security; Communities, Agencies To Share Grant For Equipment, Planning, Training," Associated Press, 20 April 2004.

30. U.S. Northern Command Web site, accessed 20 April 2004.

31. White House "Homeland Security" Web site, accessed 20 April 2004.

32. Richard Tomkins, "Rice Defends Anti-Terror Actions," UPI, 28 March 2004.

33. Tomkins, "Rice Defends Anti-Terror Actions," UPI.

34. Opening statement of National Security Advisor Condoleezza Rice to the National Commission on Terrorist Attacks, 8 April 2004.
35. Hope Yen, "Rice Says Bush Understood Al Qaeda Threat," Associated Press, 8 April 2004.
36. Ann Coulter, "How 9/11 Happened," *Universal Press Syndicate*, 31 March 2004.
37. "Kerry Pledges Return To Clinton Terrorism Policies," NewsMax.com, 31 January 2004.
38. "Jamie Gorelick's Wall," *Washington Times* Op-Ed, 16 April 2004.
39. "Jamie Gorelick's Wall," *Washington Times* Op-Ed.

CHAPTER 7—MAN OF THE PEOPLE?

1. Kerry for President Web site, "Protect The Right To Choose," www.johnkerry.com, accessed 24 January 2004.
2. Kerry As Quoted In "John Kerry On The Issues," *Lowell Sun*, 11 October 1972.
3. Kerry for President Web site, "Protect The Right To Choose," www.johnkerry.com.
4. Kerry, *A Call to Service*, p. 182.
5. Kerry, Congressional Record, 3 February 1986, p. S 864.
6. Johnson, "Kerry Vows Court Picks To Be Abortion-Rights Supporters," *Boston Globe*, 9 April 2003, emphasis added.
7. Kerry, *A Call to Service*, 182.
8. Johnson, "Kerry Vows Court Picks To Be Abortion-Rights Supporters."
9. Amy Fagan, "House To Vote On Fetal Homicide," *Washington Times*, 26 February 2004.
10. President George W. Bush, statement issued by the White House, accessed on-line at http://www.whitehouse.gov/news/releases/2004/03/20040325-9.html, 25 March 2004.
11. Kerry for President Web site, "Women's Rights," www.johnkerry.com, accessed 28 March 2004.
12. Gary Langer, "Support For Legal Abortion Wobbles; Religion Informs Much Opposition," *ABC News*, 2 July 2001.
13. Dalia Sussman, "Conditional Support; Poll: 30 years After Roe v. Wade, American Support Is Conditional," *ABC News*, 22 January 2003.
14. Johnson, "Kerry Hits Ban On Abortion Procedure," *Boston Globe*, 6 November 2003.
15. "Poll: Abortion Is Murder But Up To The Mother," Newsmax.com, 18 June 2000.
16. Karen Tumulty and Perry Bacon Jr., "A Test Of Kerry's Faith," *Time*, 5 April, 2004.
17. Patricia Rice, "Archbishop Burke Says He Would Refuse Communion To Kerry," *St. Louis Post-Dispatch*, 31 January 2004.
18. Kerry As Quoted In "John Kerry On The Issues," *Lowell Sun*.

19. Kerry for President Web site, "Protect Gay And Lesbian Families," www.johnkerry.com, accessed 24 January 2004.

20. Patrick Healy, "Kerry Treads Cautiously On Gay Marriage Ban," *Boston Globe*, 10 February 2004.

21. Kerry for President Web site, "Support For Civil Unions," www.johnkerry.com, accessed 28 March 2004.

22. Dana Blanton, "Majority Opposes Same-Sex Marriages," Fox News, 21 November 2003.

23. Blanton, "Majority Opposes Same-Sex Marriages," Fox News.

24. "Poll: Few Favor Same-Sex Marriage," *CBS News*, 15 March 2003.

25. Sussman, "Gay Marriage opposition; Poll: Most Americans Are Against Same-Sex Marriages, But Don't Want Constitutional Amendment," *ABC News*, 22 September 2003.

26. Owens, "Military Ethos And The Politics Of 'Don't Ask, Don't Tell,'" The Ashbrook Center for Public Affairs, February 2000; accessed online at http://www.ashbrook.org/publicat/onprin/v8n1/owens.html.

27. Charlie Cain and Mark Hornbeck, "Michigan Voters Want Affirmative Action Ban," *Detroit News*, 20 January 2004.

28. Pew Research Center for the People and Press, "Conflicted Views On Affirmative Action," 14 May 2003.

29. Langer, "Assistance, But Not Preference; Poll: Most Share Bush's View On Affirmative Action," *ABC News*, 27 January 2003.

30. Farrell, "Affirmative Action Flawed, Kerry Declares," *Boston Globe*, 31 March 1992.

31. Lynne Duke, "Senators Seek Serious Dialogue On Race," *Washington Post*, 8 April 1992.

32. MASS PAX-C.P.P. Candidate Questionnaire, 1972.

33. Michael Janofsky, "Massachusetts Senate Candidates Debate Again," *New York Times*, 5 June 1996.

34. VandeHei, "A Spiritual Struggle For Democrats," *Washington Post*, 27 November 2003.

35. Kerry, Congressional Record, 23 June 1989, p. S7465.

36. Matthew Cooper, "The New Choirboys," *Newsweek*, 4 May 1998.

37. George W. Bush, "Statement By The President," 16 August 2001.

38. Miga, "Bush Boosts Faith-Based Charities," *Boston Herald*, 30 January 2001.

39. Scot Lehigh, "Kerry Is Focused - On 2004?" *Boston Globe*, 9 February 2001, emphasis added.

40. Kate McCann, "Kerry Vows Separation Of Church And State," Associated Press, 18 December 2003.

41. S.J. Res. 180, CQ Vote #251: Rejected 51–48: R 33–11; D 18–37, 19 October 1989, Kerry voted nay; S. J. Res. 31, CQ Vote #600: Rejected 63–36: R 49–4; D 14–32, 12 December 1995, Kerry voted nay; S. J. Res. 14, CQ Vote #48: Rejected 63–37: R 51–4; D 12–33, 29 March 2000, Kerry voted nay.

42. Lehigh, "Issue Splits Bay State Candidates," *Boston Globe*, 20 June 1990.

43. Kerry As Quoted In "Candidates On The Issues: The Flag," Associated Press, 23 January 2004.

44. Sussman, "Sect Appeal; Support For Faith-Based Initiative Depends On The Recipient," *ABC News*, 6 May 2001.

45. Jeffrey M. Jones, "Public Favors Bush's Faith-Based Charities Initiative; Strongest Support Among Republicans, Conservatives, Churchgoers," The Gallup Organization, 31 July 2001.

46. Black, "Senate Vote Looms On Amendment Banning Flag Burning," CNN, 28 March 2000.

CHAPTER 8—SHOW ME THE MONEY!

1. Kerry, Democrat Presidential Candidates Debate, Milwaukee, WI, 15 February 2004.

2. Ed O'Keefe, "Field Notes: John Kerry; Reports From The Campaign Trail," *ABC News*, 5 February 2004.

3. VandeHei, "Kerry Leads In Lobby Money," *Washington Post*, 31 January 2004.

4. John Solomon and Aparna H. Kumar, "Kerry Pocketed Speaking Fees," Associated Press, 9 February 2004.

5. Michael Isikoff, "Cash And Kerry," *Newsweek*, 9 February 2004 issue.

6. Isikoff, "Cash And Kerry," *Newsweek*.

7. David Brooks, "Kerry's Special Friends," *New York Times*, 7 February 2004.

8. Brooks, "Kerry's Special Friends," *New York Times*.

9. Isikoff, "Cash And Kerry."

10. Isikoff, "Cash And Kerry."

11. "The Insider," *Insight Magazine*, 17 February–1 March 2004 issue.

12. Federal Election Commission Web site, accessed 16 February 2004.

13. Ruth Marcus and John Mintz, "Big Donor Calls Favorable Treatment A 'Coincidence,'" *Washington Post*, 25 May 1998.

14. Marcus and Mintz, "Big Donor Calls Favorable Treatment A 'Coincidence,'" *Washington Post*.

15. Marcus and Mintz, "Big Donor Calls Favorable Treatment A 'Coincidence.'"

16. Federal Election Commission Web site, accessed 16 February 2004.

17. Brooks, "Kerry's Special Friends."

18. John Solomon, "Kerry, Edwards Boasts About Special Interest Money Don't Tell Whole Story," Associated Press, 2 February 2004.

19. Solomon, "Kerry, Edwards Boasts About Special Interest Money Don't Tell Whole Story," Associated Press.

20. Solomon, "Kerry, Edwards Boasts About Special Interest Money Don't Tell Whole Story."

21. Solomon, "Kerry, Edwards Boasts About Special Interest Money Don't Tell Whole Story."

22. Center for Responsive Politics statistics, "Member Money: Top Committee-Related Industries for Committee Members," Commerce, Science and Transportation Committee figures for the 107th Congress, 2002.

23. Center for Responsive Politics statistics, "Member Money: Top Committee-Related Industries for Committee Members," Small Business Committee figures for the 107th Congress.
24. Owen Gibson, "Media Chiefs Back Kerry Campaign," *London Guardian*, 10 February 2004.
25. Gibson, "Media Chiefs Back Kerry Campaign," *London Guardian*.
26. Gibson, "Media Chiefs Back Kerry Campaign."
27. Center for Responsive Politics Web site, http://www.opensecrets.org, accessed 2 February 2004.
28. Center for Responsive Politics Web site, http://www.opensecrets.org.
29. Charles Lewis and The Center For Public Integrity, *Buying Of Presidency 2004*, 2004, pp. 364–365.
30. Isikoff, "Cash And Kerry."
31. Isikoff, "Cash And Kerry."
32. Isikoff, "Cash And Kerry."
33. S. 27, CQ Vote #64: Passed 59–41: R 12–38; D 47–3, 2 April 2001, Kerry voted yea; Year End 2001 Report For Citizen Soldier Fund–Non-Federal Account, IRS Web site, www.irs.gov, accessed 29 January 2004; Glen Johnson, "In A Switch, Kerry Is Launching A PAC," *Boston Globe*, 15 December 2001.
34. Isikoff, "Cash And Kerry."
35. Isikoff, "Cash And Kerry."
36. Solomon, "Kerry, Edwards Boasts About Special Interest Money Don't Tell Whole Story."
37. Kerry for President, "Kerry Ranks 92nd Out Of The 100 Senators In Contributions From Special Interest PACS And Lobbyists," Press release, 4 February 2004.
38. VandeHei, "Kerry Leads In Lobby Money."
39. U.S. Sen. Zell Miller, statement made on Fox News' *Hannity & Colmes*, 3 February 2004.
40. John Solomon, "Kerry Got $120,000 In Speaker's Fees," Associated Press, 11 February 2004.
41. Solomon, "Kerry Got $120,000 In Speaker's Fees," Associated Press.
42. Solomon, "Kerry Got $120,000 In Speaker's Fees."
43. Solomon, "Kerry Got $120,000 In Speaker's Fees."
44. Solomon, "Kerry Got $120,000 In Speaker's Fees."
45. Solomon, "Kerry Got $120,000 In Speaker's Fees."
46. John Solomon, "Torricelli Has Raised Cash For John Kerry," Associated Press, 7 February 2004.
47. Solomon, "Torricelli Has Raised Cash For John Kerry," Associated Press.
48. Solomon, "Torricelli Has Raised Cash For John Kerry."
49. Solomon, "Torricelli Has Raised Cash For John Kerry."
50. Sharon Theimer, "Unions, Torricelli Finance Anti-Dean Ads," Associated Press, 11 February 2004.
51. Theimer, "Unions, Torricelli Finance Anti-Dean Ads," Associated Press.

52. Tapper, "Kerry Funds Raise Questions; Donations from Tech Firm Spark Controversy for Candidate," *ABC News*, 9 February 2004.

53. Tapper, "Kerry Funds Raise Questions; Donations from Tech Firm Spark Controversy for Candidate," *ABC News*.

54. Tapper, "Kerry Funds Raise Questions; Donations from Tech Firm Spark Controversy for Candidate."

55. Lisa Getter, "Kerry Denies Donations Fueled Lobbying for Contractor," *Los Angeles Times*, 20 February 2004.

56. Getter, "Kerry Denies Donations Fueled Lobbying for Contractor," *Los Angeles Times*.

57. Getter, "Kerry Denies Donations Fueled Lobbying for Contractor."

58. Getter, "Kerry Denies Donations Fueled Lobbying for Contractor."

59. Getter, "Kerry Denies Donations Fueled Lobbying for Contractor."

60. Getter, "Corporate Ally Helped Few Workers In Kerry's State," *Los Angeles Times*, 22 February 2004.

61. Getter, "Corporate Ally Helped Few Workers In Kerry's State," *Los Angeles Times*.

62. Johnson, "Doubt Cast On Kerry's 'Pac-Free' Claim," *Boston Globe*, 12 June 2003.

63. Johnson, "Doubt Cast On Kerry's 'Pac-Free' Claim."

64. Solomon and Kumar, "Kerry Pocketed Speaking Fees," Associated Press.

65. Solomon and Kumar, "Kerry Pocketed Speaking Fees," Associated Press.

66. VandeHei, "Kerry Fundraiser Helped Finance Anti-Dean Ads," *Washington Post*, 11 February 2004.

67. Solomon, "Three Times, Kerry Nominations And Donations Coincided," Associated Press, 5 February 2004.

68. Solomon, "Three Times, Kerry Nominations And Donations Coincided," Associated Press.

69. Solomon, "Three Times, Kerry Nominations And Donations Coincided."

70. Solomon, "Three Times, Kerry Nominations And Donations Coincided."

71 Solomon, "Three Times, Kerry Nominations And Donations Coincided."

72. Solomon, "Three Times, Kerry Nominations And Donations Coincided."

73. Solomon, "Three Times, Kerry Nominations And Donations Coincided."

74. Mooney, "Bundling Benefits Kerry Coffers," *Boston Globe*, 28 January 1996.

75. Thomas Edsall And Dan Balz, "Sen. Kerry Not Banking On His Wife's Fortune," *Washington Post*, 24 March 2003.

76. Howard Fineman, "Having A Gay Old Time," *Newsweek*, 5 May 2003.

77. Charles Donefer, "Campaign 2004: LCV Goes On The Air For Kerry," *Greenwire*, 2 February 2004.

78. Deborah Orin and Brian Blomquist, "John's Eco-Pals Got Wife's Greenbacking," *New York Post*, 10 February 2004.

79. Christopher C. Horner, Op-Ed, "Playing Ketchup: Recipients Of Heinz Money Making Strong Kerry Pitch," *National Review* Online, 28 January 2004.

80. Glover, "Kerry Nets Environmental Endorsement," Associated Press, 24 January 2004.

81. Ellen J. Silberman, Jack Meyers, "Kerry Loan Twice As Nice," *Boston Herald*, 25 February 2004.
82. Silberman, Meyers, "Kerry Loan Twice As Nice," *Boston Herald*.
83. Silberman, Meyers, "Kerry Loan Twice As Nice."
84. Silberman, Meyers, "Kerry Loan Twice As Nice."
85. Kerry for President Web site, www.johnkerry.com, accessed 3 February 2004.
86. Balz, "Team Bush: The 'Iron Triangle,'" *Washington Post*, © 1999.
87. Kerry for President Web site, www.johnkerry.com, accessed 3 February 2004.
88. Kerry, Congressional Record, 3 April 2001, pp. S3335–S3336.
89. Kerry, Congressional Record, 3 April 2001, pp. S3335.
90. Kerry, Democrat presidential candidates debate, Milwaukee, WI, 15 February 2004.
91. Kerry for President, press release, "Kerry Statement Opting Out Of The Public Finance System," 3 November 2003.
92. Miga, "Kennedy Rallies Dems, Up Donors for Kerry," *Boston Herald*, 17 February 2004.
93. Center for Responsive Politics, data accessed online at http://www.opensecrets.org/presidential/summary.asp?ID=N00000245, 7 March 2004.
94. NBC, Nightly News, 17 February 2004.
95. Kerry, remarks on the campaign trail in Boston, 2 December 2003.
96. Kerry, remarks to the Florida Democratic Party State Convention, Orlando, FL, 6 December 2003.
97. NBC, *Meet the Press*, 31 August 2003.
98. Kerry, remarks to Florida Democratic Party State Convention, Orlando, FL.
99. Kerry, Democratic presidential candidates debate, Durham, NH, 9 December 2003.
100. Kerry, remarks in Nashua, NH, 10 December 2003.
101. CNN, *Late Edition With Wolf Blitzer*, 21 December 2003.
102. Kerry, remarks in Nashua, NH.
103. Kerry, campaign event, Merrimack, NH, 7 January 2004.
104. Jill Lawrence, "Kerry Takes Cut At Republicans, Then Buries Hatchet With Dean," *USA Today*, 11 March 2004.
105. Alexander Bolton, "Kerry Rips K Street," *The Hill*, 14 January 2004.
106. VandeHei, "Kerry Leads In Lobby Money."

CHAPTER 9—CORPORATE CORRUPTION

1. Sam Dealy, "Kerry Gets A Pass?" *National Review*, 28 April 2004.
2. Dealy, "Kerry Gets A Pass?" *National Review*.
3. Dealy, "Kerry Gets A Pass?"
4. Dealy, "Kerry Gets A Pass?"
5. Dealy, "Kerry Gets A Pass?"

6. Dealy, "Kerry Gets A Pass?"
7. "The BCCI Affair," Executive Summary, A Report to the Committee on Foreign Relations United States Senate by Senator John Kerry and Senator Hank Brown, December 1992.
8. James Ring Adams and Douglas Frantz, *A Full Service Bank: How BCCI Stole Billions Around the World* (New York: Pocket Books, 1992), p.171.
9. Adams and Frantz, "A Full Service Bank: How BCCI Stole Billions Around the World," p.170.
10. Adams and Frantz, p.170.
11. Adams and Frantz, p.170.
12. Adams and Frantz, p. 254.
13. Ponte, "Cash-And-Kerry," *Frontpage Magazine.*
14. Jonathan Beaty and S.C. Gwynne, *The Outlaw Bank: A Wild Ride into the Secret Heart of BCCI*, p. 185.
15. On December 7, 2002, Wooldridge contributed to a *Miami Herald* story about John Kerry's presidential campaign.

CHAPTER 10—WELFARE, CRIME, JOBS, AND VETS

1. U.S. Census Bureau figures.
2. Michael Grunwald, "Facts Tell Half Story In Race For Senate," *Boston Globe*, 21 August 1996.
3. Grunwald, "Facts Tell Half Story In Race For Senate," *Boston Globe.*
4. Grunwald, "Facts Tell Half Story In Race For Senate."
5. Bob Hohler, "Kerry Defining Voice, Vision While Looking Ahead To 1996," *Boston Globe*, 11 December 1994.
6. James M. O'Neill, "The First 100 Days," *Providence Journal-Bulletin*, 9 April 1995.
7. Senate Republican Policy Committee, "Welfare Reform Bill/Voucher Guarantee If Cash Is Denied," 13 September 1995; H.R. 4, CQ Vote #413: Rejected 42–58: R 1–53; D 41–5, 13 September 1995, Kerry voted yea.
8. Senate Republican Policy Committee, "Welfare Reform Bill/No 5-Year Limit If No Jobs-Child Care Programs," 13 September 1995; H.R. 4, CQ Vote #414: Rejected 40–60: R 0–54; D 40–6, 13 September 1995 Kerry voted yea.
9. Hohler, "Weld Backs Welfare Cash Ban," *Boston Globe*, 29 September 1995.
10. S. Amdt. 2661, Introduced 8 September 1995; S. Amdt. 2679, Introduced 8 September 1995.
11. Meg Vaillancourt, "Weld, Kerry Press Issue Of Benefits," *Boston Globe*, 18 September 1996.
12. S. Amdt. 2661, Introduced 8 September 1995; S. Amdt. 2679, Introduced 8 September 1995.
13. Doris Sue Wong, "Advocates Blast Kerry For Voting For Welfare Bill," *Boston Globe*, 3 August 1996.

14. John Perazzo, "John Kerry: Further Left Than He Lets On," *Frontpage Magazine*, online at http://www.frontpagemag.com, 17 February 2004.

15. Alberta Cook, "Kerry's Resignation Didn't Surprise Droney," *Lowell Sun*, 23 May 1979; Brian C. Mooney, "First Campaign Ends In Defeat," *Boston Globe*, 18 June 2003.

16. Mooney, "First Campaign Ends In Defeat."

17. "Guy Carbone Wants To Be D.A., Hits At Kerry As 'Inexperienced' First Assistant," *Lowell Sun*, 14 May 1978.

18. Cook, "Kerry's Departure Spur To Droney," *Lowell Sun*, 11 June 1979.

19. *Lowell Sun*, 24 September 1978.

20. Cook, "Kerry's Resignation Didn't Surprise Droney," *Lowell Sun*.

21. Black, "Ambition And Growth Mark Life Of John Kerry, Democrat," *Boston Globe*, 9 October 1984.

22. Cook, "DA's Office Didn't Fight Sedach's Release," *Lowell Sun*, 24 August 1979.

23. Commonwealth Of Massachusetts, Executive Office Of Public Safety, Fax, 2 May 1996.

24. NOTE: Parole Rate Is Percentage Of Inmates Paroled That Were Interviewed By Parole Board. Commonwealth Of Massachusetts, Executive Office Public Safety, Fax, 28 March 1996.

25. Disaster Center Index Page, www.disastercenter.com/crime/macrime.htm, accessed 9 February 2004.

26. George B. Merry, "Auto Theft Is Still 'Big Business,'" *Christian Science Monitor*, 22 November 1983.

27. S. 1607, CQ Vote #360: Adopted 60–38: R 39–5; D 21–33, 9 November 1993, Kerry voted nay.

28. S. 1607, CQ Vote #361: Adopted 65–34: R 34–11; D 31–23, 9 November 1993, Kerry voted nay.

29. S. 254, CQ Vote #118: Adopted 48–47: R 47–7; D 1–40, 14 May 1999, Kerry voted nay.

30. Statements by Ed Gillespie, chairman of the Republican National Committee, press conference, 25 February 2004.

31. Kerry, Congressional Record, 13 June 1988, p. S7692

32. NBC, *Meet the Press*, 1 December 2002.

33. Mooney, "Democrats Shift On Death Penalty," *Boston Globe*, 7 December 2003.

34. CNN, *Late Edition*, 17 April 1994.

35. S. 2455, CQ Vote #175: Passed 65–29: R 37–6; D 28–23, 10 June 1988, Kerry voted nay. H.R. 5210, CQ Vote #368: Rejected 25–64: R 6–33; D 19–31, 13 October 1988, Kerry voted yea. H.R. 4404, CQ Vote #71: Rejected 27–60: R 7–30; D 20–30, 27 April 1990, Kerry voted yea. S. 1798, CQ Vote #275: Passed 79–20: R 40–5; D 39–15, 26 October 1989, Kerry voted nay.

36. William Tucker, "Deterring Homicides/With The Death Penalty," *Human Events*, Vol. 59, No. 12, April 2003.

37. "Death Penalty Deters Murder," National Center For Policy Analysis, Daily Policy Digest, 7 May 2003.

38. Tucker, "Deterring Homicides/With the Death Penalty," *Human Events*, Vol. 59, No. 12.

39. CNN, "Kerry Pledge: 10 Million Jobs In Four Years," 26 March 2004.

40. CNN, "Kerry Pledge: 10 Million Jobs In Four Years."

41. CNN, *Late Edition*, 7 November 1993, emphasis added.

42. Kerry, Congressional Record, 15 July 2003, p. S9400.

43. Kerry et al, Letter To President Bush, 11 June 2001.

44. Kerry, Congressional Record.

45. H.R. 5110, CQ Vote #329: Passed 76–24: R 35–11; D 41–13, 1 December 1994, Kerry voted yea.

46. H.R. 4444, CQ Vote #251: Passed 83–15: R 46–8; D 37–7, 19 September 2000, Kerry voted yea.

47. Kerry, AFL-CIO Working Families Presidential Forum, Chicago, IL, 5 August 2003.

48. Kerry, AFL-CIO Working Families Presidential Forum, Chicago, IL.

49. Kerry, remarks at town hall meeting, Vinton, IA, 13 January 2004.

50. Kerry, Congressional Record, p. S9400.

51. Martin Crutsinger, "Greenspan Warns Against 'Protectionist Cures' To Deal With U.S. Job Losses," Associated Press, 20 February 2004.

52. David Ignatius, Op/Ed, "Dishonest Trade Talk," *Washington Post*, 24 February 2004.

53. David Crane, "New Waves Of Trade War Talk In Wake Of U.S. Protectionism," *Toronto Star*, 1 February 1993.

54. "Kerry, Kennedy For Free Trade," *Boston Globe*, 29 June 1999.

55. Denis Paiste, "The Talk Turns To Trade," [Manchester] *Union Leader*, 12 January 2004, emphasis added.

56. Adrian Walker, "Kerry Announces He Will Back Pact," *Boston Globe*, 14 November 1993.

57. Daniel Griswold, "NAFTA At 10: An Economic And Foreign Policy Success," *CATO Institute's Center For Trade Policy Studies*, December 2002.

58. Griswold, "NAFTA At 10: An Economic And Foreign Policy Success," *Center For Trade Policy Studies*.

59. "New Kerry Ad Rips Bush On Jobs," Associated Press, 2 April 2004.

60. Organization For International Investment, "'Insourcing' American Jobs Lost In 'Outsourcing' Debate," Press Release, 13 February 2004.

61. Joel Millman, "Foreign Firms Also Outsource—To The U.S.," *Wall Street Journal*, 23 February 2004.

62. "Kerry Says China Trade Bill Will Help Massachusetts Businesses," *PR Newswire*, 4 June 1987.

63. "John-Kerry/China-Bill," *Business Wire*, 12 March 1987.

64. Farrell, "Kerry Breaks Party Ranks To Back China Trade Status," *Boston Globe*, 15 June 1991.

65. H.R. 4444, CQ Vote #251: Passed 83–15: R 46–8; D 37–7, 19 September 2000, Kerry voted yea.

66. Rothstein, "PNTR Vote Painful To Friends And Foes," *The Hill*, 20 September 2000.

67. Kerry, Democrat Presidential Candidates Debate, Milwaukee, WI.

68. Daniel Sneider, "Focus On Foreign Policy Plays To Kerry's Strength," *San Jose Mercury News*, 16 December 2003.

69. Kerry for President, www.johnkerry.com, accessed 6 April 2004.

70. Kerry for President Web site, www.johnkerry.com/issues/veterans/, accessed 18 February 2004.

71. *Union Leader/ABC News*, Democrat Presidential Candidate Debate, Manchester, NH, 22 January 2004.

72. FactCheck.org Web site, www.factcheck.org/article.aspx?docid=144, accessed 18 February 2004.

73. "Funding For Veterans Up 27 percent, But Democrats Call It A Cut," FactCheck.org Web site, www.factcheck.org, accessed 18 February 2004.

74. Senate Republican Policy Committee, "VA-HUD Appropriations/Allocation of VA Resources," 4 September 1996.

75. H.R. 3666, CQ Vote #268: Adopted 79–18: R 50–0; D 29–18, 4 September 1996, Kerry voted nay.

76. H.R. 2620, CQ Vote #263: Motion rejected 25–75: R 8–41; D 16–34; I 1–0, 1 August 2001, Kerry voted nay; H.R. 2684, CQ Vote #286: Motion agreed to 61–38: R 16–37; D 45–0; I 0–1, 22 September 1999, Kerry voted yea.

77. H.R. 2673, CQ Vote #3: Adopted 65–28: R 44–4; D 21–23; I 0–1, 22 January 2004, Kerry did not vote.

CHAPTER 11—GAS, OIL, AND HOT AIR

1. Kerry for President Web site, "Enter Into A 'Conservation Covenant' With The American People," www.johnkerry.com/issues/energy/, accessed 30 January 2004, emphasis added.

2. Kerry for President Web site, "Restoring America's Waters," www.johnkerry.com/issues/energy/, accessed 31 January 2004.

3. Kerry for President Web site, "Reassert U.S. Leadership In Global Environmental Progress," www.johnkerry.com/issues/energy/, accessed 31 January 2004, emphasis added.

4. Kerry for President Web site, "Promoting Smart Growth And Livable Communities," www.johnkerry.com/issues/energy/, accessed 31 January 2004, emphasis added.

5. "Bush Administration Actions To Promote Healthy Forests," White House press release, accessed online at http://www.whitehouse.gov/infocus/healthyforests/restor-act-pg2.htmi on 25 April 2004.

6. "President Bush Signs Healthy Forests Restoration Act into Law," White House press release, accessed online at http://www.whitehouse.gov/infocus/healthyforests/ on 26 April 2004.

7. Kerry, press release, 3 December 2003.
8. "Pumped up," *National Public Radio*, accessed online at http://www.pbs.org/newshour/bb/transportation/jan-june01/gas_05-14.html, 14 May 2001.
9. Christopher Ruddy, "Election Scorecard," NewsMax.com, 12 April 2004.
10. Kerry for President Web site, "Reduce Our Dependence On Foreign Oil," www.johnkerry.com/issues/energy/, accessed 30 January 2004, emphasis added.
11. H.R. 2084, CQ Vote #275: Rejected 40–55: R 6–45; D 34–9; I 0–1, 15 September 1999, Kerry voted yea; S. 517, CQ Vote #47, Adopted 62–38: R 43–6; D 19–31; I 0–1, 13 March 2002, Kerry voted nay; S.1926, Introduced 8 February 2002; Peter Cohn and John Godfrey, "Another Committee Loses Voice On Energy Overhaul," *Congressional Quarterly Daily Monitor*, 12 February 2002.
12. Andrew Kleit, "Modeling Increases In CAFE Standards Proposed By Senator Kerry," Competitive Enterprise Institute, 10 February 2002, emphasis added.
13. "Are Lives Really An Acceptable Price For Fuel Efficiency?" *USA Today*, 8 July 1999.
14. Henry Payne, Op-Ed, "What Would President Jesus Drive?" *National Review* Online, www.nationalreview.com, accessed 7 February 2004.
15. Robert B. Bluey, "Bush Administration To Renew Fight For ANWR Drilling," CNSNews.com, 9 January 2003.
16. Kerry, remarks at John F. Kennedy Library, Boston, MA, 9 February 2003.
17. Kerry, remarks in Cedar Rapids, IA, 13 June 2003.
18. Kerry for President Web site, "Developing Alaska Natural Gas Pipeline," www.johnkerry.com/issues/energy/, accessed 1 February 2004, emphasis added.
19. NPR, *Morning Edition*, 31 December 2003.
20. H.R. 6, CQ Vote #456: Motion rejected 57–40: R 44–7; D 13–32, 21 November 2003, Kerry did not vote.
21. NPR, *Morning Edition*, 31 December 2003.
22. Kevin Landrigan, "Kerry Offers Ways To Fight Pollution," [Nashua, NH] *Telegraph*, 23 April 2003.
23. Landrigan, "Kerry Offers Ways To Fight Pollution," *Telegraph*.
24. Editorial, "Divers Ruminations," *Providence Journal-Bulletin*, 8 April 2003.
25. Dealey, "Wind Farm Is An Issue For Kerry," *The Hill*, 18 June 2003.
26. Myron Ebell and Marlo Lewis Jr., "An Open Letter To Selected Senators On Their Support For The Renewable Portfolio Standard," Competitive Enterprise Institute, 25 September 2002.
27. NPR, *Morning Edition*, 31 December 2003.
28. "Last Year's Oil Imports More Than Half Of U.S. Supplies," *Energy Wire*, accessed online at http://www.anwr.org/features/imprthlf.htm, ANWR.org.
29. Neal Gabler, "Bush's Scorched-Earth Campaign," *Los Angeles Times*, 8 June 2003.

30. Center for Responsive Politics Web site, www.opensecrets.org, accessed 25 February 2004.

31. Center for Responsive Politics Web site, www.opensecrets.org, accessed 25 February 2004.

32. Center for Responsive Politics, www.opensecrets.org, accessed 2 February 2004.

33. American Tort Reform Association President Sherman Joyce, statement, accessed online at http://www.atra.org/about/ on April 14, 2003.

34. "Oval Office Dreams," *Miami Daily Business Review*, 19 May 2003.

35. Carolyn Lochhead, "Silicon Valley's Y2K Lawsuit Limit Gaining In Senate," *San Francisco Chronicle*, 10 June 1999, emphasis added.

36. Elizabeth Austin and Jim Day, "Rising Awards Adds Fuel To Debate On Tort Reform," *Chicago Lawyer*, November 2003.

37. Kerry for President Web site, "Kerry Talks Health To City Employees," www.johnkerry.com/pressroom/clips/news_2003_0710a.html, accessed 11 November 2003; Congressional voting record.

38. S. 1415, CQ Vote #160: Adopted 49–48: R 45–8; D 4–40, 16 June 1998, Kerry voted nay; S. 1415, CQ Vote #158: Motion agreed to 50–45: R 12–41; D 38–4, 11 June 1998, Kerry voted yea; S. 648, CQ Vote #188: Motion rejected 51–47: R 51–2; D 0–45, 9 July 1998, Kerry voted nay; S. 240, CQ Vote #290: Rejected 32–61: R 3–45; D 29–16, 27 June 1995, Kerry voted nay.

39. H.R. 956, CQ Vote #140: Motion agreed to 65–35: R 24–30; D 41–5, 2 May 1995, Kerry voted yea; S. 640, CQ Vote #199: Motion rejected 58–38: R 40–3; D 18–35, 10 October 1992, Kerry voted nay; S. 640, CQ Vote #198: Motion agreed to 57–39: R 39–3; D 18–36, 10 October 1992, Kerry voted nay; S. 640, CQ Vote #197: Motion rejected 57–39: R 39–4; D 18–35, 10 October 1992, Kerry voted nay.

40. Susan Jones, "Tort Reform Group Warns Kerry To Avoid Edwards," CNSNews.com, 3 March 2004.

41. Jones, "Tort Reform Group Warns Kerry To Avoid Edwards," CNSNews.com.

42. Pam Smith, "Lawyers Gird For Battle," *Recorder*, 18 July 2003; http://www.law.com/jsp/article.jsp?id=1058416388549.

43. ATLA Web site, http://www.atla.org/cle_con/sf03/ch.pdf, accessed 17 July 2003.

CHAPTER 12—KERRY ON GUNS

1. Noah Webster, "An Examination Of The Leading Principles Of The Federal Constitution," Philadelphia circa 1787.

2. Thomas Jefferson, Draft Virginia Constitution, 1776.

3. "On The Issues: John F. Kerry On Gun Control," *New York Times*, accessed online at http://www.nytimes.com/ref/politics/campaigns/issue_gun_control.html.

4. Halbfinger, "Shotgun In Hand, Kerry Defines His Gun Control Stance," *New York Times*, 1 November 2003.

5. Halbfinger, "Shotgun In Hand, Kerry Defines His Gun Control Stance," *New York Times*.

6. Halbfinger, "Shotgun In Hand, Kerry Defines His Gun Control Stance."

7. Halbfinger, "Shotgun In Hand, Kerry Defines His Gun Control Stance."

8. Thomas M. Moncure Jr., "The Second Amendment Ain't About Hunting," *Howard Law Journal*, 1991.

9. George Will, *Washington Post*, p. A–21, 21 March 1991.

10. Dan Springer, "Study: Guns No Safer When Locked Up," Fox News, 8 July 2002.

11. Wayne LaPierre, "John Kerry's Hidden Agenda," *America's Freedom*, p. 38, May 2004.

12. LaPierre, "John Kerry's Hidden Agenda," *America's Freedom*, p. 38.

13. Humane Society of the United States, accessed online at http://www.hsus.org on 25 April 2004; LaPierre, "John Kerry's Hidden Agenda," *America's Freedom*, p. 38.

14. Humane Society of the United States, accessed online at http://www.hsus.org.

15. "A Third Way On Guns," *New Dem Daily*, 2 August 2001, accessed online at http://www.ndol.org/ ndol_ci.cfm?contentid=3678&kaid=131&subid=192.

16. "A Third Way On Guns," *New Dem Daily*, 2 August 2001.

17. LaPierre, "John Kerry's Hidden Agenda," *America's Freedom*, p. 38.

18. Kerry, "Protect the right to choose," accessed online at http://www.johnkerry.com.

19. Kerry, "A Record Of Working On Behalf Of Gay And Lesbian Americans," accessed online at http://www.johnkerry.com.

20. Kerry, "Open College Opportunities For Women," accessed online at http://www.johnkerry.com.

21. Zacharia Johnson, statement to the Virginia Ratifying Convention, June 12, 1788.

CHAPTER 13—BAD MEDICINE

1. "Numbers Of Americans With And Without Health Insurance Rise, Census Bureau Reports," U.S. Census Bureau press release, 30 September 2003.

2. "Numbers Of Americans With And Without Health Insurance Rise, Census Bureau Reports," U.S. Census Bureau press release.

3. Sally C. Pipes, "Some Choose To Forego Health Insurance Plans," *Investor's Business Daily*, 9 January 2004.

4. Kerry for President Web site, www.johnkerry.com, accessed 28 January 2004.

5. Kerry for President Web site, http://www.johnkerry.com, accessed 28 January 2004.

6. Kerry for President Web site, http://www.johnkerry.com.

7. ABC, *This Week with George Stephanopoulos*, 22 February 2004.

8. Kerry, remarks at town hall meeting, Manchester, NH, 6 August 2003.

9. Kerry, "Affordable Health Care For All Americans," remarks at Mercy Medical, Cedar Rapids, IA, 14 December 2003.

10. Kenneth E. Thorpe, "An Overview And Analysis Of The Democratic Presidential Candidates' Health Care Reform Proposals"; "Health Insurance Coverage In The United States: 2002," U.S. Census Bureau, 7 September 2003.
11. Calvin Woodward, "Price Tag Of Kerry Health Plan Drops In New Analysis," Associated Press, 4 April 2004.
12. Woodward, "Price Tag Of Kerry Health Plan Drops In New Analysis," Associated Press.
13. PBS, *The NewsHour with Jim Lehrer*, 2 July 2003.
14. Ronald Brownstein, "Bush Replays Themes That Worked In 2000 Election," *Los Angeles Times*, 24 February 2004.
15. Sue A. Blevins, "Debunking Medicare Myths: How A New Prescription Drug Program Could Affect American Taxpayers And Seniors," *Institute For Health Freedom*, 8 December 2000.
16. "Modernizing And Improving Health Care," White House press release, accessed online at http://www.whitehouse.gov/infocus/medicare/, 8 December 2003.
17. Kerry for President, http://www.johnkerry.com, accessed 28 January 2004, emphasis added.
18. "Medical Care Cost Doubles In 3 Years," *New York Times*, 9 September 1968.
19. Blevins, "Debunking Medicare Myths: How A New Prescription Drug Program Could Affect American Taxpayers And Seniors," *Institute For Health Freedom*.
20. Kerry, U.S. Congress, campaign brochure, 1972.
21. John Kerry, remarks at Massachusetts Democratic Party State Issues Convention, Springfield, MA, 1 June 2001.
22. H.R. 1, CQ Vote #457: Motion agreed to 70–29: R 47–3; D 22–26; I 1–0, 24 November 2003, Kerry voted nay; H.R.1, CQ Vote #458: Motion agreed to 61–39: R 49–2; D 11–37; I 1–0, 24 November 2003, Kerry voted nay.
23. Jennifer C. Kerr, "Kerry To Skip Iowa Debate For Medicare Filibuster," Associated Press, 22 November 2003.
24. S. 1, Vote #5: Passed 16–5: R 9–2; D 6–3; I 1–0, 12 June 2003, Kerry voted nay.
25. Kerry for President, "John Kerry Launches New Television Ad In Iowa Today," Press Release, 12 December 2003.
26. Congressional Record.
27. Sam Hananel, "Kerry, Lieberman Skip Final Medicare Vote To Return To Campaign Trail," Associated Press, 25 November 2003.
28. Hananel, "Kerry, Lieberman Skip Final Medicare Vote To Return To Campaign Trail," Associated Press.
29. Kerry, "Kerry Offers Amendment To Help Seniors In Prescription Drug Coverage Gap," Press Release, 20 June 2003.
30. S. Amdt. 958, Withdrawn By Unanimous Consent 6/26/03; Lolita C. Baldor, "Lieberman, Kerry Miss Medicare Vote," Associated Press, 27 June 2003.
31. Kerry for President, "John Kerry Announces He Will Return To Washington To Stand With Seniors For A Real Medicare Bill," Press Release, 23 November 2003.

32. Fact Sheet, "The Bipartisan Medicare Agreement," White House, 17 November 2003.
33. Fact Sheet, Office of the Majority Leader, 18 November 2003.
34. Woodward, "In Latest Presidential Debate, Stories Not Fully Told," Associated Press, 22 January 2004.
35. Woodward, "In Latest Presidential Debate, Stories Not Fully Told," Associated Press.
36. MSNBC/DNC Democrat Candidate Debate, Des Moines, IA, 24 November 2003.
37. Editorial, "Seniors Now Know Their True Friends," *Boston Herald*, 25 November 2003.
38. Glover, "Kerry Criticizes Bush On High Drug Costs," Associated Press, 1 February 2004.
39. Center For Responsive Politics Web site, www.opensecrets.org, accessed 2 February 2004.
40. Fox News, *On the Record*, 10 October 2003.
41. AARP Democrat Candidate Debate, Bedford, NH, 18 November 2003.
42. Stacy Forster, "Personal Health (A Special Report)," *Wall Street Journal Online*, 21 October 2003.
43. Congressional Record.
44. H.R. 2015, CQ Vote #209: Adopted 85–15: R 43–12; D 42–3, 31 July 1997, Kerry voted yea.
45. S. Con. Res. 57, CQ Vote #119: Rejected 45–53: R 0–52; D 45–1, 16 May 1996, Kerry voted yea.
46. H.R. 2264, CQ Vote #247: Adopted 51–50: R 0–44; D 50–6, with Vice President Al Gore casting a yea vote, 6 August 1993, Kerry voted yea.
47. Kerry for President Web site, www.johnkerry.com, accessed 21 January 2004.
48. AARP Democrat Candidate Debate, Bedford, NH.
49. PBS, *The NewsHour with Jim Lehrer*, 2 July 2003.
50. Brownstein, "Kerry Unveils Health-Care Overhaul Plan," *Los Angeles Times*, 17 May 2003.
51. Serafini, "Targeting The 'Worried Insured'," *National Journal*.
52. Johnson, "Kerry Proposes Health Care Plan," *Boston Globe*, 17 May 2003.
53. Michael F. Cannon, "Mrs. Clinton Has Entered The Race: The 2004 Democratic Presidential Candidates' Proposals To Reform Health Insurance," Cato Institute, 5 February 2004.
54. Cannon, "Mrs. Clinton Has Entered The Race: The 2004 Democratic Presidential Candidates' Proposals To Reform Health Insurance," Cato Institute, emphasis added.
55. Michael Cousineau, "Kerry Hammers Bush Drug Plan," [Manchester] *Union Leader*, 22 January 2004.
56. Kelly Field, "H.R.1, Medicare Prescription Drug, Improvement, And Modernization Act Of 2003" *CQ BillAnalysis*, 8 December 2003.
57. CBS, *Face the Nation*, 25 January 2004.

58. Lauran Neergaard, "AP Interview: FDA Chief Says Agency Means Business On Drug Importation Ban," Associated Press, 9 January 2004.

59. Morton M. Kondracke, "Bush, Kerry Make A Deadly Duo For Health Research," *Roll Call*, 23 February 2004.

60. Editorial, "Pricing Drugs," *Washington Post*, 17 February 2004.

61. Holman W. Jenkins Jr., Op-Ed, "In A Year Divisible By Four, Pharma Is The Enemy," *Wall Street Journal*, 4 February 2004.

62. Douglas Holtz-Eakin, director, Congressional Budget Office, letter to Senate Majority Leader Bill Frist, 23 January 2004.

63. William K. Scheuber and Bradford P. Cohn, MD, "California MICRA, The National Model In Tort Reform," San Francisco Medical Society, available online at http://www.sfms.org/sfm/sfm303e.htm.

64. Jane Ann Morrison, "Supporters, Opponents Of Tort Reform Bill Present Arguments," *Las Vegas Review-Journal*, 30 May, 2002.

65. Kerry, Congressional Record.

66. S. 11, CQ Vote #264: Motion rejected 49–48: R 49–2; D 0–45; I 0–1, 9 July 2003, Kerry did not vote; S. 2061, CQ Vote #15: Motion rejected 48–45: R 47–3: D 1–41; I 0–1, 24 February 2004, Kerry did not vote.

67. S. 1052, CQ Vote #219: Rejected 36–59: R 34–10; D 1–49; I 1–0, 29 June 2001, Kerry voted nay.

68. Kerry for President Web site, "John Kerry's Plan To Make Health Care Affordable To Every American," www.johnkerry.com, accessed 21 January 2004.

69. Cost Estimate Of H.R. 5, Help Efficient, Accessible, Low-Cost, Timely Healthcare (HEALTH) Act Of 2003," Congressional Budget Office, 10 March 2003.

70. "Confronting The New Health Care Crisis: Improving Health Care Quality And Lowering Costs By Fixing Our Medical Liability System," Department of Health and Human Services, 24 July 2002.

71. Center for Responsive Politics, http://www.opensecrets.org, Citizen Soldier Fund, Affiliate: John Kerry (D), accessed 10 April 2004 online at http://www.opensecrets.org/presidential/leadpac_ind.asp?id=N00000245&cycle=2004.

72. Kerry, *A Call to Service*, pp. 143–144.

73. Johnson, "Kerry Makes Bid For Veterans," *Boston Globe*, 24 August 2003.

74. H.R. 588, CQ Vote #447: Adopted 95–3: R 51–0; D 44–2; I 0–1, 12 November 2003, Kerry did not vote; S. 1050, Q Vote #185: Adopted 85–10: R 39–10; D 45–0; I 1–0, 20 May 2003, Kerry did not vote.

75. S. 1689, CQ Vote #400: Passed 87–12: R 50–0; D 37–11; I 0–1, 17 October 2003, Kerry voted nay.

76. H.R. 2673, CQ Vote #3: Adopted 65–28: R 44–4; D 21–23; I 0–1, 22 January 2004, Kerry did not vote; U.S. House Committee On Appropriations, "House Passes FY04 Consolidated Appropriations," Press Release, http://appropriations.house.gov/index.cfm?FuseAction=PressReleases.Detail&PressRelease_id=342, 8 December 2003.

77. H.R. 2620, CQ Vote #263: Motion rejected 25–75: R 8–41; D 16–34; I 1–0, 1 August 2001, Kerry voted nay.

78. H.R. 2684, CQ Vote #286: Motion agreed to 61–38: R 16–37; D 45–0; I 0–1, 22 September 1999, Kerry voted yea.

79. H.R. 3666, CQ Vote #268: Adopted 79–18: R 50–0; D 29–18, 4 September 1996.

CHAPTER 14—DUMBING DOWN EDUCATION

1. Walter Williams, "Washington's Education Establishment," *Creators Syndicate*, 8 January 2003.

2. Williams, "Washington's Education Establishment," *Creators Syndicate*.

3. "Public Education In The United States," Microsoft® Encarta® Online Encyclopedia 2004 http://encarta.msn.com © 1997-2004 Microsoft Corporation.

4. "Public Education In The United States," Microsoft® Encarta® Online Encyclopedia 2004 http://encarta.msn.com ©.

5. "Public Education In The United States," Microsoft® Encarta® Online Encyclopedia 2004 http://encarta.msn.com ©.

6. "Public Education In The United States," Microsoft® Encarta® Online Encyclopedia 2004 http://encarta.msn.com ©.

7. J. H. Snider, "From Public School To Welfare Service," *Washington Post*, 2 September 2003.

8. Home School Legal Defense Association figure, citing research by Dr. Brian Ray, president of the National Home Education Research Institute, accessed online at http://www.hslda.org/research/faq.asp 10 April 2004.

9. Thomas Jefferson, 1816, emphasis added.

10. Kerry for President Web site, "A Real Deal For Education: John Kerry Outlines Detailed Plan To Strengthen Public Schools," www.johnkerry.com, accessed 31 January 2004.

11. Kerry for President Web site, "Strengthening America's Schools For The 21st Century," www.johnkerry.com, accessed 31 January 2004.

12. Kerry for President Web site, "Kerry Unveils Higher Education Proposals To Help Students Pay For College, Succeed In The New Economy," www.johnkerry.com, accessed 31 January 2004.

13. Kerry for President Web site, "Strengthening America's Schools For The 21st Century," accessed 29 January 2004.

14. Ben Feller, "U.S. Tops In School Spending, Not Scores," Associated Press, 16 September 2003.

15. Feller, "U.S. Tops In School Spending, Not Scores," Associated Press.

16. Heritage Foundation, education talking points, http://www.heritage.org, accessed online 10 April 2004.

17. Heritage Foundation, education talking points, http://www.heritage.org.

18. Grunwald, "Weld, Kerry Split On Help For Aging Cities," *Boston Globe*, 11 August 1996.

19. Kerry, remarks at Northeastern University, Boston, MA, 16 June 1998.
20. Kerry, remarks at Democrat Presidential Debate, Baltimore, MD, 9 September 2003.
21. Matt Leon, "Sen. Kerry In Tune With Educators," [Quincy, MA] *Patriot Ledger*, 11 July 2003.
22. Kerry, remarks at Thomas Jefferson High School, Council Bluffs, IA, 25 November 2003.
23. Kerry, remarks at Thomas Jefferson High School, Council Bluffs, IA.
24. Kerry, American Federation of Teachers Web site, "Response To AFT Questionnaire From Sen. John Kerry," www.aft.org, accessed 4 February 2004, emphasis added.
25. Kerry, remarks in Iowa City, IA, 22 October 2003, emphasis added.
26. Kerry, remarks in Iowa City, IA.
27. Kerry, remarks in Iowa City, IA.
28. Kerry, American Federation of Teachers Web site, "Response To AFT Questionnaire From Sen. John Kerry," www.aft.org.
29. H.R. 2546, CQ Vote #20: Rejected 54–44: R 50–2; D 4–42, 27 February 1996, Kerry voted nay; H.R. 2546, CQ Vote #21: Rejected 52–42: R 48–1; D 4–41, 29 February 1996, Kerry voted nay; H.R. 2546, CQ Vote #23: Rejected 53–43: R 49–2; D 4–41, 5 March 1996, Kerry voted nay; H.R. 2546, CQ Vote #25: Rejected 56–44: R 51–2; D 5–42, 12 March 1996, Kerry voted nay.
30. John Leo, Op-Ed, "Choice Words For Teacher Unions," *U.S. News & World Report*, 11 March 1996.
31. Leo, "Choice Words For Teacher Unions," *U.S. News & World Report*.
32. Kerry, remarks at Northeastern University, 16 June 1998.
33. Kristen Gerencher, "Senate Ups Education IRA Limit," *CBS MarketWatch*, 24 May 2001.
34. Dana Milbank, "Bush Likely To Drop Vouchers," *Washington Post*, 2 January 2001.
35. Miga, "Classmates—Ted K Backs Bush's Ed Plan," *Boston Herald*, 24 January 2001.
36. Kerry, Congressional Black Caucus Institute Debate, 9 September 2003.
37. Kerry, remarks in Council Bluffs, IA, 25 November 2003.
38. Center for Responsive Politics, John Kerry, (D), Top Industries as 2004 presidential campaign donors, http://www.opensecrets.org, accessed online 11 April 2004.
39. Kerry, Congressional Record, 10 September 1985, p. S 11148.
40. S. 1150, CQ Vote #22: Adopted 75–22: R 35–6; D 40–16, 3 February 1994, Kerry voted yea
41. S. 1513, CQ Vote #236: Rejected 47–53: R 35–9; D 12–44, 27 July 1994, Kerry voted nay.
42. S. 1513, CQ Vote #237: Adopted 93–7: R 39–5; D 54–2, 27 July 1994, Kerry voted yea.
43. Senate Republican Policy Committee, "Elementary & Secondary Education/School Prayer, Violating Constitution," 27 July 1994.

44. Christopher Wankjek, "Program Seeks To Cut Pregnancies In Urban Youth," *Columbia University Record*, 6 March 1998.
45. "Talking Points 2004: The Candidates' Briefing Room," Heritage Foundation, accessed online at http://www.heritage.org/Research/Features/Issues2004/Abstinence.cfm on 23 April 2004.
46. Personal Responsibility, Work Opportunity, and Medicaid Restructuring Act of 1996, #1996-231, Kerry voted nay.

AFTERWORD
1. The Iowa Brown & Black Coalition Presidential Forum, Des Moines, IA, 11 January 2004.
2. Brian C. Mooney, "Taking One Prize, Then A Bigger One," *Boston Globe*, 19 June 2003.
3. Mooney, "Taking One Prize, Then A Bigger One," *Boston Globe*.
4. Susan Jones, "Kerry's Campaign Uses Photos Of Prisoners To Raise Money, GOP Says," CNSNews.com, 10 May 2004.
5. Mike Glover, "Kerry Bashes Bush On Health Care Costs," Associated Press, 10 May 2004.
6. Gov. Howard Dean, Democrat Candidate Debate, Greenville, SC, 29 January 2004.